Action Learning

Krystyna Weinstein wears several 'hats'. Her main work interests are action learning and 'communication', and she has worked with many major UK companies. She also has strong ties with Eastern Europe, where action learning is beginning to take hold.

As an ex-journalist and editor, she also runs writing workshops along action learning lines (her book on writing is also published in 1995). She is coordinating editor of *Organisations and People*, the AMED journal, and publishes a quarterly newsletter for the International Foundation for Action Learning, an organization for which she acts as secretary.

Before this, she spent several years as a research fellow at Manchester Business School, where she gained an MSc in organizational behaviour.

Other titles available from HarperCollins in the Successful Manager Series

Managing Your Own Career – Dave Francis
Learning to Lead – Bob Garratt
Superteams – Colin Hastings, Peter Bixby, Rani Chaudry-Lawton
Managing Yourself – Mike Pedler and Tom Boydell
Manage Your Time – Sally Garratt
Finance for the Perplexed Executive – Ray Proctor
Managing People – Vivien Whitaker

Krystyna Weinstein

Action Learning

A Journey in Discovery and Development

HarperCollins*Publishers*

HarperCollins*Publishers*
77–85 Fulham Palace Road,
Hammersmith, London W6 8JB

A Paperback Original 1995
1 3 5 7 9 8 6 4 2

A catalogue record for this book
is available from the British Library

ISBN 0 00 638224 X

Set in Linotron Palatino by
Rowland Phototypesetting Ltd
Bury St Edmunds, Suffolk

Printed in Great Britain by
HarperCollinsManufacturing Glasgow

Contents

Preface

This book emerged from my frustration at never having anything easy and readable on action learning to give people when they asked me if I could recommend a basic introduction to the subject.

I've attempted to write it simply, to put myself in the place of readers who know little, and to ask some of the basic questions in the hope of supplying straightforward answers and explanations. I hope I have succeeded!

For giving me access to participants on their action learning programmes, I would particularly like to thank W H Smith, TSB, Motorola, Lever Brothers, BUPA, Seagrams, Surrey and Hampshire County Councils, Brighton Borough Council, Vygon and Sun Life. I would also like to thank IMC (International Management Centres), Nottingham Trent University, Manchester Metropolitan University, and Brighton University, for giving me access to students on their post-graduate management-by-action learning programmes.

I would also like to thank the many colleagues running mixed-company programmes, and all the participants on these programmes, who were willing to let me come and talk to them. And finally all those participants on the various mixed-company programmes which I myself have run in the past few years (and one in-company programme for Nationwide-Anglia), whose thoughts and comments feature widely.

I proffer my thanks to David Boddy and Catherine Jubb, both of whom read the manuscript for 'sense' and readability. Their ideas have contributed immensely to the final shape of the book. My thanks also to Bob Garratt who suggested several important amendments. And finally, I need to acknowledge the influence of Jean Lawrence, who first introduced

Action Learning

me to action learning, and whose experience and knowledge
I greatly value – some of which I hope is reflected in this
book.

Krystyna Weinstein, London, July 1994

Background and Material for the Book

Action learning has a particular attraction and relevance for us today. Programmes are currently operating in a range of sectors – local government, the police force and the NHS, small businesses and non-profit-making organizations – not only in the UK but right across Europe (including Eastern Europe), the USA, Australia, several countries of the Far East, and in South Africa. There is a great deal of talk and interest in the idea of a 'learning company', and many questions are being asked about how we can make this seductive idea come about. How can we make sure that all the learning, all the experience each of us gains, can be shared with others, to everyone's mutual benefit? How can we, in fact, take learning out of the classroom and anchor it firmly in our everyday lives, at work, in leisure – anywhere?

Action learning has one of the more potent answers to the question: 'How can we become a learning company?' because its structure and processes create a learning company in miniature.

The idea for this book arose out of my experiences – as a set adviser, and as Secretary to IFAL (the International Foundation for Action Learning) – of people wanting to know more about action learning. Not the theory, or how to be a practitioner, but what happened in such programmes: what did participants do, what did they gain – and learn – and how did they do this. In particular, how is it possible to learn without teachers and experts; what did a project consist of; why does it take so long (other courses are no longer than one week, normally). And, of course, who are such programmes for, and what purposes did organizations using action learning specify as their reasons for using it.

The experiences documented here were collected in the summer of 1993. My aim was to hear from those who'd done it what it was like to participate in an action learning programme, and what they had learnt. This last point, in particular, is the key to any programme.

I asked participants whether they would prefer to be interviewed or to write down their impressions. They almost all opted for the former. I interviewed – in face-to-face interviews or by telephone – 69 people on sixteen different programmes. Of these, nine were in-company programmes, seven were mixed-company, and five had academic links. Of the individuals I spoke to, 18 (in five sets) were involved in working on group projects, and the rest on their own individual ones. To give a further breakdown: I met with five sets (20 individuals) in the sets they had been working in. The interviews lasted anything from half an hour with individuals to three hours with some of the sets.

In addition, I spoke informally to a few individuals who are currently on programmes which include an action learning element, and I was given access to some written documentation – largely from the programmes with academic links, but also some reflective documents from one of the other programmes.

The range of companies and organizations who were running in-house programmes – and whose participants I spoke to – was varied. Among those included were: W H Smith, TSB, Motorola, Lever Brothers, Nottingham Trent University, BUPA, Seagrams and Vygon (these last three on academic programmes run by the International Management Centres), Surrey and Hampshire County Councils, Brighton Borough Council, and Sun Life.

Other participants were on mixed-company programmes run by independent consultants. The organizations they came from included finance institutions (pensions, insurance and merchant banking), the Civil Service, and a wide range of small businesses.

A third category consisted of mixed-company programmes linked to study for MSc and MBA degrees in Management, using action learning, run at Brighton University and Manchester Metropolitan University. Here, too, participants came from a variety of organizations: universities, the NHS, telecommunications, and other businesses.

The functions and positions of those taking part covered the entire spectrum: from managing directors and chief executives to senior functional managers, from engineers and IT specialists to marketing and sales personnel, retail and banking employees, lecturers and teachers, along with staff responsible for administration, training and personnel.

On concluding the research I was left with the following observations and insights:

- The excitement of the participants in describing their learning was for me one of the advantages of meeting face to face rather than reading scripts. Hearing how they talked gave me further insights into their experiences.
- The majority felt that they had learnt a great deal more than either they or the organizers of the programmes had anticipated. This led me to divide the learning into two component parts: *anticipated learning* (what participants had planned or hoped to learn – because they had, in most but not all instances, relatively clear ideas of why they were on the programmes); and *unanticipated learning* (what they gained as a result of this programme and its elements, many of which were not what participants had been expecting).
- In the course of tackling such issues as effective management of people, events and issues, participants gain new insights about themselves. The creation and putting into place of new strategies was obviously important to participants, but what they mostly talked of was the personal development they were experiencing as a result of learning to manage themselves.
- Action learning legitimizes, and brings out the value of, giving people space and time to stand back, think, reflect, see things in perspective. Two participants' insights here: 'I know I need to sit back and reflect, but unfortunately our time sheets don't allocate space for this'; and 'Reflecting, stopping to think, has saved me from plunging in and making mistakes as I go along'.

- As a result of action learning, action-based managers tend to become more reflective and pragmatic, while reflectors and theorists find that they become more active as the programme gives them the tools to work with.
- It brings out the value of sharing doubts, successes, questions and mistakes with others.
- The longer the programme, the more the participants felt they had benefited, because this allowed their development to take place and their confidence to grow.
- The depth and breadth of learning was greatest where: individuals worked on their own projects rather than on group projects; the participants were responsible for or participated to some degree in implementing what they had proposed; the set adviser was 'qualified'; there was some action learning related input taught as part of the programme (in addition to a one-day introduction to action learning at the beginning of a programme), or where some other development programme had preceded it.
- Most outstanding of all, everyone mentioned that their self confidence had increased.

HOW THIS BOOK IS STRUCTURED

This book is intended to cater for people with different levels of knowledge of action learning, and hence different interests.

If you know very little about action learning and want to know more, but keep it brief and practical, you may find it best to begin with Part 1, **Action Learning in a Nutshell**, which records in detail the vital elements that constitute a successful action learning programme, and then move on to Part 3, **The Experience of Action Learning**.

If you want to know about the theory of action learning and to take time to reflect on the philosophy that underpins it, you may want to read Part 2, **What is Action Learning: A Reflective Piece**, first. Alternatively, you may find that reading Parts 1 and 3 gives you a better grounding before returning to Part 2.

Those who know something about action learning already and have formulated a number of questions about it, such as: 'what happens on an action learning programme?' and 'what do people get from it?' will find in Part 3 the responses of participants to such questions, detailing their own first-hand experience of action learning.

If, after reading Parts 1–3, you want to plunge in and try running a programme, turn to Part 4, *Putting an Effective Action Learning Programme into Practice*, for what you need to do to start up and run a successful programme. You will also find further recommended reading that will give you more details than this book has space for.

Action learning at its best is capable of 'reaching those parts that other programmes do not reach'. My research left me with a very strong impression that for a programme to succeed certain elements need to be present. If some elements are missing, the programmes are that much the poorer, and the participants and their organizations the losers. A few of the programmes attended by the participants interviewed for this book did not fully meet what I would now define as the criteria for successful action learning. Nevertheless, it is only in uncovering the limitations of some programmes, and in analysing why they were less than successful – as described in participants' own words in this book – that we will know what makes for programmes which will 'deliver the goodies', and which ones merely scratch the surface and never reveal the full depth, breadth and complexity that is the potential of a well-run programme.

Ultimately, this book can do no more than attempt to describe the experience of action learning. It is an attempt, because even the participants in programmes, whose words form the main bulk of this book, sometimes found it difficult to express in words what it was they had gained and learnt – or even how it had come about. 'I know I've changed – that I'm not the person I was . . . but I'm not really sure how it happened' was how one participant put it. Others went into details – which are catalogued throughout – about a more effective way of communicating, working and generally relating to others, as well as a greater intellectual and emotional honesty. These are not 'road to Damascus' revelations. It is just that words – although adequate to describe specific skills and achievements gained – often prove inadequate to chronicle how we feel changed, how we sense we are different. There is also a sense in which words cannot convey 'experience' – they convey only information about it. It is, after all, a paradox to try to write a book about action learning, a subject which places 'action' and the 'experience' of that action as the starting point for learners.

PART 1

Action Learning in a Nutshell

This part of the book is a brief and practical introduction to action learning (unlike Part 2 which is more reflective). Its aim is to provide a digest for those readers who either know little about the subject or feel they are not yet ready for a more theoretical/philosophical piece. In addition to describing the various types of programmes, it also explores the reasons why organizations run such programmes, why individuals attend them, and what both hope to gain.

WHAT IS ACTION LEARNING?

Action learning is a 'process' underpinned by a belief in individual potential: a way of learning from our actions (and from what happens to us and around us) by taking the time to question and reflect on this in order to gain insights and consider how to act in future.

There are two other important elements to action learning: it involves a group of people who work together on their 'doing' and their 'learning'; and it requires regular and rigorous meetings of the group, to allow space and time for this process of questioning and reflection.

So, when applied at work, action learning means working and learning simultaneously. Participants on an action learning programme will focus on work-based issues, problems and questions. These might involve an individual's managerial and personal development; teamwork or staff-management; consulting; managing change . . . or indeed any other issue that is of concern to them. In other, non-work, situations, the same applies: learning from what we do.

This sounds simple and obvious – and in a way it is . . . rather like learning to ride a bicycle. But there's a great deal more to it – hence the scope for a book!

It is precisely because action learning involves a group of people that it is so effective for introducing 'change' into organizations: change in the way people work together, in the way they behave and think, ie a culture change. Changes also occur because participants attending a programme begin to influence others, which may in turn bring about changes in the structures, systems and processes within an organization.

Endless opportunities to learn

The belief underlying action learning is that our daily activities provide us with endless opportunities to learn. Nowhere is this more true than at work – in the organizations where so many of us spend at least a third of our waking hours. The same is true of learning opportunities when we 'play'. Yet we persist in thinking that learning is something that takes place only in a lecture room or on a course.

In fact we are learning all the time – be it at work or elsewhere. We learn as much from our mistakes as from our successes. But we do not make learning a conscious activity. Nor do we make it explicit. Moreover, we rarely share our learning with others so that they can benefit. Neither do we question whether the conclusions we are individually drawing all the time, and subsequently acting on, are valid. We don't always check out our assumptions or prejudices. We tend to act purely on our own judgements. And yet others' insights can prove very valuable – if we create the opportunity to work and share with them in a constructive manner.

Action learning creates an opportunity to become conscious of what we do, how we think, and what we believe. In so doing it eventually encourages a climate of learning within an organization.

What constitutes an action learning programme?

In an action learning programme:

- everyone works on a work-based project, or series of tasks
- the group of people who join a programme and work together learn to work in a constructive and effective way
- the emphasis throughout the programme is as much on achieving visible results as on learning.

The five main elements of an action learning programme are:

1 *the set*: a small group of people – five or six – who meet regularly, ideally once a month for a day;
2 *the projects or tasks* that each person works on during the programme;
3 *the 'processes'* that the group adopts when working, which

differ in many ways from the way we normally work in other groups;

4 *a set adviser* who helps the group as it works and learns;

5 *the duration of a programme* – normally from three to six months.

Each of these five elements is explored in greater detail in Part 3, where a question-and-answer approach is used to describe the main aspects of each element, illustrated by the experiences of participants in their own words. Thus I hope not only to convey the flavour but also to explain the value of each of these key elements.

WHAT'S SO SPECIAL ABOUT ACTION LEARNING?

The thinking behind action learning is that learning is not solely about acquiring knowledge or a skill by reading a book or listening to a lecture. Learning is about doing something differently, or behaving differently; about applying and making use of a skill or of new knowledge; or about thinking differently, or having a new set of values and beliefs. Only when we can transfer our knowledge, skill, behaviour or beliefs and insights to something practical, thus providing evidence that we are able to apply it, can we claim that we have really learnt. In other words, learning is about changing.

The best way to learn to do something differently is to focus on that 'doing' – in an area we have an interest in, an issue we need to tackle, an opportunity to grasp, or a problem we need to resolve – and learn from that experience, discovering as much from our successes as we do from our mistakes.

We learn best and most effectively when we learn in the company of others who are also learning. None of us has a monopoly on knowledge, insights, perspectives. And we all have a host of questions. By working and learning with others, we are able to share in their knowledge, insights and perspectives, and hear their questions. The more we share, the more we learn and realize our own potential.

We learn best when we ask questions and try to seek not answers but an understanding. So, in response to questions beginning with 'why . . .' we don't need to give explanations and justifications, but rather stop and think, and reflect.

Time to stop, think, ask questions and reflect is crucial to learning; as is the regularity of that process and the rigour applied.

Going back to work after a set meeting, and doing something differently, and then coming back to the set and talking about what we've achieved or have failed to achieve – this 'rhythm' is essential to anchoring the learning.

The impulse to give advice, pass judgement on anyone, or to try to find easy solutions to problems should be resisted. Problems are normally symptoms of other underlying problems. It is those that action learning aims to get at.

Action learning takes time. It takes time to learn; it takes time to build up trust among a group working and learning together so that members feel free to discuss some issues that they've maybe never discussed before; it takes time to build up confidence to do things differently; finally, it takes time to practise and perfect what we are doing differently.

(For those readers interested, the thinking behind each of these aspects of action learning is described in much greater detail in Part 2.)

Learning is about doing something differently. This can involve:

- gaining new knowledge and information
- reasoning differently
- behaving differently
- becoming more aware
- gaining greater understanding of their own and others' motives

---

- altering beliefs and values
- acknowledging feelings and their impact

All of this plays a part in action learning. A good set adviser (see Part 3) will encourage participants to become aware of these changes

Who is it for?

Action learning is for everyone. Programmes have operated in every type of organization: education and health services, charities, local government, banks and building societies, manufacturing companies, service companies.

People who have attended programmes include shop-floor staff, social workers, secretaries and managing directors; marketing, finance and personnel teams; IT specialists and engineers.

Sets are selected so that people within them are able to help one another, even if they perform different functions – sometimes coming from different organizations. Thus it is most beneficial if sets are made up of people from the same level of responsibility; in other words, a very senior manager and a junior person would be unlikely to work in the same set.

Managing – and action learning

We all manage something, whether it be a switchboard, a shop, a million-dollar organization, an IT department or an engineering workshop, a clerical section or personnel department. It might be managing a customer or managing a project. It might be managing others, be it a team of six or sixty, it might simply be managing ourselves or our careers.

Whatever it is we manage, we need to manage it effectively. Questions and queries, dilemmas and quandaries will arise; we will face minor hiccups or major problems. We will have – even if we don't always recognize them – chances and opportunities, challenges and openings.

To manage better, we need to learn. And we learn by stopping and taking note of everything that impinges on our managing, by reflecting on this and gaining insights and clues about how to manage better next time. For no matter what we manage, we will have successes and we'll make mistakes. And we can learn from both.

We can also learn from other people and their experiences, if we're willing to share.

And then we need the confidence to recognize all this, and maybe to take some personal, even professional, risks. Above all, we need to learn to think and to ask questions.

Action learning helps participants tackle all this.

When is it useful?

Action learning, because it is a process, is useful in a whole range of circumstances:

- in 'development' programmes
- as a follow-up to more traditional courses, to anchor and consolidate the learning
- as a vehicle for helping people manage and cope with change of any sort
- to provide a useful opportunity for networking across an organization, helping members to understand the wider aspects of that organization

Above all, it is a forum where people can share difficulties and problems, without fear.

Its strength is that, as already stated, it is a process which encourages particular ways of communicating which often prove to be more helpful than our everyday discussions. For it emphasizes rather a 'dialogue' with others (see p. 47 for a more detailed explanation of the distinction). Thus participants learn to listen (not as easy as it sounds!), to ask helpful questions, to help others resolve their own queries and issues through encouraging them to think and reflect. In fact several participants have likened the set to a group of mentors.

The 'magic' for some participants:

'You become aware of yourself and others. You become aware of your qualities and skills.'

'You learn to value good productive communication and you want to transfer it back to work.'

'It gives you space for you – it values and respects the individual, and hence gives you confidence.'

More pragmatically: 'It's about problem solving – a firm structure to help you tackle projects, problems, any issue you face at work, where you have to take decisions, find solutions, evaluate them. It encompasses all of these.'

One engineer expressed amazement that 'the common issue we all had, regardless of how our projects were defined, was dealing with people – staff colleagues or bosses.' Which in turn gave 'comfort that I'm not alone with this problem. Others experience it as well.' And having a common issue means everyone's insights are likely to be helpful and a source of good ideas.

A sales manager said simply: 'It's the best course I've ever been on.'

For a chief executive in a local authority, who admitted to having few peers to talk to at work, there was 'nothing else like it . . . It's a holistic approach – you bring the whole person to it, not just a person in a role – and it encourages you to be a whole person wherever you are, so you use not just your knowledge but your whole experience and your emotions. It can be draining, but it's powerful. You come and talk of a "disaster" at

---

work, and you go away feeling the confidence to deal with it.'

'I always come away revitalized and re-energized' said another senior manager. And he went on to say 'It gives you time and space to stand back and reflect . . . unfreeze your thoughts, rise above everyday problems . . . brings things into perspective in a non-judgemental, supportive yet challenging way, and it says "what can I do about . . . ?" which makes you take responsibility and ownership. It's very exciting but at times daunting. But you get a great sense of achievement.'

'It's the only meeting you go to where you're not "in role" and expected to play a part. You're expected – in fact pushed – to be the real you.'

Another participant commented how 'It produces a radical change in how you operate. You are personally challenged. The onus is on you as a person, and not simply you as a role-player in some large organizational theatre. It makes you confront who you are, how you want to be, what's stopping you and what you're doing to yourself and to others.'

For one participant it was '. . . like putting together your own programme . . . You find that in addition to your project, the ostensible learning vehicle, you're simultaneously working on time management, empowerment, presentation skills, assertiveness . . .'

So, as one manager put it: 'It's a process that allows managers to blossom. It shows them the power of discovery and gives them greater sophistication as managers.'

To many it was '. . . a programme which forces you to face up to and tackle the real problems – and not the symptoms.'

And to a young manager in his first job it was 'magic . . . in that it draws on everything you know, and uses it.'

Is anything taught on an action learning programme?

On a classic action learning programme there is no teaching. This is probably one of the most difficult aspects of action learning for new participants to understand. How can you learn without being taught?

It *is* possible, as participants come to realize. They each bring so much experience and knowledge, and as they share with one another they gradually perceive that between them they often have insights and even answers, and do not need experts to come along and tell them. (For more on the thinking behind this, see Part 2.)

This is not to dismiss experts or expert knowledge: there is a time and place for them. So, action learning programmes are often run after taught courses, to help consolidate the knowledge that participants have acquired – either through lectures, case studies or reading.

Some action learning programmes do in fact incorporate a measure of taught input on subjects that are either of direct relevance to the projects or the learning that the programme is hoping to achieve.

How is the programme structured?

The programme begins with an introduction to action learning itself. Thus participants will be introduced to a bit of the theory of action learning, and will be told of the importance of projects, and how these are chosen and managed. Participants will also be introduced to the action learning way of working in a set which, as we've already said, differs quite considerably from the way we are used to working with others in different settings.

Briefly, the action learning way of working involves focusing at any one time on each individual member of the set in turn, giving them what is called 'airspace'. During this time it is the task of fellow set members to focus on that one person

17

and his or her issues, questions or project, and concentrate on helping them. Ideally, each set member will be given their own airspace in the course of each meeting.

The way the set works is by asking good, helpful questions, and by providing feedback or sharing insights. What it does not do is give advice. Participants say it takes time to learn to work in this new way, but that once learnt it is very productive.

So, on an introductory day, participants will be given the opportunity to experience – even if only for a short time – working in this way. (For more on how a set works, see pp. 88–9.)

DIFFERENT TYPES OF PROGRAMMES

Programmes are normally run in-company*, so that the participants are all drawn from one organization (albeit from different offices up and down the country). Mixed-company programmes, on the other hand, include participants from different companies and organizations.

Within these programmes there are four types of projects:

- in-company ones where everyone works in a familiar setting, ie within their own department or section
- in-company programmes where projects are undertaken in unfamiliar departments or sections
- mixed-company programmes where projects are based in the participants' own work area
- mixed-company ones where the project is not only in a different company but also in an unfamiliar department or section.

The most common are the first two. The third option – mixed-company with participants working on their own projects – is normally reserved for more senior people.

---

* The term 'in-company' refers to any organization, whether a limited company or not.

An example of the fourth are programmes run in multi-national organizations. One recently run programme, for instance, took place in a ferry company with operations in many European countries. The participants came from each of these countries and represented a variety of functions; each set then focused on an issue to be resolved in one particular field of activity – such as finance and freight. Another possibility is a 'mixed-company' set drawn from separately managed companies within a vast conglomerate (indeed, one of the sets interviewed for this book was made up of employees from separate businesses which came under one large umbrella organization).

In-company programmes

In-company programmes are run for people at all levels of responsibility, with the possible exception of the most senior managers and chief executives. The involvement of such very senior people would depend on the purpose of the programme (eg culture change). Because senior managers have no obvious peers within an organization, experience has shown that the issues they are working on and confronting daily are best tackled in the company of other managing directors and chief executives, and in an environment where they feel free to express their doubts and queries. (For more on programmes run specifically for senior managers, see p. 277.)

An in-company programme of action learning tends to be championed and hence introduced by the management-development or training manager, a line manager, or a senior manager. Precisely who will participate depends very much on the aims of the programme. If it is a company-wide initiative – such as culture change or TQM (Total Quality Management) – then a wide cross-section of staff is likely to be involved. If it is for more loosely defined management development in general, eg a graduate development programme, then participants may be more specifically selected. And if it is for some other issue, such as creating a new staff appraisal system, participants will be selected according to their interest and, perhaps, knowledge.

Then there are programmes in which everyone has to be involved if the stated objectives are to be achieved, eg a team performance improvement programme. As a section manager in a major international electronics company pointed out, such programmes depend on including all members of staff. 'A rolling stone gathers moss,' he said. 'If you want to use action learning for a company-wide project – as we did – you need to involve everyone. Our programme was about improving performance – and that meant everyone. We involved everyone, 94 people in all. Those who were more motivated are now showing real results in terms of output, and that in turn is motivating those who were more negative or cynical about the programme, saying, "we've seen it all before." They now feel left behind – although it's caused some friction among those who don't want to, for whatever reason.'

In the words of a sales manager, company-wide programmes 'begin to remove tribalism from a company. You build teams into bigger teams, and create huge networks, whether you're in a big company or a small one. In a small one it's easier because you already know people better. But you still need to identify a common issue, such as TQM, for instance.'

'And if you want to introduce a culture change into a company, you've got to have a company-wide programme, with everyone involved, even though they begin by involving senior managers first, and then cascading down,' was the observation of an IT manager from a major insurance company.

Thus, programmes, and hence sets, can be made up of people from any level, whatever their function. They may then work either in mixed-function sets, or single-function sets. By and large it is usual to place people in sets with others of similar levels of responsibility, though this is not vital.

Participants on one of the largest in-company programmes in the UK (run some ten years ago by the
Prudential Assurance Company) listed, among a host of
other insights, the following:

'I realized that I did not have to toe the party line. I
was my own person and could make things happen.'

'Old style status takes a long time to change. Action
learning helped to build the foundation from which we
could make this change.

'It gave me a lot of self-confidence, realizing that I
could demand things of the organization if well argued,
rather than just accepting demands of the organization.'

'It stretched our thinking and made us go well outside
our normal perimeters.'

'I know of no other form of management training
activity which transformed line managers into zealots –
missionaries wanting to get their staff involved.'

Mixed-company programmes

In mixed-company programmes, participants will, as the
name implies, come from different organizations: public and
private, large and small. But programmes run for separate
businesses who nevertheless belong to the same parent company are also, in a sense, mixed-company programmes. As
with in-company sets, participants can be drawn from different functions or all from the same one.

Mixed-company programmes are often attended not only
by more senior people, but also those who are investigating
the benefits of action learning with a view to running in-
company programmes within their own organization. One
newcomer to action learning – a senior manager in a small
building firm that was becoming involved in Investors in
People – after participating in a mixed-company programme
decided, on the basis of his own experience, to lobby for the

introduction of a company-wide programme for his firm's employees because 'it values everyone, includes them actively, they're listened to, they can ask questions . . . and everyone will begin to take pride at work and have a sense of achievement. But I do need to persuade the boss that it will be cost-effective – since even people coming to set meetings have to be "costed" in some way. But he's already in favour, because he's seen that those already in a pilot programme are beginning to deliver the goods and we're having much less aggro from our customers since we began.'

(For more on the advantages and/or disadvantages of mixed-company versus in-company programmes, see pp. 102–104.)

There are now a number of university-based management MSc and MBA programmes run along action learning lines. These by and large consist of mixed-company sets; although sometimes personnel from one organization may all attend the same management programme and hence choose to work in the same set (as is the case, for instance, with action learning based programmes being run for National Health Service personnel).[1]

WHY UNDERTAKE AN ACTION LEARNING PROGRAMME?

The reasons for organizations running – or individuals attending – action learning programmes are many and varied.

Some individuals on mixed-company sets were, as we have seen, simply curious to find out what it was about, and whether it was appropriate and of interest for their organization or department.

One senior manager in a small firm had come on a mixed-company programme because he had found no other programme that catered for his needs or questions. He came, however, in trepidation: 'I'd had no formal education and thought I'd be out of my depth. I soon found I wasn't, and it was one of the most interesting and rewarding experiences of my life.'

In that same set was an IT manager from a large insurance company. He had some doubts about a mixed-function, mixed-company set. 'I came to investigate whether it was a programme that we could usefully use. I think we – my staff – would gain more by working together in an in-company set, and resolving our own specific issues.' This manager also felt that he would want a more 'focused' approach to the programme, probably with his staff working on a group project.

Participants on another mixed-company set came because they had all taken part in a week-long management development programme, and the issues raised by it were of such impact that they wanted to continue or '. . . to consolidate our learning,' as some of them put it. In fact several of them stated that they personally could not imagine joining an action learning programme other than as a sequel to a taught course. Few organizations, however, use action learning in this way – although it is of course ideal for such consolidation and for testing out and experimenting with the new knowledge and ideas gained on courses.

One major building society decided to investigate action learning following an intensive investment in more traditional one- and two-day courses on all the subjects available for managers (from 'how to motivate your staff' to time management). They concluded that although some people benefited from such programmes, overall they were not seeing the results they had hoped for in terms of higher performance and more effective management. They felt that action learning might 'pull things together'. The response, after the programme, was that it had done just that: given their managers much greater insights, much greater self-confidence, an increased commitment to their work, and much better rapport with their staff.

To 'increase team performance' was the aim of another major organization, this time in the international telecommunications sector. They felt action learning would give their entire staff the scope for working together – the ultimate goal – on real-life projects, hence providing a much greater learning curve. Their programme was specifically designed to achieve this aim. The sets – mostly made up of people from different though work-related sections – were, they felt, also an ideal way of introducing the concept of teamworking.

A major retailer's reasons for using action learning – in a programme that had encompassed staff in all parts of its multi-outlet business – were that it was simply the best form of developmental training they knew of.

An institution of higher education, where departments formed very separate entities, created a programme with the aim of '. . . engaging senior managers in real management problems, and changing the culture.'

And another organization used action learning as a 'radical' approach to tackling the issue of erstwhile site engineers having, because of reorganization and a rationalizing of work, to become 'consultant' engineers. No role model existed for them to follow, there were no previous job descriptions to pick up. Faced with the problem of enabling the engineers to tackle the unknown, their solution was an action learning programme which allowed all those engineers to work together – 'comrades in adversity' as much as 'comrades in opportunity' – and by working on the job and sharing their experiences and insights, to establish what the new role was about.

Surrey County Council which runs many action learning programmes for all its staff, listed the following reasons:
- it is a good support mechanism for managers
- provides very useful thinking time
- provides space for reflection
- counteracts stress – slows down pace of work
- highlights experiential learning
- very empowering

- good for self- and manager-development, working on real management issues
- very powerful for individuals
- enables the development of counselling skills
- enables the development of consultancy skills, analytical questioning and problem solving
- provides space for self-discovery
- produces ways forward on work issues
- unlocking, unfreezing
- helps with the management of change
- provides cross-departmental and external exchange opportunities

For a survey of participants' experiences of action learning – What did they learn and gain? How useful was a programme? – skip to Part 3, which examines in detail all the elements that make up an action learning programme. Alternatively, if you want to explore more of the thinking behind action learning first, turn to Part 2.

PART 2

What is Action Learning? A Reflective Piece

In a book on action learning, it's obviously critical to state, right at the outset, what action learning is about and to give some definitions. As a starting point this in fact proves to be difficult. It is elusive. Reg Revans, the founding father of action learning, said that 'action learning takes so long to describe because it is so simple.'

SOME DEFINITIONS OF
ACTION LEARNING

Revans's original definitions talk about 'managers' learning; but the approach he has propounded is applicable and available to everyone and anyone. Various other 'action learners' have tried defining it, and perhaps a selection of their definitions will begin to give an insight into what action learning is:

It is learning by doing . . . We learn by doing from the cradle on. In action learning we go further by making arrangements – often very simple arrangements – to enhance the opportunities to learn from our experiences, and to speed up the process.

Jean Lawrence[1]

Action learning is an approach to the development of people in organizations which takes the task as the vehicle for learning. It is based on the premise that there is no learning without action and no sober and deliberate action without learning. On the whole our education system has not been based upon this principle. The method has been pioneered in work organizations and has three main components: people who accept responsibility for taking action on a particular issue; problems, or the task that people set themselves; and a set of six or so colleagues who support and challenge each other to make progress on problems. Action learning implies both self-development and organization development.

Mike Pedler[2]

A manager's tools are knowledge, skills and an accumulation of years of thinking, acting and discovery. Together these make up 'experience', with which he

29

or she faces the problems of management . . . Every problem tackled adds to that experience and from it he/she acquires a new mix of experience to take forward into the future. By sharing problems with others . . . every manager can use their experience and their perception to enlarge their own experience and enrich their learning.

David Sutton[3]

And Reg Revans writes: 'Action learning suggests that we may best master whatsoever unknown challenge appears, by working with others who seek to triumph in the same way'. He goes on to say that this is the prime reason why 'programmes should be collectively designed and launched by those who hope to profit from them.'

Furthermore:

The primary occupation of managers is to treat their problems (or to seize their opportunities) . . . in other words, managers must make up their minds about what to do and settle for doing it. All secondary activity should be linked as closely as possible to this everyday task. For this simple reason, action learning is cradled in the very task itself . . .[4]

When participants on action learning programmes were asked to define action learning, or explain what it meant to them, they too found it difficult to encapsulate this in one brief phrase or sentence.

'It's difficult to explain,' said one young scientific research officer. 'It seems very simple at the outset: a group of people who each have a real work project which they work on and learn from that, with the help and support of the other participants . . . but then it begins to get more complex.'

'It's about doing something and learning from it,' was another participant's response, though she went to say: 'but that's too simple because it's how you approach that action and how you learn that are important . . . and that's when defining action learning begins to get complicated!'

'It's a process of looking at an issue in front of others – of trying things out and reporting back,' was another attempt at a definition.

A managing director who has been involved with action learning for the past ten years explained what it was for him:

> There are a great many things that I learnt as fact, but they only have curiosity value until I can find ways of applying them. Learning by doing takes care of that and the experience provides a much more indelible memory than a transient fact.

THE FLAVOUR AND 'SPIRIT' OF ACTION LEARNING

The comments listed above came from people who – in spite of their inability to put into precise words a definition of action learning – had spent several months on action learning programmes, gaining and learning. 'I wish I could bottle it – it's so difficult to describe' was one participant's cry, implying that maybe you can't fully understand what action learning is about until you've tried it. It's like driving past a beautiful landscape: from the car you can describe the hills, streams, and trees, but until you stop the car, get out of it, walk, smell, feel and sense it . . . you don't really experience it. It's neither tourism nor voyeurism. Yet in order to tempt people into tasting it, something of the 'flavour' of action learning needs to be captured in words first, despite their limitations.

The participants' accounts in this book will convey some of that flavour. But words and even deeds alone do not convey the 'spirit' of action learning. That spirit has more to do with the energy and confidence that such a programme can give participants. 'I always come away full of energy and revitalized,' is a common observation. Yet the spirit of action learning that provides this energy demands that we put a stop to the 'busyness' we are so embroiled in and recognize the value of 'simply having the time to stand back and gain a perspective, to have time to think', a sentiment echoed by almost everyone on an action learning programme.

Others will tell you that the spirit has something to do with being honest and open, valuing others, having courage, and developing self-confidence – particularly after working with people, being listened to, being valued, being supported and yet pushed intellectually and emotionally.

One of the problems of describing action learning is that it means different things to different people. Yet there *is* a great deal that is common to all participants, and the best way for me to convey this is by using some simple signposting. Becoming involved in action learning is like going on a journey: you begin with the clear signposts and the route seems straightforward, but the further on the journey you go, the more the side routes and detours become significant. It is in this sense that action learning is a journey of discovery and development.

WHAT IS ACTION LEARNING ABOUT?

Action learning is a process that young children use continuously: they learn by doing something, by testing it out. They learn to walk by taking the risk of testing what it's like to stand hazardously on two legs rather than four. Later, they learn to ride a bicycle. But they only learn when they get on it and try out the balance, veer around crazily, probably fall off, until through practice they get to the stage of being so good at balancing that they can steer without even having their hands on the handlebars! But as we get older our learning by doing seems to get shelved, shunted to the sidelines. Instead we read, we listen to others (lecturers) talk about things. Gradually we begin to believe that because we have taken information/knowledge in 'cognitively', we have learned. And so we have, at one level. As a result, we know *about* – but this in itself doesn't mean we know *how* and *when* and *what if*.

Some of the participants I spoke to had taken this 'adult' approach to action learning. They had read about it – rather like the reader of this book! And their comments? As one said:

> I'd read quite a bit about action learning before coming on the programme, and it all seemed logical, pretty straightforward, almost commonsense. But 'it' didn't happen as I'd anticipated. As an engineer I'd expected to solve my 'problems' in a 'straight-line' approach – here's the problem, here's a solution – but it's not like that. You begin to work on whether what you have identified as the problem really is the problem . . . and that's when the real work of action learning begins.

Hands-on experience is in the end the only way to acquire the answers to these questions. Craftsmen take this approach when they learn a skill; training for certain professions (eg medicine) contains elements of this approach to learning. But training for the rest of us has been slow in taking up this practical approach.

Instead we go on one- and two-day courses or workshops which may even include some role-playing to help consolidate and anchor our learning. When we return to work, we are often still left with those nagging questions about how we can really apply what we've learnt; we may still feel there are questions we have which weren't covered, or parts of the course that we didn't take down sufficiently clearly in our notes.

We try out some of the new ideas we've memorized, and if we're lucky we feel we've been successful. On the other hand, we may not achieve what we hoped to and yet not quite understand why. Meanwhile, at the back of the mind, that list of gnawing questions remains. But what can we do about them, who can we ask?

Too often the temptation is to put this newly acquired

theoretical knowledge into a metaphorical drawer, file the beautiful binder we were given during the course on a bookshelf, and carry on as before.

Such was the experience of one manager on his return from a course on 'motivating your staff'. He didn't know how to begin to tackle his staff's lack of motivation. Should he talk to them each individually? Do something collectively? Where to start? So he did nothing. And it wasn't until he joined an action learning programme to help put this acquired knowledge into action that he came to the realization that in fact the issue was not how to motivate his staff, but how to motivate himself!

Cognitive learning no more makes a manager than a swimmer. The latter will drown the first time she jumps into the water if her coach never takes her out of the lecture hall, gets her wet, and gives her feedback on her performance.

H. Mintzberg

Anybody in management education can tell you that lectures and bookwork alone are not sufficient for developing people who have to take decisions in the real world.

Reg Revans

I hear and I forget . . . I see and I remember . . . I do and I understand.

Chinese proverb

Action learning is the opposite of chalk and talk

'It's the opposite of chalk and talk' is one way I often describe action learning. From chalk and talk we gain knowledge, but we can't know whether we're able to transfer that knowledge into practice until we try. That's where the action comes in – action on some work-focused issue that is close to the participant's heart. And it's through applying what we think we know, or behaving in ways that we think will be effective, by making mistakes and thus discovering what we don't know or understand, and by celebrating our successes and understanding how they came about – ie through recalling, reflecting on, asking questions about, and analysing all of this – that we gain insights, and understanding . . . and learn. We gain insights into how to be, how to behave, and what might be useful next time we find ourselves in a similar situation – 'similar', because nothing is ever the same again!

This process lies at the heart of action learning.

> It's a process that encourages and allows managers to blossom. It shows them the power of discovery and gives them greater sophistication as managers.

As one participant put it: 'It's unlike traditional courses where you work on make-believe projects and then, come Friday, you go back to reality and you're not sure what, if anything, you can take back, until you've tried it.'

So, back to the subject of this book, and the paradox of writing a book about it. You will learn *about* action learning by reading; you will become aware of the steps and stages of an action learning programme, and what you might learn and gain by participating in such a programme. But you won't really know the *how* of it until you've tested it, run a programme, been part of one yourself – experienced the 'how it works' in practice. It's the experience of living through it that consolidates book-based or course-based knowledge.

Action learning is about working on real issues, taking actions – not merely talking about them – and learning while doing so

It was during lecture-based courses that Reg Revans originally, and others subsequently, became aware that their student managers were relatively passive and lacking in energy in the classroom. They came to life, however, when they discussed their own 'back home' problems with one another. The message came over loud and clear: managers are people of action who learn from action (unlike lecturers and academics, whose action and learning is based around thoughts and ideas). The other message was that managers will help each other in the right environment; they are prepared to share their experience and insights; and they represent a great seam of untapped wealth. Any one room of, say, ten middle managers, or ten functionally experienced staff, has within it over 100 years' experience – often untapped and unshared.

And this, in a sense, is where the essential message of action learning originates: we learn best when we have a real work (or other) issue to resolve. We are more involved in, and committed to, the action (and the subsequent learning) if what we are trying to resolve, change or manage is something we are responsible for, something we have to tackle – maybe something we have never had to do before. Our tasks should therefore be based on such issues as how to get a team working well together, how to involve people in issues that affect their lives, how to introduce new working practices, how to tackle a new work role, how to increase sales, how to reduce costs, and so on.

Thus an action learning programme requires everyone to work on a real project. In this sense action learning is about working and learning simultaneously, so that work provides a valuable learning opportunity.

The essential idea in an action learning programme is that participants mustn't simply come up with a feasible, elegant solution on paper – as in a case study. As with any real actionable project, they have to work through various stages, such as investigating, talking with people, planning, designing, resourcing, evaluating as they go along, recommending and, if possible, implementing what they are recommending. In this way participants take responsibility from start to finish. Only by testing their ideas in practice will they know whether or not those ideas are effective and practical, whether any issues have been overlooked, what problems occur as a result, how to tackle them in turn, what to do differently in the future, and so on.

We're all aware that the skills and knowledge we have aren't always sufficient to help us with uncertainties, questions, challenges and opportunities that we face. In so many instances we find ourselves feeling unsure, puzzled, juggling with several options. An issue we are tackling suddenly appears less straightforward than it seemed at the outset; simple techniques don't work, our body of knowledge or skills seems unable or inadequate to provide easy solutions. The answers elude us.

Reg Revans makes a useful distinction to help – at one level – with such dilemmas. He points out that there is a difference between what he calls 'puzzles' and 'problems'. We are dealing with *puzzles* when there is a known 'answer' to our questioning and probing though we don't yet know it. Probably another course of study or some more reading will give us the solution. By contrast, *problems* are those issues, challenges, opportunities where there is no single solution, no one way of doing things. It's a question of juggling with insights, ideas, experience, and deciding what is the best solution in these particular circumstances.

Puzzle – an embarrassment to which a solution already exists, where there is one right answer
Problem – no existing solution; different people in different circumstances will suggest different courses of action

---

Action learning is geared to helping people deal with problems, not puzzles. And if the word 'problem' sounds too negative – as many participants claim – there is a host of other words that perhaps define more clearly the issues that action learning deals with best: quandaries and questions, uncertainties, irritations, challenges or opportunities.

So, as you come face to face with some issue or challenge, you become aware of your own questions, uncertainties, even doubts. That's the time when you are most likely to learn, because resolving those issues is central to your being effective and successful. In other words, you learn best when you have some concrete issue on which to 'hang' your learning, rather than trying to learn in abstract.

As George Bernard Shaw said: 'Activity is the only road to knowledge.'

Thus, in action learning, participants focus on tasks or projects which in turn become the vehicle for learning (or rather, *one* of the vehicles!).

The real voyage of discovery consists not in seeking new lands, but seeing with new eyes.

Proust

A person does not gather learnings as possessions but rather becomes a new person.

Gib Atkin

When you read, you gain knowledge; when you 'do', you gain experience; when you reflect, you gain an understanding of both.

Anon

LEARNING WITH OTHERS

'Learning with and from others similarly engaged' is one of the basic tenets of action learning. It is built into the nature of the programmes. A group of people will resolve issues in a more effective and imaginative way – if they work effectively together – than one person.

Reg Revans has always said that managerial learning is 'a social exchange in which managers learn with and from one another during the diagnosis and treatment of real problems'.

We none of us have a monopoly on good ideas, insights, or even information – there is now too much of it for any one person to grasp, possibly even to understand. Moreover, we always bring our own perspective to everything – inevitably! That perspective will colour what we see and do; it may not alter from year to year, and so may prevent us from growing and changing; it can also create a block for others who wish to develop and change.

But when we work with others who are also concerned with trying to understand what is really happening around us, we gain from the searching and questioning that each one of us goes through. Improbable as this may sound initially, it is something that participants referred to time and time again: how beneficial it is to work with others . . . even on *their* issues.

Reg Revans is fond of quoting Lord Rutherford, with whom he worked at the Cavendish Laboratory in Cambridge during the late 1920s: after an afternoon's 'action learning' (the term was not yet coined) with a group of colleagues whose task was to find some means of financing their laboratory and its research at a time when the threat of closure loomed large, Lord Rutherford exclaimed: 'Gentlemen, I have in the course of this afternoon become aware of the depth of my own ignorance. What does yours look like to you?'

So, the challenge of others revealing their doubts and their areas of ignorance, and working with them to create more insight and clarity is as helpful to those examining their actions as it is to the rest of the 'comrades in adversity'

(Revans' term for this group of learners – others have coined more positive-sounding terms, such as A. Mumford's 'comrades in opportunity').

I was asked, while preparing this book, whether it was possible to undertake action learning as a solo activity – on your own. Intellectually it clearly is, though only up to a point. We are, after all, thinking beings. 'It's something that I need to learn to do without others – on my own' was the comment of one young participant after her colleagues in adversity had quizzed her, pushed her, and made her think of issues that hadn't occurred to her. But doing so on our own is weaker, because we lose the benefit of others. How can we guarantee that on our own we won't merely pursue our own inclinations, that we will challenge ourselves as much as a group of others will force us to? Do we really have such faith in ourselves?[5]

The set

The action learning term for such a focused group is a *set*. It differs in a number of fundamental ways from a group of people gathered together around a table, or in the pub, to talk about an issue. Briefly (for the rest of this book will go into the details) its characteristics are:

- it is always a small group – of no more (ideally) than five or six people
- it meets regularly and frequently
- each member has a task or project (the *action*)
- each member is given *airspace* – their own time for talking
- it uses primarily a *questioning* approach to working (ie no advice and few solutions)
- it focuses on learning as much as on action
- it probably works with a set adviser present
- it does not judge, but is there to support – and also to challenge everyone in the set

Such a set, once it begins to work effectively, will increase everyone's learning, and repertoire of responses to the various situations and circumstances the participants face.

LEARNING WITHOUT EXPERT INSTRUCTION

Action learning places a high value on each individual, so you can learn without experts, lecturers, and specialists. This may seem like heresy to many – and such a bold statement does require some modifying.

In a 'classic' action learning programme there is no taught element. The programme centres on the combined expertise of the set members. The thinking behind this is that we all of us have a great deal of knowledge and experience which, when combined with others' knowledge, experiences, and perspectives is often as valuable as having an expert come in to teach.

> . . . in true action learning it is not what a man already knows and tells that sharpens the countenance of his friend, but what he does not know and what his friend does not know either. It is recognized ignorance not programmed knowledge that is the key to action learning: men start to learn with and from each other only when they discover that no-one knows the answer but all are obliged to find it.
>
> Revans

We have been brought up to believe that experts know best. We undervalue ourselves, are in turn undervalued, and lose confidence in our own insights and abilities. And so we bring in experts who often confirm what we have been thinking – which is in itself useful! There are, of course, areas of specific knowledge where an expert can add considerable insight. But frequently someone within a set has that expertise already. And when it comes to knowing our own situations and circumstances, each of us is the expert on that.

Action learning stresses the value of the so-called non-experts, thus handing back to each of us our own 'power'. Reg Revans is provocative when talking about experts, for they are mostly, as he puts it, experts of past knowledge. The past, however, is not necessarily a guide to what will be useful or relevant in the future. Moreover, experts are frequently pedlars of packages and solutions that fit all problems! More useful, according to Revans, is the ability to ask questions, and thus to see where past expertise may have some relevance, but also where it is of little use.

How often do we go on a course, hear ideas and suggestions that we feel might be effective or relevant but which we subsequently fail to implement for a number of complex reasons – there wasn't time, we didn't want to stick our necks out, it would be rejected anyway, we'd be told it had been tried before, no one ever listens, and so on. Alternatively, we go on a course only to find that much of what we hear is only of marginal relevance to our own circumstances. Or, we are told so much, we simply forget whole chunks of it – remembering only bits that are relevant today, not knowing what may be relevant tomorrow, by which time it's too late because the lecture's been forgotten. Or, worse still, we don't fully follow or understand what we've been told but there is no chance to stop, examine it, ask questions and try to understand. Anyway, maybe everyone else present fully understands and we're alone in failing to grasp it. So, we remain silent – and confused.

What happens in an action learning programme is that our belief in ourselves is restored. We realize – through having to think and work through issues we face – that we often have the answers to our questions and problems. With the help and support of the group with whom we work, we test out our own ideas in practice, evaluate them and learn from so doing. 'I kept asking questions and seeking others' answers, until I realized that the answers were in me.'

Action learning programmes create an environment where participants go through this process of recalling, analysing and thinking in the company of others, similarly engaged. Such a group becomes a supportive, challenging team, ready to give participants feedback, to help, and to question . . . and it is when this begins to happen that action learning becomes complex and very rich.

Our own experience is the best teacher

Action learning is based on the premise that our own experience is one of the most useful 'teachers' – if we know how, and are prepared, to make the most of it.

Over a lifetime we gather a huge mass of data about our work, our relationships at work (and elsewhere), and about our own and others' behaviour. This accumulation of experience forms the basis of our opinions, generalizations, convictions – our 'theories in use'. But, in the words of one participant, 'experiences, like dreams, need interpreting'; or as T.S. Eliot said, 'We had the experience but missed the meaning.'

Interpreting our own experiences and actions

To realize the true value of our experience we need to learn to reflect on it, to put our 'theories in use' to the test by sharing them with fellow set members who will respond with insights and questions of their own. Together we can learn from our multiple experiences, both 'good' and 'bad', successful and less successful. It is a process that requires time, openness – and often courage.

It is for this reason – the stress on the learning – that sets usually need to work with a set adviser, at least in the initial stages of a programme. Without the set adviser pulling the set back from rushing into action, constantly asking them 'what have you learnt?', action learning becomes merely another action-focused programme where the experience and the action are not fully explored and reflected on. Without such feedback, we learn little.

$$L = P + Q$$

This is action learning shorthand for: learning consists of programmed knowledge plus questions.

- **P** – *programmed knowledge* – is the expert knowledge, the knowledge in books, what we are told to do because that is how it has been done for decades.
- **Q** – *questioning* – is just that: questioning what aspect of this previous knowledge and experience is useful, relevant or helpful here and now as we deal with our immediate issue.
- **L** – *learning* – results from the combination of the two, ie all the knowledge we accumulate through reading or going on courses and listening to lectures (the knowledge of the experts) and Q (asking questions about that programmed knowledge and about the circumstances you find yourself in).

Hence $L = P + Q$.

Q is the important part of the equation, for it means we test out each situation we find ourselves in, to try and understand it better, and see if the P we know is relevant or whether we are facing a new situation where past knowledge and life encounters are not going to be of much help.

Each of us has a mass of accumulated life encounters from which we create our own theories and on which we then proceed to act. Returning to the equation: this mass of accumulated encounters is a form of P. It represents our own programmed knowledge and it is this, as much as the knowledge in books, that we need to question.

Reg Revans then has another equation:

$$L > C$$

In other words, learning has to be greater than change. What he means is that to survive, to keep up with changes around us, our learning, and the speed at which we learn, has to be greater than change. This obviously has implications for the world in the 1990s. We hear everywhere that change is accelerating, that nothing is static, everything is constantly changing. So, if we accept the equation that $L > C$, it means we have to learn ($P + Q$) at a fast rate. But the faster the change, the more rapidly P will become outdated. That leaves us with Q. The better our questions, the more opportunity of accelerated learning.

Asking questions – examining, thinking – these are fundamental aspects of action learning.

Action learning is therefore an excellent complement to standard teaching courses where you learn about X, Y and Z, because real life isn't so neat and tidy. When you're back at work and you begin to wonder how to use what you have learned, what would be useful, you find you forgot some parts of it or don't seem to be applying others as effectively as you hoped – that's when action learning programmes come into their own: to help you apply your learning and consolidate the knowledge.

We know that we have learnt when we can do something differently.

This may result from seeing things differently, gaining a different understanding of them, being able to think differently or ask different questions.

Put simply, learning – as we use the word in everyday language – is often applied to memorizing (as the *Brain of Britain* programme implies), or to merely understanding intellectually after reading something or hearing a lecture; or applying some newly acquired skill, ie doing something differently; or developing and changing in some way, after an experience.

L = *Memorizing*

L = *Understanding* something intellectually

L = *Applying* some newly acquired skill, ie taking action and doing something differently

L = *Experiencing*: an inner development which touches on beliefs and attitudes, and which leads to development

Said one branch manager from a major building society:

I was sent on this programme because, although I'd attended every management course available in the company, I still wasn't performing or achieving. And that was because, although I knew a great deal 'about' various managerial topics, I was unsure of how to apply them, and what to do if I didn't get things quite right . . . And then I'd lose confidence, or find it was easier to simply behave as I had before . . . This programme has enabled me to use – to test out and apply – all that 'chalk and talk' that I'd absorbed and kept in my head, but not really applied in any coherent fashion.

We need to be able to examine and ask ourselves questions about these expert or theoretical solutions or ways of doing things. We need to apply our own critical assessments and insights, and either choose what we think will be helpful, or devise some other ways of resolving the issues we face.

Participants on action learning programmes are made to focus primarily on asking questions, and are discouraged from giving advice (a form of programmed knowledge).

Questioning oneself and others who are on the programme, not to find answers but rather to explore, uncover, unpeel (as the skins of an onion), to get at the core issue, and to get insights and begin to understand.

Through being asked questions and having to give explanations or answers, you hear yourself talk, you hear your own inconsistencies or doubts, or you confirm what you think . . . but doing it out aloud is different from asking yourself 'in your head'. You hear things – in fact you say things – you don't necessarily think in the silence of your head.

Through this focus on one person, and the asking of questions, to try and unravel meaning, a set is engaging in 'dialogue' with that person, rather than having a 'discussion'. David Bohm makes a useful distinction between dialogue and discussion.

Dialogue from the Greek 'logos' meaning 'word', and 'dia' meaning 'through'. A dialogue emphasizes the idea of a 'meaning' that flows between people from which emerges a greater understanding – possibly even a shared meaning.

Discussion (same root as percussion and concussion) emphasizes analysis, breaking up/down, and different viewpoints.

'A discussion', says David Bohm, 'is like a ping-pong match, with people batting ideas around in order to win a game . . . In a dialogue there is no attempt to gain points . . . in a dialogue everyone wins.'[6]

Action learning is about questioning

Questioning – learning to ask the right questions – is the fundamental aspect of action learning.

Questioning – more and more discriminating questioning – is at the heart of action learning . . . The simple nudge of a question occurring as one responds to another can change the way we see ourselves and be a permanent unrepeatable eye-opener.

And:

Questions always lead to more questions, and perhaps to more discriminating questions. It seems unlikely we will be able to make progress on the vast organizational problems in businesses, government and society without developing the skills of asking and responding to more and more discriminating questions. It is certain that we will not find in any book an answer to how to distribute food to the starving; how to enable computers to arrange to do heavy, dangerous and repetitive work without causing hardship to people; how to ensure that we give adequate health care to all new born babies; or how to house even our present population.[7]

Jean Lawrence

THE REFLECTIVE ELEMENT

Built into the processes of action learning is a large reflective element. As we are asked – or ask ourselves – questions, we are pulled back or propelled forward in our thoughts. Participants on a programme are made to look back and reflect on what they did (the action) or did not do, and on what happened. But equally importantly, participants are also made to look back at what they said and felt; and on what others said or did, or did not do. It is by replaying events, conversations, and feelings that we can begin to understand why we did, or did not, achieve something, or what was stopping us. We may also reflect on what else we could have done, or what we could have done differently – and what results that might have brought.

The reflection is also about examining what we believe and value, our understanding and insights, and how we see ourselves changing and moving – or unable to because we seem stuck. Being questioned by others, or hearing their own reflections on themselves, is a powerful way of examining those parts of us which, in the end, drive our actions and behaviours.

Reflecting – recalling, thinking about, pulling apart, making sense, trying to understand – is crucial to our learning. It makes us more aware of ourselves, of others, and of what is happening around us. The process of action learning gives us the time to do this. It also legitimizes reflection; points up the benefits. Reflection is a stage in the *learning cycles* (eg Kolb and Revans, see p. 51) which participants in action learning (and indeed any other learning experiences) are introduced to and encouraged to follow to a greater or lesser degree (see pp. 167–9).

We can begin to build up the basic action learning equation (see above) to look like this:

$$L = P + Q + A + R$$

Here A represents the action (or the conversation or thoughts and feelings); and R is the reflection.

As one participant said:

> It gives you time and space to stand back and reflect, unfreeze your thoughts, rise above everyday problems, bring things into perspective, get others' perspectives – all in a non-judgemental, supportive yet challenging way . . . and say 'so what can I/you/do about it?', ie take responsibility and ownership. It's very exciting if at times daunting. But you get a great sense of achievement.

And another said:

> It gives you the time and ability to move away from tasks and activities and see and understand and learn about – and learn from – what you're doing. At work we're simply achievers of activity.

I've realized that the time out for thinking and reflecting is crucial. I now often go out for a quick walk and take my 'problem' with me for a walk!

LEARNING, DEVELOPING AND CHANGING

It is this constant emphasis on learning and how it is achieved which is one of the distinguishing hall-marks of action learning – the asking of the question 'so what did I learn from that?' which becomes second-nature. (There are other learning and experiential programmes that bear some resemblance to action learning, but which differ in many fundamental ways, see below.)

Thus the task or project (the action) part of a programme provides – at least initially – the main vehicle for learning. As time goes by, participants find more learning opportunities. In fact, the set and its process become major sources of learning (see below).

The Kolb and Revans 'learning cycles'

Learning from our actions thus involves undertaking some actions (a *project* which consists of various tasks to be carried out, behaviours, conversations, and so on), recalling them, being questioned about them, reflecting on them, trying to understand what was happening, coming to some conclusions or having some insights, preparing to do something differently next time, and then beginning on some 'new' actions (a continuation of a task or project).

Diagrammatically such learning cycles are represented in fig. 1.

In a sense, though, they need to be shown as spirals for hopefully we do not return to the same place from which we started – that would not be learning. Instead we move to a different place, hence the notion of something moving and changing, ie a spiral.

Strictly speaking, reflecting is something we should be

fig. 1

Kolb and Revans Learning Cycles

Kolb Cycle

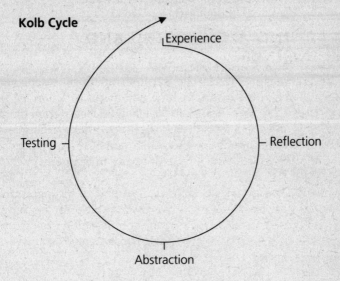

Experience

Testing

Reflection

Abstraction

Revans Cycle

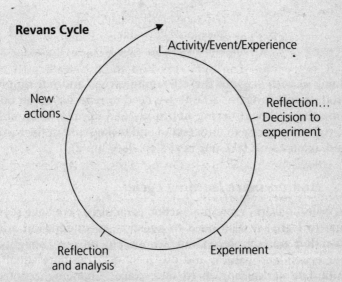

Activity/Event/Experience

New actions

Reflection…
Decision to experiment

Reflection and analysis

Experiment

51

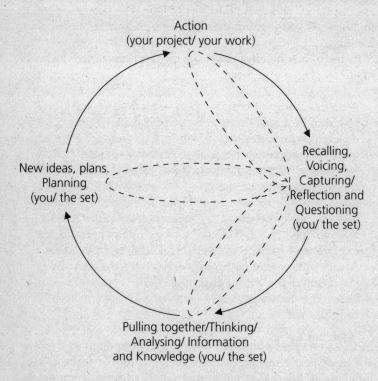

Action
(your project/ your work)

Recalling,
Voicing,
Capturing/
Reflection and
Questioning
(you/ the set)

New ideas, plans.
Planning
(you/ the set)

Pulling together/Thinking/
Analysing/ Information
and Knowledge (you/ the set)

doing at each stage of these learning cycles, and not simply
after undertaking an 'action': we need to reflect even on our
reflections (though trying not to get tied up in knots!), and
to reflect as we try to understand and make sense of theories,
and again as we take our next steps (see fig. 2).

... And an inner learning cycle:

In order to learn, more than action is required. We have seen
that to learn we also need to question, to understand and
to reflect not simply on our actions but on our thoughts,
our beliefs and values, and our feelings. These are equally
important if learning is to take place. Changing actions,

ie behaviours, without changing underlying beliefs and assumptions, will be a short-term affair. To change we need to undergo more fundamental shifts in our thoughts and feelings.

A useful distinction between *action* and *experience* has been made by Logan and Stuart:[8]

> A distinction can be drawn between an outer and inner world of human existence. Activity is focused upon and enacted in an outer world, whilst experience is located in an individual's inner world . . . Juch comments that '. . . those who devote their major attention and efforts to the world outside them . . . dealing with people and tasks and situations in the environment . . . may become out of touch with their inner capacities or purpose in life . . .' That inner focus – which characterizes experience – may be bypassed or short-cut by predominantly outer-oriented activity. The more that activity is characterized by the 'busyness' and flitting about behaviour typical of action managers, the more likely that this will occur.

In addition to recalling and reflecting on our actions, there is an 'inner' experiencing – more to do with our feelings and inner thoughts – that we also need to address if we are to truly learn and change. 'Confronting our own ignorance', owning up to the fact that we don't know, maybe even admitting to the fear this causes and how we therefore cover it up by bluster or even aggression or by remaining silent – these are examples of inner experience.

Diagrammatically, then, there is an inner learning cycle or spiral (see fig. 3).

It is only by tackling our inner experiences that we begin to gain the full value of action learning and see its potential. If we don't face up to these very common and human experiences we diminish ourselves and others. It's at this level – if participants are willing to explore these inner caverns – that action learning becomes truly powerful.

fig. 3   *Inner Experiential Cycle*

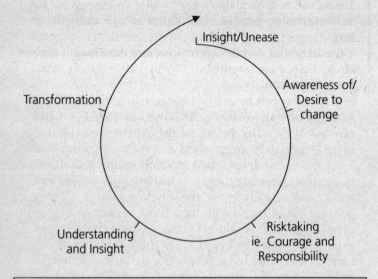

It is not hard to stand behind one's successes. But to accept responsibility for one's failures, to accept them unreservedly as failures that are truly one's own, that cannot be shifted somewhere else or onto something else, and actively to accept . . . the price that has to be paid for it: that is devilishly hard.'[9]

Vaclav Havel

We will only begin to learn when we become aware of – admit to – our own ignorance and are prepared to do something about it.

Revans

We do not see things as they, we see them as we are.

Talmud

Denial is a way of life. More accurately, it is a way of diminishing life, of making it seem more manageable. Denial is the alternative to transformation.

> Personal denial, mutual denial, collective denial. Denial of facts and feelings. Denial of experience, a deliberate forgetting of what we see and hear. Denial of our capabilities. Politicians deny problems, parents deny their vulnerability, teachers deny their biases, children deny their intentions. Most of all we deny what we know in our bones . . .
>
> M. Ferguson[10]

Learning how to learn

The challenge for action learning is to enable people to be more effective, not simply for the duration of the programme but for the rest of their lives. The power of action learning is that in tackling the set project we acquire tools to help us face future problems and challenges more confidently and effectively.

Learning is concerned with accumulating new facts and figures, new skills and behaviours. It is also about gaining new understanding and becoming more aware. It may lead to us changing our beliefs and attitudes. In this sense, learning carries with it the implication of doing things differently, of changing, be it our actions, beliefs, behaviour or attitudes – ourselves, in fact.

By going around the learning spirals – by 'doing', by stopping to reflect, by trying to understand – we explore different approaches and experience various stages in learning. Each of us is better at, or has a preference for, certain ways of learning.

Learning preferences and styles:

To paraphrase a whole volume of work, Honey and Mumford in their *The Manual of Learning Styles* divided those who learn from experience into four categories (these categories are not exclusive but serve merely as an indicator of preference and whichever preference is currently dominant):

- *activists* who prefer immediate action, perhaps stopping to consider after the event;
- *reflectors* who prefer to stop and think, and tend to be cautious;
- *theorists* who integrate what they have seen or done into sound rational schemes;
- *pragmatists* who are keen on trying out ideas, theories and techniques.

The 'styles' of learning of these four types of learner coincide with stages in the learning cycles/spirals:

- doing something – *experiencing*;
- thinking about what happened – *reviewing*;
- drawing some conclusions – *concluding*;
- deciding what to do in a similar situation – *planning*.

According to Honey and Mumford:

> . . . [if you are] an all-round learner, you are likely to manage each stage of this process consciously and well. Your activist tendencies will ensure you have plenty of experiences. Your reflector and theorist tendencies will ensure that afterwards you review and reach conclusions. Your pragmatist tendencies will ensure that you plan future implementation.

We tend to opt for activities that are most congruent with our individual style of working/learning. But as the authors point out, '. . . if you want to be fully equipped to learn from experience, you will need to develop styles which at present you do not use.'

One way of doing this is by working in a set, seeing how others work and studying how their approach differs from our own – the way they tackle their learning, the way they behave in the set, and the language and concepts they use. Thus set members can learn from colleagues with differing styles. Activists, for example, by being asked questions which force them to weigh the pros and cons before piling into the next activity, will discover the benefits of a more reflective approach.

In order to gain the most from others, we need to acquire learning skills: those behaviours that help us learn. Mumford has listed a number of factors which aid the learning process:

- establishing effective criteria for yourself
- measuring your effectiveness
- identifying your own learning needs
- planning your personal learning
- taking advantage of learning opportunities
- reviewing your own learning process
- listening to others
- accepting help
- facing unwelcome information
- taking risks and tolerating anxieties
- analysing what other successful performers do
- knowing yourself
- sharing information

A further distinction between types of learner identified by Honey and Mumford rests upon attitudes to learning:

- Incidental learners learn when shocked or jolted into a realization;
- Intuitive learners just somehow learn but aren't quite sure how it happened;
- Retrospective learners as the term implies learn by recalling and reflecting;
- Prospective learners plan to learn.

This emphasis on 'conscious learning' is interesting, for it implies that maybe the best learners are simply that – forever

Conscious Competence

Conscious Awareness and Reflection ⟶ Learning

Unconscious Incompetence	Conscious Incompetence
Unconscious Competence	Conscious Competence

fig. 4

awake and aware. Many participants in action learning programmes talk of the greater awareness and consciousness they now have of what is happening around them. To adapt the 'Johari window' analogy: rather than becoming 'unconsciously competent' they are implying that they remain 'consciously competent' (see fig. 4).

As one participant wrote in a reflective document: 'What I am trying to do now is control which learning style I adopt through recognizing at a given point what is happening, and adopting a style that I feel is most appropriate to the situation. For example, at meetings where I am genuinely enthused by ideas and discussion, my activist and pragmatist roles dominate. I am consciously forcing myself to adopt a more reflective style in these situations. And I'm doing the same in my decision-making process back at work.'

More important for action learning, however, is this notion of 'opportunistic' learning (see p. 300). For that is what action learners become – as witnessed by the remarks quoted in this book. They have begun to learn from a whole variety of opportunities. Life, and work, are their classroom.

A wise person learns when he or she can. A fool learns when he or she must.

Duke of Wellington (*paraphrased*)

To a great experience one thing is essential – an experiencing nature.

Walter Bagehot

We are all surrounded by opportunities. But they only exist once seen. And they are only seen if they are looked for.

Edward De Bono (*paraphrased*)

So, coming back to action learning. Action learning makes people aware of their style – but also encourages people to become prospective and opportunistic learners. 'I have realized', said one participant, 'that everything is data. I now expect to learn from any situation I'm in.'

By focusing on work-centred projects and action, action learning takes learning out of the classroom and into the workplace (or anywhere else, for that matter). In this way it opens our eyes to the fact that we can learn from anything, anywhere, and anytime – by overhearing conversations, reading a book, taking time out to reflect, experimenting, observing some activity, the possibilities are endless.

By becoming opportunistic learners, we also begin to gain insights into how and in what circumstances we best learn – a useful insight to have when we face new challenges or worries, for it means we can reproduce the circumstances which will help us learn faster and better in the future. And the faster we learn, the more effective we become. So, if I discover that I learn best by being asked questions, I create circumstances where I will be asked; if I discover I learn best by listening to others, I again create those circumstances, and so on.

Too old to learn?

For many people learning stops at 18, or at most 21. 'We're too old to learn,' they say.

Are we ever too old to learn – and change? The answer has to be yes, so long as we shut our minds to the possibility. Learning demands a certain humility. Reg Revans's statement that it is only when we recognize our own ignorance that we begin to learn implies that we need to overcome our own internal barriers – and those of others – if we are to continue learning.

Learning is our ticket to survival. Indeed, Revans maintains that if we are to survive our rate of learning needs to be greater than the rate of change.

Learning is fundamental to growth, adaptation, change and progress. By not learning we remain as we are, we stay in the same place – which may of course be the most comfortable place to be. And it may, on reflection, also be the 'right' place for us to be at any one point in time, provided we opt to remain after considering the alternatives rather than out of habit or fear. Facing up to the fact that we could be doing things differently – not how we've always done them in the past, perhaps – often demands courage. Similarly, to admit that we do not know or understand something, that we need help and insights from others, can be a fearsome experience. What will people think of us? Will they laugh at us?

> When something becomes a habit we stop paying attention to it . . . All of us learned things about how to be when we were growing up . . . [But] much of that learning has now passed into habit and so getting in touch with what we are really doing now, is making what is habitual conscious. This gives us a chance to discard that which no longer fits.
>
> Virginia Satir

> The unexamined life is not worth living.
>
> Socrates

I do not teach my pupils, but I provide conditions in which they can learn.

Albert Einstein

Re-organizing and enlarging one's experience is the basis of all problem-centred learning.

David Sutton

How do you learn to work in an action learning sort of way – and how do you know when you're working well?

True to its philosophy, you learn about action learning by doing it! This is the paradox of writing a book about it and the experiences of participants. Until you've experienced it, you won't really understand it!

All programmes begin with some form of introduction to the basic concepts – such as the set, its processes, the set adviser and the use of a project. Such introductions may last a day or two. Thereafter it is usual to throw people in at the deep end, form them into sets, and with the guidance of a set adviser, begin. And it isn't necessarily easy. We are not used to listening, asking questions rather than telling anecdotes, hijacking another's story, giving advice, or launching into a discussion on some subject, with everyone having a free-for-all. Giving someone airspace, and not being able to take it over, can be very difficult and frustrating for many.

As for how you know when you're working well – you know, you sense the difference, and you see how you're working differently. Gone are the general, often competitive discussions; gone is the advice and the interrupting. One member commented after just one meeting: 'We've become less competitive with each other – against each other – and we're working more effectively now with one another.'

There is also a new sense of achievement and satisfaction, a greater awareness, and for many a release of new energy:

'You sense a greater awareness of everything.'

'You find you're asking questions – concentrating on someone and their issue, totally focused and engrossed, and you no longer give advice.'

Another participant commented that 'You think about the responses you're given to questions – and you don't just accept them.'

'You look at what you're doing, thinking and feeling and reflect on them all. It becomes a way of life outside the set as well.'

ACTION LEARNING IS A PROGRAMME, NOT A COURSE

One of the key advantages of action learning is that the programme is spread over a number of months. Some may argue that this is impractical, that there simply isn't the time; at this stage I am usually reminded of a Frenchman who said: 'We never have any time to stop and think now. But we always find the time to stop and put things right when they've gone wrong.' In other words, we do have the time, but we choose how we're going to use it.

In a world of instant coffee, instant dessert, microwave ovens, push-button entertainment on TV, anything that takes just a little bit longer is viewed as suspect.

Comments from participants on action learning programmes indicate that it is precisely the element of time that is so crucial. By spending more time we give ourselves the chance to learn, we gain understanding, we consolidate and 'internalize'. Learning is never instant. It is because of the time spent in recalling, reflecting, thinking about subsequent actions and next steps, testing out, reflecting again, becoming aware, and continuing on a learning spiral that we consolidate and anchor our learning. This stress on recalling, revisiting and reflecting – what so many participants refer to as the 'discipline' of action learning – can only be experienced over a period of time. One participant was typically adamant: 'A week is not the same, you need the longer period.'

WHAT DOES AN ACTION LEARNING PROGRAMME CONSIST OF?

Briefly – because the rest of this book goes into the details of the various elements that make up a programme – it consists of the following:

- A small group of five or six people – the set – who meet regularly to work and learn together. Their task is to focus mainly on the action and learning of each individual, rather than the group as a whole (this focus may, however, be slightly different where the group is aiming to learn about teamwork).
- Each person tackles a work-centred task or project which is essentially the 'learning vehicle'. As such, it might be a specific task that the participant undertakes to gain insights into how to 'manage' such tasks more effectively; or how to handle, or work with, others better; or how to develop certain personal qualities and skills.
- The set adopts a strict question-based process (no advice, no discussions, no anecdotes), and offers everyone their own airspace during which the focus of the other set members is on them and what they are achieving and learning.
- Participants revisit their project (ie the action bit of the programme) and assess what they are learning at regular intervals – ideally at each set meeting.
- Each set is facilitated by a set adviser whose main skills are 'process' skills (ie he/she is not required to be an expert in any particular field). Their task is to help individuals in the set to learn by taking responsibility for their own learning.
- Programmes are run over a minimum of three months. This

'Pots' Diagram

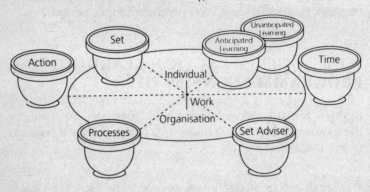

fig. 5

time element is crucial for achieving both the learning and action (ie outcomes on projects).

- Each participant (or the set as a whole if they are working on a group project) has a client – someone in a senior position who can claim ownership of the programme; someone who, in Reg Revans's terms, 'knows, cares and can'. The client is a champion of the programme, committed to it and believing in its value; he or she must ensure that participants are given time by their managers to work on their projects and to attend set meetings. Clients are the senior people who will in some way assess the results of the programme, either through being given a report or presentation – written or verbal – at the end of a programme, or by some form of discussion with the participants.

(See fig. 5)

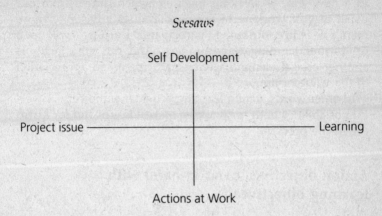

Seesaws

fig. 6

The simultaneous achievement of concrete benefits and learning

In action learning, the learning is as important as the action. The action seems straightforward: most participants are used to focusing on projects and taking certain actions to complete the job. Learning, however, is often overlooked. Action learning places equal emphasis on accomplishing a task and developing oneself in the process (see fig. 6.)

The action, which consists of a project or tasks to be achieved, has a double focus: a specific action outcome and some defined learning. In other words, actions must focused around achieving the participant's learning needs (or those of the group, in the case of a group project).

But as fig. 5 indicates, each element is integral and contributes to the overall success of a programme in all the breadth, depth and complexity that action learning offers.

Working in the set provides many instances for participants to learn about working within a group. However, the processes that the set adopts (listening, questioning, giving everyone airspace, not giving advice) introduce participants to a new way of working together which differs from our usual way of working in a group. The set adviser – whose main role is to contribute to participants' learning – will open up further learning opportunities. And the time factor is another crucial element, giving participants an appreciation of the value of time.

In other words, action learning provides some very powerful possibilities both for working on real issues and for learning in the process.

Action objectives hand in hand with learning objectives

A programme may thus be instigated because there is an issue an organization (or rather, the people who make up an organization!) wants resolved. People with foresight realize that this provides an ideal opportunity for learning to take place.

Alternatively, the development of staff is taken as the key focus, and projects are chosen with a view to providing opportunities for that development to take place.

> That which can be taught directly to another is relatively trivial whereas things of significance can only be learnt.
> Carl Rogers
>
> The difficulty lies not in new ideas, but in escaping from old ones which ramify into every corner of our minds.
> John Maynard Keynes

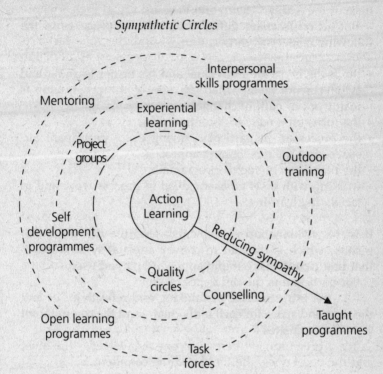

fig. 7

Ways in which action learning differs from other action or experiential programmes

There are other programmes which have much in common with action learning. The highly complementary relationship of action learning with other 'sympathetic' approaches is outlined in fig. 7. Such approaches or programmes are all forms of 'experiential' learning, which has been defined as 'the process that links education, work and personal development'

(Kolb), and 'learning which arises from the first-hand experience of the learner' (Boud and Pascoe).

But action learning differs from other approaches in the following respects:

- the focus is on the individual and his or her learning and achievements (even when the aim of the programme is teamwork or culture change);
- the focus on a real work-centred project
- the processes: in particular, giving every participant airspace, and the questioning approach;
- the time-span of such a programme;
- working with a set adviser skilled in process work and in facilitating learning.

It is this combination of elements – and the rich brew that results, which is difficult to convey adequately in words – that participants have found so rewarding and useful.

For participants the differences were:

'. . . the infrastructure of thinking and reflecting . . . and the time and space for each individual – and the commitment that all this creates.'

'It's a programme where everyone is involved – the quiet and the vocal ones, the timid and the confident.'

'. . . working on a real project – not an imaginary one – and having to do something about it.'

'The emphasis on learning – all the time, not just at the end of the programme.'

'It's the discipline of the processes – of listening and of not giving advice.'

'It involves the "whole" person and who you are and what you value and want to be, not simply the "role" person you are at work.'

For others it was: '. . . unlike other courses where you're told what you'll learn, you're given outcomes to expect and told what you'll be able to do after them. Here, the learning is much more up to you . . . it's your own individual learning.'

Going on to describe, rather than define, action learning,

one participant said it was '. . . like putting a mirror in front of you and confronting issues you'd prefer to ignore or avoid.'

Another participant came at it from a different angle: 'It's like putting together your own programme. You find that in addition to your own project – the ostensible learning vehicle – you're simultaneously working on time-management, empowerment, presentation skills, assertiveness . . .' Another agreed: 'It uses elements of lots of courses we've been on but never used.'

For another participant it was '. . . about management development – and developing people generally'.

'It's about professional development – and to be that it also has to be about personal development. You can't separate the two. To be professional you have to have competence to do a good job, meet new environments. It's not just a question of your knowledge and skills. So, put personal growth on top of these and you're doing more than relying simply on experience – which could simply look like twenty times one year's experience, rather than growth and change.'

For others it was an injection of energy: 'I don't know how it happens, but it gives you energy.'

Some referred to an action learning spirit, which they defined as being 'not about finding answers to questions or problems, but taking the time and space to talk and think and reflect on what you're being asked. It somehow releases you, gives you a sense of freedom.'

Others agreed: 'It's not about finding solutions to symptoms but about identifying the real problems.'

More graphically, a managing director of a small software company said it was 'like shining a light into the corners – or lancing a boil that's been irritating you.'

'I wish I could bottle it,' was one wishful thought. And even Reg Revans, the founding father of action learning, found himself stuck: 'It's so simple, it's difficult to describe.'

Let us however continue and attempt to do so!

'Undoubtedly other groups could help in achieving many of the benefits of action learning, but I'm not sure I'd have had the same confidence in their objectiveness or their level of understanding. Action learning really is different. It's about really listening . . . and its underlying structure and common 'experiencing' by everyone present make the individuals want to participate more than in many other programmes. At work, for instance, we often listen, but we're really disinterested. At the pub it's more mates chatting and giving advice. Neither of these happens in action learning. You have your own airspace – everyone concentrates on helping you, in the knowledge that their turn will come. It's the discipline that is powerful – you have to explain a problem or issue to the set, and in itself it's useful to have to articulate and get it into an order in your own mind . . . and if you get lost, the set asks you to be more precise, or explain more. And it's really hard work.'

DIFFERENT TYPES OF ACTION LEARNING PROGRAMMES

Broadly speaking, programmes fall into two categories: in-company and mixed-company. In-company programmes are the most common, encompassing all functions and all levels of responsibility. Mixed-company programmes are more likely to be attended by more senior staff, who have fewer if any peers within their own organization. Alternatively, they may be attended by individuals who are there to investigate and assess the value of such a programme for their particular organization.

A further difference lies in the focus of work within a programme: projects may involve individuals or the entire group.

Types of Projects

	F Setting Un F	
F **Task**	Both familiar	Task familiar Setting unfamiliar
Un F	Task unfamiliar Setting familiar	Both unfamiliar

fig. 8

Reg Revans postulated that there are four main programme variations and hence types of projects (see fig. 8). Of these four variations, the least common – for logistic and 'intelligence' reasons – is that involving participants engaged on projects in a company which has no relationship with their own. There are several instances, however, of programmes run for businesses which, though separate, belong to the same parent company.

Projects thus undertaken will vary as to:

- whether they will be carried out in the participants' own department and hence sphere of knowledge, or whether they will be tackling something that is completely outside a participant's normal activities and functions – possibly even in another company;
- whether the projects undertaken are individual or group ones. The latter are most likely to be adopted where the goal is team-building, or where (as was the case in one company) the set acted as consultants to a client's brief.

WHEN CAN ACTION LEARNING BE 'USED'?

Action learning is helpful where people face what Reg Revans calls 'problems', ie issues, quandaries, dilemmas, irritations. Those occasions when there is no one solution but a range of possibilities, thereby opening the door to choice and decisions. Alternatively, as is increasingly the case, people in all walks of life, and in most organizations, are faced with issues and hence decisions that they have not had to take before. Nor are they aware of anyone else having faced a dilemma of this kind; and even if they had, each situation is unique. It is in these circumstances, where something entirely new is being tackled, and where so-called expert knowledge can't help – except maybe in offering a few possible directions – that action learning is helpful.

Someone who is learning to use a word processor would gain little from attending an action learning programme. But someone given the task of determining whether staff in a particular department would benefit by having individual word-processing facilities would find that a useful project to work on in an action learning programme. The first form of learning is what Reg Revans defines as a *puzzle*; the latter, which has no one answer or solution, is thus what he terms a *problem*.

Thus action learning is useful where there is no one way forward, no single answer; where the solution will depend on circumstances, people, on history, on what is to be achieved – on a host of often unpredictable forces. Likewise, action learning is helpful where change of any sort is involved, because change brings in its wake uncertainties, doubts, fears and hence 'problems'.

As one old-timer said: 'Action learning is explorative and inquisitive – it encourages that spirit in participants.'

By bringing together a group of people, each with their own experiences, knowledge and perspectives, and encouraging them to adopt a 'questioning approach', action learning enables participants to begin to pose the 'right' questions when faced with dilemmas. The right questions being those which lead to new avenues to explore, and ultimately to possible solutions. As another participant put it: 'Someone who isn't prepared to ask questions, to investigate and explore, is probably part of the problem.'

An action learning approach could thus be applied to the following circumstances:

- when we are confronting a new situation we have never been in before;
- when we are working with a new group of people we have never dealt with before;
- when we want to test out new ways of working with people we already know;
- when our jobs or roles change and we're not sure what our responsibilities are, or how to relate to other staff;
- when the organization we work for is facing a major dilemma and needs to move forward;
- when we feel there are untapped human resources around us that we are ignoring;
- when the organization we work for is faced with challenges and needs to establish strategies and plans for the future;
- when we want to change the way things have been before;
- when we want to change something in our own personal make up: the way we do things, the way we react – ie personal development;
- when, as part of an NVQ or MCI initiative, we must attain competence in a given area

So, to use organizational terminology, action learning is effective for organizational development, team development and personal development. In reality, the three intertwine, and it is often difficult to know where one ends and another begins: without individual development there is no team development; without the latter, there is little organizational development.

THE BENEFITS OF ACTION LEARNING

What are the benefits of action learning? A task achieved, and a great deal of learning! Participants in most instances (but not all) complete a project which has some tangible outcome for the organization, department or section within which they work, and along the way they learn.

What they learn may be what they set out to learn (ie their anticipated learning). However, participants also gain, learn and develop in ways they had not anticipated – as a result of the way such a programme is constructed. Many comment that their learning:

(a) was broader than they had anticipated, that it touched on and encompassed everyday work issues they had not expected, and that it came about in unforeseen ways;
(b) went deeper, addressing attitudes and beliefs which affect behaviours, but had maybe not been looked at before; hence the learning became anchored and more deeply rooted.

Part 3 of this book details the experiences of participants in their own words – what they gained, learned, thought and felt about action learning. So, to simply preview the main findings, there are six principal gains that participants talked of:

1 learning a more 'disciplined' way of working
2 learning to network
3 learning to relate to, and communicate with, others more effectively
4 gaining increased self-confidence
5 gaining increased awareness
6 gaining increased readiness to take responsibility and initiative

ACTION LEARNING IS FOR EVERYBODY

Action learning is for everyone and anyone, old or young – regardless of job, status, profession or role in life.

The participants quoted in this book are probably the best guide to who it is aimed at. They included engineers, shop-floor staff, sales and marketing personnel, bankers, trainers and developers, teachers and lecturers, middle managers of a variety of hues and in different functions, clerical assistants, senior managers and managing directors, hospital administrators, nurses, paramedical staff, social workers, shop retail staff, a baker, a builder, and several people in IT.

But the possibilities don't stop there: it is for secretaries and supervisors, students and accountants, trainers and farmers. Programmes have run in every conceivable type of organization from local government, education, and the health service to blue-chip finance, service and manufacturing companies, from small companies to individual business entrepreneurs.

But is everyone 'suitable'?

The answer is no. Action learning is very much a programme for those who want to explore, to investigate; for those who are inquisitive; for those who want to understand, to gain insights, to go on learning; and for those who are prepared to change.

On the other hand, those who avoid or choose not to come on such programmes may be the very people who would stand to gain the most.

When participants were asked whether they thought everyone was suitable, their views were mixed:

'No, it's not for someone who is selfish and won't listen to others. He or she will pose problems. On the other hand, both they and the set may learn: the former to change and learn to listen and consider others; the latter to tackle someone like that – who may be like people they come across elsewhere and don't know how to deal with.'

Some felt 'you need a certain empathy with others'. Others thought it was not for those who are very self-opinionated, authoritarian and dismissive of others. The philosophy of action learning is about valuing everyone, learning to be tolerant while still being intellectually rigorous and challenging. Nevertheless, several participants pointed out, it could be an interesting experience for participants to be given the chance to 'tackle' such a person in the safe environment of a set – and it would give the individual so tackled some food for thought!

Thus one participant felt that 'some may find it difficult to participate in the process [of the set], particularly if some members dominate. You need a good set adviser, otherwise the set will move to where there the loudest noise is coming from.'

There will be those who have a strong preference for solutions and clear-cut answers, and for treating everything as a puzzle. They may initially feel very unhappy with some of the more 'right-brained' activity that occurs in the set. Alternatively, they could have their minds opened and stretched by such a programme.

And then there are those who genuinely prefer to work alone, who do so successfully, and perhaps should not be coerced into being different.

Interestingly, all those participants who said they found the programme of limited use and were unsure whether everyone would benefit from it, pinpointed the way the set worked as their stumbling block. It seems that this is the most difficult aspect of action learning for some, if not most, to grasp. It is also one of the main distinguishing features of action learning. (For more about the processes and participants' experiences of them, see p. 155.)

To choose or not to choose?

There might seem to be a risk of falling into a trap where those who go on action learning programmes are self-selected. This raises the question of whether participants should be compelled to attend such programmes. I would say that the right to choose is in line with the philosophy of action learning and should therefore be built into a programme. Those who choose not to take part, for whatever reason, may later be more willing when they see that participants are not eaten alive or mauled to pieces!

Joining an action learning programme presupposes a wish – and a belief in, or at least a willingness – to test out the value of working with others in a more open, effective and constructive way than we are usually wont to do, for a host of reasons, often allied with issues of authority, status, power, lack of confidence and fear.

It also presupposes that participants want to explore and investigate.

One participant on a mixed-company set – a senior manager in a government quango – admitted that he had learnt little:

> I didn't really get involved. I felt I didn't want to. I could see others gaining and becoming enthusiastic. But it just wasn't me to be as open as the programme demanded, which would have been the way to really gain from it.

It is therefore important that people are provided with information about the nature of an action learning programme before being given the option of not joining if they feel strongly opposed. There may, however, be some benefit in the 'shock of the new'. One participant – an engineer, now totally committed to action learning – described his first experiences of the set as being full of horror at the thought of having to talk about himself in front of a group of people. Initially he was adamant that he would do no such thing.

Someone who is coerced or denied the right to opt out can make the programme difficult for everyone else – although a great deal can be learnt by tackling and coping with a negative or disruptive member of a set. But it could in the end prove to be counter-productive, destroying the wider aim of the programme.

Thus, in action learning terms, this question is a typical problem and not a puzzle!

'ACTION LEARNING CAN DAMAGE AN ORGANIZATION'S HEALTH'

Perhaps it might be more apt to use a homeopathic image and say that applying drops of what may appear to be poison to a particular organization will ultimately cure it. Likewise, because of its investigative, questioning approach, action learning can be dangerous for some organizations.

Action learning cannot be viewed simply as just another form of workshop – a bolt-on – because it changes the way people work, think and view each other. In that it takes a questioning approach and 'empowers' set members by encouraging them to take responsibility, to become accountable, and to value themselves, it is based on a profoundly democratic philosophy. As such, it may be deeply disturbing for those who fear any change in existing structures, status and beliefs.

An action learning programme – if effectively managed – highlights the benefits of a questioning, democratic, networking form of organization. It turns out people who are able to think clearly, who challenge, who have gained in self-confidence, who question, seek responsibility and a sense of achievement, who listen to and value different perspectives, and who know the benefits of collaboration rather than confrontation.

> 'It's not only radical . . . it's the most dangerous course I've been on. Dangerous because it makes you question everything.'
>
> 'It's about empowering people. It hands responsibility and power back to staff.'
>
> 'It's part of the feminization of management . . .'
>
> 'It produces a radical change in how you operate. You are personally challenged. The onus is on you as a person, and not simply on you as a role-player in some larger organizational theatre. It makes you confront who you are, how you want to be – what's stopping you, what you're doing to yourself and to others.'
>
> For those who want to take more control of, and responsibility for, their lives and their work, it is an ideal opportunity to learn how to do so more effectively, with more personal power, and with greater confidence:
>
> 'It releases you, it creates a sense of freedom'.
>
> 'It brings you conscious awareness. It makes your brain work at a different level and speed.'
>
> 'It's about empowering yourself and hence others. It pushes responsibility and duties – even power – back to you, and to others.'

Interestingly, three of the programmes investigated for this book were in companies which by and large did not espouse the values and processes of action learning. The problem this posed was that after attending the programme, the participants became dissatisfied with their employers, and many admitted that they were looking for an opportunity to leave.

'It changes you, the participant, but if the company you work for doesn't really want to change, you end up feeling frustrated.'

This was what happened to a group of clerical staff in a Civil Service department. The participants were given a responsible project to work on, came up with interesting ideas and solutions, gained in self-confidence and realized their own potential – only to then be returned to their old desk-bound structurally limited jobs.

As several participants said: 'Organizations need to be aware that they will not get back the same people they sent on the programme.' Those responsible for introducing action learning need to make this clear to those who back the programme. It changes people, and they can become disillusioned and unhappy if their organization fails to realize this.

In fact, many participants from action learning programmes make career changes and other work-related moves very soon after such programmes. This is partially because they have developed, have gained visibility through being on the programme, and have made new contacts while working on their projects (just one of the unanticipated gains!).

In the case of another company running a programme to 'change the culture', it seemed to the three sets of young managers involved that the culture change had gone no further than them. As they tackled their projects, contacts with other managers were conducted along 'old' lines, and all the barriers and fears were there. Another set – a group of young graduates on a programme as part of their training – also found the 'messages' of action learning totally at odds with the culture of the organization. 'Here you play the "game" which means you see nothing and ask no questions. Action learning has given us the skills to both see and ask questions.' The result – disillusionment.

These are but a few instances, but they point to issues that need to be addressed before running an action learning programme. So, although taken to its logical conclusions action learning can prove to be too revolutionary for many organizations, taken slowly it begins to change the culture of an organization and build a very different, more committed and more fulfilled work force.

Action learning is subversive

- it values everyone
- it's democratic
- it stresses questioning
- it stresses listening
- it insists on actions
- it gives courage
- it encourages responsibility
- it examines everything

Action learning offers insights on how to create a learning organization

A great deal is currently being written about the value of a 'learning organization' – one where learning is a way of life. Yesterday's answers are not necessarily those for tomorrow, and the challenge is to enable the entire organization, ie all the individuals within it, to share their learning – their knowledge, experiences and insights – with others.

As Bob Garratt, author of *The Learning Organization*, has put it: 'Action learning is a process for the reform of organizations and the liberation of human vision within organizations.'

The authors of *The Learning Company*,[12] state that 'Action in the learning company always has two purposes: to resolve the immediate problem, and to learn from that process.' It sounds suspiciously like action learning in action! And the action learning set begins to resemble a learning company/organization in microcosm. The challenge, therefore, is how to create an action learning ethos throughout an organization!

Peter Honey, in an article entitled 'Establishing a Learning Regime'[13] postulates ten learning behaviours, which are remarkably similar to the learning that participants claim to acquire on action learning programmes (see p. 299).

But this alone is not sufficient to create a learning organization. It merely creates the behaviours that 'oil its wheels'. A learning organization also needs:

- the will to become one;
- the 'structures' that enable it to function as a learning company;
- opportunities to work on a daily basis as one.

Action learning provides a programme for developing the behaviours and skills. But it also provides some insights into the will, structures and opportunities. By demonstrating the benefits of such working it can provide the impetus or 'will' to become such an organization. It also supplies a model of the structures that enable working and learning to occur simultaneously, and a matrix for a networking form of organization rather than a hierarchical one. Furthermore, it provides an insight into how to create 'opportunities' that enable learning to be 'extracted' from the work process.

One could, in a sense, claim that the basis of a learning company is a network of like-minded people who enjoy the challenge of working in an action learning way. They form a powerful network which will share and exchange insights and information, provide help and support for each other in their work and personal 'experiments', will ask questions and challenge supportively, and give feedback. They will, in other words, learn with and from one another, and in the process 'transform' themselves and the organization they work for.

*

What's it like to take part in an action learning programme?

If you have read through to this point you should be beginning to form a picture of action learning. Part 3 explores in greater detail the experience of taking part in an action learning programme. It poses the questions that participants raise at the outset, gives answers, and recounts the stories, the insights, and the assessments, largely in the participants' own words.

The experiences recounted include stories of personal development, team development, managing change, project management, learning to network, coping with an MSc, tackling a new job, consolidating learning after a course, helping graduates learn in their first jobs . . . and so on.

And what about setting up and running effective programmes?

Part 4 of this book is devoted entirely to the practical issues of creating and running an action learning programme. It offers simple guidelines and summarizes the main points to remember.

PART 3

The Experience of Action Learning

This part of this book deals with the practicalities of action learning: the set, the action (projects and tasks), how the set works, the set adviser, the time-span, plus the learning and how it is evaluated.

Each element is discussed separately, using firstly a question-and-answer approach to address some of the questions most commonly asked by participants before, or in the early days of, a programme. Then, in their own words, participants describe their experiences.

The Set

SOME QUESTIONS ANSWERED

What exactly is the 'set'?

The set is the small group of people who meet regularly during a programme to work with each other. A set should have no more than five or six people in it. If it is larger, there is room for people to opt out and not participate.

Set members act as a resource to one another, and as a 'support and challenge' group. Each member is in turn supported and challenged by the other set members as they tackle their allotted project and focus on their learning. 'Comrades in adversity', is how Reg Revans described the set; others have been more upbeat, referring to them as 'comrades in opportunity' (Alan Mumford).

'Pots' Diagram

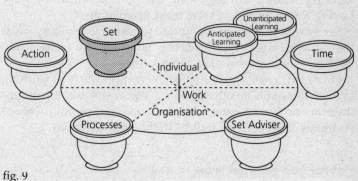

fig. 9

How does a set differ from any other group of people gathered together to work?

The set differs in several ways. Primarily it differs because its task is different. The aim of the set is not to resolve issues together. It is to help each individual member resolve his or her own issues with the support and challenge of the rest. This will, of course, be somewhat modified if the set is working on a group project. But even in this instance each member should be allocated a mini-project, and hence the same process will apply for at least part of the meeting. At some point, the whole project will need to be addressed and other processes will then be more effective.

In this sense the work of a set focuses on one person and his/her issues, rather than simply on the issues. So, when a set is working, what takes place could be described as a dialogue with one person, rather than a discussion amongst a group. However, if the person who is the focal point decides that a discussion or a brainstorm would be useful – possibly before resuming again the one-person format – then the set is free to do so. Sets are thus able to set their own agendas. Set advisers in such an instance will follow their 'sense' of how to respond (see p. 206).

One set I interviewed did in fact try out different ways of working before returning to the 'classic' action learning way, having found that it was the most productive.

Set members are also committed to meeting regularly, with the same members in attendance, and with the focus firmly on their learning as well as their actions.

One participant, a police officer, was very clear how working in a set differed from other groups: 'You're not in competition, there are no threats, you want everyone to succeed, there are no prizes and you're all pulling in the same direction.'

1 What you get from being in a set:
- time and space for your own reflections
- insights from others/with others

- different perspectives from others
- exchange of ideas with others
- others' experiences
- others' knowledge
- being questioned by others
- an opportunity to 'hear' yourself think – and respond
- support from others
- challenge by others
- sharing confusions with others
- sharing successes with others – and learning from them
- hearing yourself be helpful – and gaining in confidence

2 Ways of using a set:
- present your story/project, with the rest listening and asking questions
- an individual focuses on his/her project or task – or an issue of interest or concern – and the rest listen and ask probing questions
- the set discuss/brainstorm the individual's 'issue' – at his or her request only – while he/she listens
- the set focuses on an issue of common interest or concern – and decides how it wants to work
- the set may ask the set adviser to find an 'expert' on a particular topic related to their work; or may ask one of their own members to do a short 'input'

At any one time the learning may be focused on one person or – if it is appropriate at the time – on the set as a whole. In time, members become attuned to thinking about their learning as the action continues. At the outset, however, it is usually the set adviser who draws attention to it.

Sets rarely appoint a chairperson or other roles, although at each meeting someone may agree to take some notes for the set – most likely on individual action plans before the next meeting, or issues of common interest that arose during the day, or simply to keep an eye on time. Furthermore, sets do not have an agenda, other than to make sure that at a set meeting every member, ideally, is given an opportunity to have their airspace.

Sets are groups which, if possible, are not joined by new members. A set becomes a cohesive group where trust and openness develop as members get to know each other. A new member would disrupt this. It then takes time for the set to re-coalesce.

The set also differs from tutorial or seminar groups in that it is the responsibility of the set members to work and find solutions. The set adviser is neither a chairperson nor a teacher. He or she is there to help the individuals and the set as a whole – by asking questions and drawing the attention of the set to what is happening and how it is working.

A set is:

- a support group
- a confidential group
- a resource group
- a challenge group
- a reflecting group
- a 'contractual' group

Some people liken sets to quality circles. But, as several participants mentioned, they saw great differences and were in fact planning to introduce an action learning way of working into their quality circles!

Sets are also *confidential* groups. What happens in a set is confidential to that group of people and may not be discussed elsewhere with others. Only in this way will participants feel free to be open and honest. They need to be able to trust the other set members. And it is only when we can be open and honest that we will address those issues that will help us develop and learn.

Finally, sets are both support and challenge groups. In their supportive role, sets will be non-judgemental of others, providing a place where people can come and be open and honest about themselves and others, and give and receive honest feedback. Feedback is essential if development and change are to occur. In their challenging role they will explore the gaps and inconsistencies in a participant's story, or will challenge their beliefs and attitudes, their thinking and actions . . . but still non-judgementally. (See **The Processes in the Set**, p. 155, for more on this.)

Over time, the set becomes a group of people who build up trust among themselves. It is the trust that enables them to begin to talk about issues of real personal concern, or admit to any lurking fears. As one participant put it, the trust was essential if she was to develop her own professional competence.

'To be professionally competent requires reflection on your practice: reflection on your own, but also under the scrutiny of the set. If you don't reflect you're likely to fall into the trap of merely multiplying one year's experience over and over again. Reflecting can – should – be a natural process, but it's hard and scary to talk about your practice in front of others, to make things public. When you trust the set and their ability to help you, then things really start to happen.'

Isn't a support group rather soft?

A support group which is nothing but supportive could well become a cocoon, and as such might not be very productive. On the other hand, cocoons are also places for development. Without them caterpillars would not become butterflies!

Support need not – in fact should not – mean 'being in agreement' and sheltering. It is rather, as several participants put it, 'a safe haven' – yet another metaphor – somewhere to come in from the storm, to shelter temporarily, to take stock, regain energy and momentum.

As a support group it is unlike any other group that most participants experience. At work, groups exist not for support but to carry out a specific work-related task. Individuals in such groups are meant to be knowledgeable – and feel confident – about what they are talking about; they are expected to take stances and defend their viewpoints.

By contrast, a set is for many 'the only place I can admit to not knowing, to having doubts, to feeling worried. You're not allowed to do that at work.' For others it is, as one senior manager put it, 'the only place and time I can be "out of role".'

'By year two,' commented a participant on an 'academic' management programme incorporating action learning, 'I needed my "fix" . . . it gave me clarity and energy. The discussions bring you conscious awareness, and it's the regularity which brings that energy and will to change, and learn.'

But this is not self-indulgence, as many participants were at pains to stress. And although a few of them talked of being hooked and needing to talk to their set, they didn't see it as a drug but as something of importance. 'I found I was storing things up to tell the set,' admitted one person. Another laughed as she said that if she did something well at work, 'I'd think, "the set would be proud of me".'

One set member, a production manager with a major packaging company, created what he himself termed 'crude' categories for levels of openness in the set:

1 *The nudists*: those who are willing to expose both strengths and weaknesses to the set. The set is more important than the pride of the individual.
2 *The closets*: those who see the benefit of the open group but only practise when it suits them. They keep their frankness in the closet for when they feel it is appropriate.
3 *The voyeurs*: those who want to share in the group experiences but will only venture out when others have made the first move. They watch, but join in only when the risks are low.
4 *The flashers*: those who seem disinterested in the ideas of group learning, yet occasionally provide flashes of inspiration which improve team performance.

One participant was unabashed when he admitted that:

> There's not been a time in the past seven years when I
> haven't been a member of a set. It's useful as a sounding
> board and it 'legitimizes' the time we all need to
> stop and take stock. But we always say we haven't got
> time, and often we really don't as the pressures
> mount up. So, it's important to have that 'special'
> time. It's saved us time in the end because we didn't
> go down as many blind alleys as we would have done
> otherwise.

Another participant echoed a similar thought. 'You can, in a
set, talk about your philosophy of life, as well as about your
project. It's an opportunity to link things that are really linked
for each of us as individuals but for which there is no room
back at work.'

'It's a bit like having several mentors,' observed one
member, 'something our managers should be doing, and
aren't.'

What the set allows members to do is to talk, reflect, admit
to emotions – something not done at work, and which may
feel unnatural and scary to many. Best avoided! But when a
group of people works closely together for a length of time,
and members grow to trust each other, emotions of a more
fragile nature will emerge. Doubts and fears will be talked
about.

These doubts, fears and frustrations are not of great
psychological dimensions, but the kind that every normal
healthy human being experiences – even if they choose not
to admit to them in certain company. Yet not talking about
them doesn't make them disappear. Simply allowing them to
emerge and be talked about – by making them legitimate –
makes them less onerous, and less scary.

Potentially there is a danger that someone may be experiencing deeper emotional problems. In such a case, the set
adviser and the set themselves – not to mention the participant who is presenting these issues – needs to become aware

of and admit to the limits of their own competence to deal with these issues beyond a certain level.

Perhaps the greater danger, however, is that no emotions will be revealed and worked on, thereby severely limiting both the individual's and the set's potential for development. This again is where a professional and effective set adviser will enable and legitimize the expression of emotions in the – it has to be admitted, unlikely – event that someone in the set doesn't begin the process quite naturally.

A senior manager's thoughts:

The set is there in a sense to 'hold your hand' at difficult moments, particularly as we're all in the same boat. The others had been where I'd been, or realized that they would be at some future time. It creates a bond and unity – a network of people who understand. I was worried about the can of worms I might be opening at work, and I needed assurance that what I'd done and suggested was OK.

I need to gain more confidence in myself and my judgement. I think we all need this and seek it out, even though we may not admit to it, and do it in a roundabout way. But actually asking for feedback means you get more than you had asked for. It opens up yet other avenues. And you also realize that asking for feedback isn't as scary as you thought it was going to be. You're often told things you know already. But when others tell you, or confirm your worst fears – you take it on board.

Support without challenge, without questioning, without 'pushing' the participants to think, to take stock, to reflect, and take responsibility for themselves – this would indeed be 'soft'. Support in the action learning sense means being non-judgemental, being available to give help and insights, and giving each participant the space and time to work through issues they are facing or are puzzled about in a safe environment where they will not be criticized or held to account.

A set therefore provides a space where participants can experiment with new ways of behaving to see how comfortable they feel, and how they may become more effective back at work.

'The set was a useful sounding board. I would often arrive feeling persecuted and stressed, and left feeling good. The time and space to talk to others in a non-competitive environment would restore my own sanguinity and sense of perspective,' commented one participant.

'It's a place where you're challenged in a non-judgemental way. You realize your job isn't on the line, so you can admit to not knowing, to feeling worried – and just talking relieves the stress you feel. And by talking and being listened to you also get insights into what's causing the stress, and how to tackle or avoid it.'

'It's difficult not to make the set sound like a crutch – but it isn't. It's more like an elastic band that stretches you,' summed up the experience of most participants.

Most participants wanted to be challenged and stretched. Those who weren't challenged commented on it. 'The set was too nice, they didn't challenge me, and they missed my confusion because I gave off an aura of being and feeling OK.'

How many people should there be in a set?

The ideal number is five or six. If there are more it creates, as in any other large group, tensions and stresses that don't arise in smaller ones.

A larger group means that individuals don't get a chance to talk, or they feel their contributions have little value, or simply feel inhibited in participating and sharing with a larger group of people.

With five or six people, meeting for a day, it gives everyone time to tell their story during the session. If the meetings are shorter, this won't happen anyway – which can cause some anxieties, and it means that some participants will have to wait a few meetings for their airspace. This in turn means that the cycle of action and learning may not occur. It is questionable whether such an arrangement is, strictly speaking, action learning, no matter how useful the discussion may be. But what's the follow-through? It is the process of having to do something and then talking about what has been done, ie the 'revisiting', which leaves many participants with the greatest sense of fulfilment.

'Meetings are more productive when there are only five or six,' remarked one participant who had initially experienced a nine-member set. 'Meetings have a different dynamic with fewer people, there's more contact, more space and time.'

Another participant said: 'Our set was too big, so we've decided to break into two smaller ones. We think it will give us more of a chance to talk to one another, and we'll get to know each other better and go deeper into any issues . . . In the bigger set if an emotional issue arises, you can't go into it sufficiently to help that person – it's a combination of too little time, too many people who each want space, and, in a big group it's difficult to talk about one's problems, anyway.'

Too large a group, and too little time diminishes participation, because participants:

- may not have time to have their airspace at every meeting;
- may not get enough space to be listened to, to think, to reflect, or simply to be quiet and sit silently;
- may feel it won't matter if they don't turn up – they won't be missed;
- may not want to be open and honest in front of a larger group;
- may keep quiet because there are so many talking and asking questions already.

How is the make-up of a set determined?

The make-up of a set will be determined by a number of factors:

- whether the programme is in-company (all members drawn from the same organization) or mixed-company (participants come from different organizations);
- the objectives of the programme;
- the specific issues participants want to address;
- geography: it may not be feasible for regular meetings to take place if members have too far to travel.

Next, the make-up of the set will depend on the aim of the programme:

- Is it to gather people from different functions, to enable them to work better together?
- Is it a career development programme? If so, a mix of people from different functions will add variety and different perspectives.
- Is it to resolve one department's issues? In which case set members may all be from the same department.
- Is it to grapple with a common issue that a group of people are facing? If so, the set should be made up of all concerned.

If the programme is a mixed-company one, then the set will be made up of people who have either attended a course together and are now consolidating their learning through applying what they have been taught so far, or who have come together to be exposed to different ways of thinking and acting as they hear the experiences of people from other organizations.

In most instances, however, set members will be made up of people who are of approximately the same level of responsibility. This is deemed to be important because it means they can help each other more fully. As one participant put it: 'they understand the issues you're tackling – may even have tackled similar ones.' The question is simply whether someone in a clerical grade, for instance, would have sufficient knowledge and insight to help a senior departmental manager resolve some of his work quandaries. Of course it's possible they may, but it is an issue that needs to be considered.

This was borne out by one programme which was judged to be unsuccessful in that participants felt they gained little – indeed, some individuals left the programme. The set members consisted of head teachers and departmental managers from medium-sized companies. In searching for reasons why the set failed to gel, the set adviser found that the head teachers felt the managers didn't have the necessary experience – and hence the understanding – of their problems and challenges. Their spheres of responsibility varied too much.

Another instance of a set which worked for some participants but less for others was described by a senior hospital manager who, with other colleagues from managerial roles, was in a set with consultants (the medical variety). He recalled that although it had been interesting, and he had gained from having to help the consultants understand aspects of management that they were encountering for the first time, nevertheless he and the other managers felt they had gained less because the consultants' level of knowledge about management was so limited.

In another instance, however, a mixed-status set was created, on purpose, to recommend a new company appraisal programme (and their recommendations were subsequently put into effect with great success). Because this was an issue that affected everyone, the set included an older, senior manager, two young IT specialists, and the supervisor of a typing pool.

There are, notwithstanding, good reasons for not mixing people of different 'status' levels. On in-company programmes, for instance, both parties might feel uneasy: those in lower grades could feel intimidated or think they have nothing of use to offer; those in more senior positions might feel uneasy about 'exposing' their doubts and fears in front of people in lower grades.

If, however, a programme is being run in an organization that claims to be a 'learning' company – with all its characteristics of openness, honesty, good communication, and so on – there would appear be no reason for not having such 'vertical slice' sets. But I wonder how many organizations, irrespective of their mission and values statements, would be able to contemplate such groupings.

Sets are rarely made up on the basis of personal skills or qualities, although some juggling might occur to create a balance, say, of men and women, or to avoid having too many people from the same function (unless this serves a purpose). Where possible, a mix of abilities and styles of working is desirable: 'We had a good mix of experience – six to eight years of work on average, and a good mix of personalities,' commented one participant. By and large it is the degree of randomness that adds a rich dimension to the learning!

Why is it that some sets fail to gel?

Sets, like other groups, create their own dynamics. It may be one member who upsets the energy in the set; it may be that the participants simply never feel totally at ease with one another: 'The "chemistry" didn't work and we didn't get as close as I'd have wanted to, to feel free to really open out.'

A good set adviser will pick this up and may raise it as an issue to be looked into and discussed – each participant offering their view and understanding of what is happening. This is as 'real' an action as working on a project or task. It gives members an awareness that if the group isn't feeling comfortable, work will be affected. One participant, who experienced a set working through this issue of discomfort within the group, commented that she now feels free to comment on the processes in other groups she works with in her organization.

If set isn't helpful, have you:

- told them
- asked for help
- been clear
- attended regularly
- felt committed and involved yourself
- listened to others
- taken responsibility for working out 'why'
- helped the set or individuals to help you (by your own responses and feedback)

Some sets don't go deep enough: one or two participants remarked that the set was little more than 'a chat group, and we don't get a lot out of it. People just go on talking, like anywhere else.' A good set adviser will intervene at such times to ask the set to reflect on what is happening.

For those on in-company programmes there will sometimes be a tendency to fall back into functional roles, to wear those hats and bring to the set the attitudes and beliefs that go with them. The set provides an ideal venue in which to explore the origins and validity of these!

Inevitably office stories and gossip also occur, and fear of stories travelling back may initially prevent members from being open and honest. This is one reason for stressing confidentiality. But many participants have pointed out that such stories give them insights into other parts of the organization that they have little or no contact with.

And then some sets fail to gel because members don't attend regularly. Regular attendance is important – probably crucial. Attendance denotes commitment, for a start. If everyone is committed, this creates a working atmosphere. If some participants attend only intermittently this conveys messages to the others about the importance the non-attending member attaches to them and the work they are doing.

Given that action learning centres on evolving personal

stories, non-attendance also means that participants who miss meetings aren't able to follow what is happening, and consequently the set loses a certain amount of its energy in having to bring them up to date.

Furthermore, the non-attending member increasingly becomes a stranger who isn't present to help, support, and simply 'be' with other set members as they tackle issues, move on, and develop. Such members might also lose out when their turn comes, because their non-attendance may be interpreted as undervaluing the set experiences, and by implication the set members. Thus the set may well feel less committed to helping such a member – which creates confusing emotions for everyone, and may destroy the 'energy' of the set.

One set adviser said she starts by telling her group that set meetings are an absolute priority, to be missed and interrupted only if the participant is called away by the chief executive or managing director!

If attendance isn't regular:

- you don't get to know the other set members, which may inhibit trust and openness
- you miss out on others' stories, and it creates annoyance when they have to update you on what has been happening
- others may feel resentment, which might not be voiced but would be shown in other ways
- it indicates that you undervalue the set, and the work they're doing
- you don't get the benefit of regular 'checks' and may increasingly see the set as irrelevant

How to get the most out of a set

- Commitment
  attend regularly
  give everyone airspace
  give everyone attention

- Use set
  ask for help/feedback
  share successes, mistakes, ideas
  be honest and open

- Give feedback
  tell set what you want/need
  tell set what isn't helpful
  tell set what is helpful

- Involvement
  everyone
  the rational part of you
  the emotional part of you

- Take responsibility, courage and risks

What are the relative advantages and disadvantages of in-company and mixed-company sets?

The advantages of in-company sets are:

- the networking and inter-departmental contacts that are created;
- the 'visibility' that such a programme gives participants;
- the creation of a greater cohesiveness within an organization as people realize the benefits of working together;
- simply a greater knowledge of the organization, all the functions within it, and the issues it is coping with.

'It was useful to have a cross-functional set. We never meet otherwise. We're separate fiefdoms. Or when we do meet it's within a structure and with tight time deadlines, so we never get to know each other.'

Similarly, many participants felt that such gatherings allowed them to 'benchmark' themselves against others. 'It's often difficult to know how you "compare" with others – this is one way of checking it out.'

The advantages of mixed-company sets are:

* seeing how different organizations tackle the same issues and problems;
* feeling freer to discuss issues with strangers;
* for very senior managers, the opportunity of sharing with 'peers';

'People in different companies have different perspectives, values, and understanding. Just hearing them is valuable. It challenges your preconceived notions that things have to be a certain way.'

Said one manager: 'I feel that with a group of strangers you can be more open and honest . . . and you have no hierarchies or difficult relationships to be concerned about.'

Another talked of 'the release of being anonymous . . . no one coming with preconceived notions of you or your role, so you have the space to be honest, and to experiment with different ways of working.'

'I'd always assumed that the way we did things was naturally the best. I've realized this isn't necessarily the case. In fact I've taken away many very practical ideas on how to restructure our assessment procedures' – this from a personnel manager.

And for one participant from a blue-chip company, working with people from the public sector and realizing that they had many insights and ideas he didn't have was 'a humbling experience'.

But one IT manager commented that such mixed-company sets, although very productive in many ways, were not suitable for certain purposes. For instance, if a company wanted to introduce cultural change it would have to run an in-company programme.

A lecturer from the higher education sector remarked how 'the problems in my sector are the same as everyone else's in other organizations! That was reassuring. It meant we really could give each other insights and ideas that could be helpful, instead of repeating our own follies over and over again.'

Another manager from a large insurance company commented on the value he had derived from having in his set a manager from a small company. 'He simply brought a different, down-to-earth approach which was very refreshing.'

Conversely, a few participants found that, fascinating though it was to work with people from other companies and get their perspectives and insights, 'you still have the problem of coming back into your own company and wanting to do things differently. It's the same re-entry problem you have when you attend any other "open" course.'

Do sets always work with a set adviser?

In most instances they do – and initially it's necessary that they do, though after several meetings the set adviser may no longer attend.

The set adviser plays a useful role, helping the set to reflect and focus on learning, acting as a 'mirror' to what is happening, while at the same time asking questions and working with each individual.

To start with sets tend to be engrossed with the action and forget their learning. One of the tasks of the set adviser is to adjust the focus. Sets that work without a set adviser often comment that they think they would have gained more with one. Where a set is made up of experienced set members there is less need for an adviser, although there are many sets which continue to run for several years and find the presence of a set adviser immensely useful.

Much will depend on the set, and, of course, on the quality of the set adviser. (For more on the role of the set adviser, see pp. 205–18.)

How does a set agree on the way it is going to work?

A number of aspects of how a set works are built into the action learning process itself. Airspace and the processes of questioning are basic to a good action learning programme. A set adviser will offer guidance on these issues at the beginning of any programme – and will remind participants when they forget.

There are, however, other issues that the set members do need to be clear about, and talk about very early on in order to create some ground rules.

A prime issue is that of confidentiality in the set: whatever is said in the set must be confined to that group and not discussed elsewhere or divulged to others.

Another important ground rule is that of being non-judgemental – which is important if members are to feel free to talk about a whole host of issues they may want to explore.

Other ground rules may include not interrupting, having a timekeeper for each meeting, nominating someone to keep a note of everyone's action plans (for follow-up at subsequent meetings), whether to permit smoking or not, a prohibition on being late to meetings or having telephone interruptions from the office, and so on.

The issue of confidentiality is particularly important. One participant who admitted she 'hated the programme' explained that the main reason was that there was a 'spy in the camp' – by which she meant that what was said in the set was being passed on to her manager. As a result, she, and other members of the set, didn't feel free to be open and to really work. In another programme, a member discovered that the set adviser had discussed something she had said with her manager – and this again destroyed her confidence in the set.

Here are the ground rules that one set created for itself, along with its expectations of the set adviser (arrived at after discussion with him). These were hung on a wall at each set meeting to remind members.

Ground rules for the set

- be honest and open – say what you mean, mean what you say
- stick to agreed schedule/plan
- positive listening
- be supportive and communicative
- give – and receive – constructive criticism and feedback positively
- respect confidentiality
- keep things in proportion
- let's have fun
- in discussion, stick to the agreed issue
- come fully prepared to each meeting
- review the learning and the learning process – individually and together

Because this set was working on a group project they included a few additional items such as:

- fair distribution of work
- manage the client
- review the future

Learning agreements and contracts:

Views differ on the usefulness of having such agreements or contracts (the latter term has a legalistic connotation – something that cannot be broken and is therefore rigid; agreement has a looser meaning and feels more flexible).

Although it is important that each participant has a clear idea of what it is they hope to work on and achieve during the programme – and although these aims, together with a brief outline of how they will be achieved, can be encapsulated in words – the whole point of an action learning programme is that things should move on and change. Often, participants come with one learning objective in mind, only to find within a meeting or two that it isn't the real issue that they need to be working on.

One such example occurred in a set where a manager was focusing on his personal style and effectiveness – only to discover that deep-down he wanted a change of job.

So, agreements and contracts may serve as a focus but should be no more than reminders for learning – a means of keeping to one path and not straying too far afield.

A learning agreement

To be decided on by the participant, the client, the participant's manager, and probably the development & training manager (particularly if the programme is based around personal and managerial development with a career move in mind).

- What I want to be doing, or achieve: what I want to make happen, or be doing differently.
- How I'm going to go about it: specify plans and actions, who may be able to help, what resources I need.
- How I'll know when I've got there: outline what will be happening (ie evidence that the goal is being achieved)

Agreements are not writ in stone. They are a focus for working and learning. Most participants find that in the

---

course of a programme they develop new ideas on what they could be doing (actions), and who could help; and as they themselves develop, they are prepared to accept new ways of doing things, and their unanticipated learning becomes as significant as anything they planned to gain.

Where do sets meet?

This is not as trivial a question as may at first appear. Since the purpose of the set is to allow each member to work on his or her own issue, and to have their airspace, such meetings should take place somewhere that is convenient for everyone. This can become an issue for mixed-company sets, or for in-company sets consisting of people scattered geographically.

Ideally meetings should take place away from any of the participants' workplaces. This is to ensure that there is less likelihood of members being called away to 'vital' meetings where their presence is indispensable! The same goes for telephone calls.

A comfortable room, with coffee, lunch and tea provided, and no disturbances make for sets that are able to concentrate on the task in hand – achieving their project goals and their learning.

If the set is made up of people from different companies, they have the option of meeting at the workplace of one of the members – but this risks causing the 'host' to feel a sense of responsibility for the day, and consequently having less energy for the work of the set.

It is useful to arrange, at the first set meeting, where and when subsequent meetings are to take place. Trying to find mutually convenient dates in six busy people's diaries can otherwise become a nightmare! And once fixed, these dates should – as far as possible – remain fixed, unless there is a crisis or several members find it impossible to make a particular meeting.

How often do sets meet – and for how long?

Ideally sets meet once a month for a day. Thus a programme planned to include six meetings would take six months – a good length of a time for a serious project to be undertaken and completed by participants.

Longer intervals risk making a programme seem to drag on, with the result that members lose their momentum and enthusiasm. If more than a month elapses between meetings, too much can happen for members to remember and recall for the set. It also leaves a long gap if there is an issue that members want to talk about with the set.

With a set comprising six members (the best number – neither too large nor too small), ideally a whole day is needed to allow every member to have their airspace. If a set meeting were to last for only, say, three hours the result would be that only two or three participants, at most, could have time for airspace at any one meeting. Should a member have an urgent issue, there would obviously have to be a 'negotiation' around the allocation of time.

If, as some sets do, they meet for only one or two hours, this can be problematic in action learning terms. When only one member has time to tell their story, the others face a wait of up to five months before their turn. Strictly speaking, this is not action learning: there is no action to be revisited and learnt from with the help of the set. True, individual members may be implementing their own action and learning alone, away from the set, but this falls short of real action learning.

The other possibility where short meetings are the only option is for everyone to have 15–20 minutes. This may sound sufficient, but participants all say that it is surprising how having one whole hour per person disappears without anyone realizing how time has flown.

In order to do any in-depth work, a presenting participant needs more than a few minutes of the set's attention – up to an hour may be required, if the issue is a real problem. With less time, the work done is either superficial, or time runs out before ideas or solutions can be addressed.

If a set is working on a group project, the same issues arise. Within a group project each member needs their airspace to tell the others how they are progressing on their mini-project.

Preparing for a set meeting

To get the most out of the set meeting – as out of any other meeting – the participants need to think beforehand what it is they would like to focus on, what they want to work on, or what they would like to get from the set . . . and how they propose to achieve what they want. This exercise means that at the end of the day each participant can ask themselves whether they got what they hoped for and, if not, what was preventing it. In this way, work within the set also becomes a focus for learning.

Many participants commented on how working in the set had given them many insights on how they worked with others, and hence how they behaved in other groups (see p. 189 on processes). For this reason, a set is also a useful place to 'experiment' with different behaviours. So, if a participant is normally a dominant and talkative member of any group he or she works in, it might be useful to notice what it is like to remain more silent, and maybe listen more!

Helpful behaviour by a presenter

- prepare for meetings
- structure your time
- be clear about what you would like – or would like the set – to focus on
- learn to ask for what you want
- learn how to get an empathetic response
- learn how to receive
- learn to generate action points

What happens if I don't want to participate actively in the set?

No one can force a set member to participate. Each participant in a programme takes responsibility for themselves and their learning – and hence their participation. Undoubtedly the other set members and the set adviser would ask a non-participating member to explain what was stopping them, and might also urge greater participation. Someone who decides not to participate – for whatever reason – may create problems for other set members; this would then be an issue for the set, and the set adviser, to work on. In the end it is the individual participant who decides whether to participate or not.

Some participants admit to not having participated much – out of choice, they claim, although one or two said it was more out of shyness and diffidence. For one such member, the six-month programme was all too short. 'I was just beginning to come out of my shell, to feel confident enough to participate, when it came to an end.'

A number of participants said they didn't take part much because they felt uncomfortable with the set and its processes. They felt uneasy with other set members – 'the chemistry was wrong' – or simply didn't feel they wanted to share and be open.

'I didn't find it useful, and didn't use it to learn. I didn't want to use it and so didn't bring up my issues, though I listened to others. I admit that it was my choice and I think I'd have learnt more if I'd been willing to participate more.'

Another echoed a similar thought: 'I didn't use the opportunities offered. But I'm not sure it would have made much difference, though it might have been useful to run things through with the set.' This particular marketing manager went on to explain that he had found working with people from different functions in the set very enlightening, and working on the project very useful and beneficial. In particular, it had given him confidence and visibility within his company, and these he felt were benefits enough.

Glimpses from a set

First meeting

Bev: How do I organize myself – and motivate my staff? I feel I never achieve anything . . . and my boss keeps undermining my authority and contradicts what I tell my staff to do . . . I'm afraid of letting go and giving my staff responsibility . . . I think we need more training . . .

Peter: I want to focus on the next career move and the skills I'll need – I need to communicate better, and have more effective discipline. I also want to have a more relaxed managerial style and feel more enthusiasm . . . I've tried being autocratic and it doesn't work . . . but I like things done in a certain manner.

Paul: We have an administrative problem – one of processing all the paperwork. We've been told to find more customers, which means more paperwork. The changes are resulting in things toppling like a pack of cards.

Norman: I've just lost direction. I'm not happy, I've lost the flavour of success, and my confidence has plummeted. We have a massive turnover problem, too much work, but basically the staff are good and willing.

Matt: I'm told I'm not challenging enough, that I do my job conventionally well – I'm very task-oriented, we get through the work but we're not achieving as much as we could be.

THE VALUE OF WORKING IN A SET

It is interesting that, at the very outset of a programme, it is the project that is talked of as the learning vehicle. The set is seen as 'just another group'. Participants therefore don't give much thought to what they will learn from the group. Some enter the programme harbouring reservations about whether non-experts, and mere managers at that, will be able to help them to learn anything.

What emerges, however, is that much of their learning revolves around valuing others, changing the way they work (eg from being active to being more reflective), growing in confidence and realizing the importance of being supportive. These unanticipated learnings – for such they were – participants in fact ascribed in large measure to the set and its processes. The set becomes, unexpectedly, a crucial learning vehicle.

Realizing the value of mixing – and working closely – with colleagues from other 'functions'

Participants on in-company sets said they had come with preconceived notions about people from other departments and functions. Such mixed-functional sets allowed them to test out the extent to which these were based on fact or fiction; alternatively to begin to understand where the differences sprang from.

'You come with assumptions about people and the different parts of the organization they work in . . . you label them, but then you see the different constraints they work under, and realize they're human too.'

'It gave us the opportunity to learn about other parts of the organization – parts we'd never know about otherwise.'

For another participant it 'cleared away the cobwebs – we heard everyone's story and began to build a more robust relationship which then fed back into our work.'

'You feel much more part of the company after such a

programme,' commented one young woman. 'You begin to understand what it's all about, and that helps you feel more committed.'

For others it was an eye-opener to see how very different the various parts of their organization might be. 'Some departments were different animals, almost. Some were more "feminine", open and caring, and more closely bonded than others. Where there was a strong male director, the culture was ruthless and aggressive,' observed one marketing manager after hearing his colleagues' stories.

Some went on to say: 'We're creating a network here, in our set, – one we can call on later, when we have some issues to resolve. It will make it that much easier, knowing there's someone you know and whom you can talk to openly.'

What such in-company programmes – and particularly those involving group projects – also highlighted was the ability of a group of people to create major change within their organization, as one young lecturer at a college of further education pointed out:

> This was my first experience of working formally within a group to effect change in an organization. It was a very valuable experience, for it taught me how a small focused group with very little individual power could effect powerful and far-reaching changes. The group has been very successful in its outcomes . . .
>
> It also taught me how I can make a useful contribution to team effort. I got to know a great deal about the institution I work in and it helped me clarify my role within it. Very importantly, it also showed me how the skills I realized I had could play a part in any organization I might want to work in. As a result I was able to reframe my work experiences . . . this produced a very new and interesting picture of my job, and it was a key factor in my getting a new job.

Another set – of research scientists – was able, after one such programme, to go as a cohesive body to their manager and instigate changes which each had tried but been unable to introduce alone.

The result, as all such in-company sets said, was that they felt much more cohesive, more part of their company, more interested in what was happening, and better able to work with each other now that they understood one another's perspective.

Benefiting from working with 'non-experts': valuing everyone

'I was amazed at how the non-experts in a given field can help you by asking intelligent questions – often very simple ones . . . their lack of familiarity with my issue caused me to explain it from basics, and made me often think more laterally.'

The necessity of providing simple explanations in response to very elementary and straightforward questions from colleagues in other departments can lead to useful new insights for the 'presenter', who may in the process become aware of inconsistencies, gaps or anomalies that he or she hadn't spotted before.

A participant in a mixed-company set recalled, 'It was interesting. There was no one else in my set from finance (I'm in banking) – I was with someone from the NHS, computing, retail and telecommunications. I was able to help them spot what, to me, were glaring problems or gaps, and I had ideas on how things could be done differently . . . They did the same for me.'

Interestingly, a personnel manager who found himself in a mixed-company, mixed-function set, found that 'although one other member of the set was also from Personnel, I found the non-experts more helpful because it was in explaining to them what to me seemed so obvious that I often saw the flaws, or they would see something that I had missed because I was too close . . . as was the other "expert".'

For others, the task of having to explain to non-experts gave them clues and insights they would not otherwise have gained – often simply by hearing themselves say something out loud: 'As you talk out loud, you start saying things that you didn't know were even in your mind. It's something to do with talking out aloud. The same doesn't happen if you're merely thinking quietly to yourself.'

On the other hand, a few people felt it a drawback to have to go back to basics – they felt it wasted time and said they would have preferred single-function sets. One IT specialist in particular felt this. But then he added that he had found it immensely useful to work in the mixed-company set he was a member of, and especially to listen to the dilemmas of the general manager of a small building firm. 'It gave me a totally new perspective on many matters,' he commented. It seems there is no clear rule!

Working with non-experts had wider ramifications, as well. Once members began to realize that they were able – as a non-experts – to help the other set members it gave them confidence in themselves.

A useful anagram for sets to bear in mind, when working together:[1]

Responsibility for self and others
Experience-led
Confidential
I – the use of 'I' language
Process skills
Equality of opportunity

The value of working in a 'support' group: sharing, and helping others

When they first embark on action learning, few participants think of sharing as something that offers them the opportunity to learn. This soon begins to change:

'At the outset I was very competitive and action and results-oriented . . . and very isolated. It's helped me work differently. I began to talk to others. It made me more professional at work. In the set I'd watch the dominant personalities and realize they're not necessarily always right, and when others were given – or rather, took – space to speak, we all became more creative. I've transferred this back to work.'

Sharing also brings out the diversity that exists among people, and with it the realization that 'it is this diversity which is the richness'. As another manager put it: 'One of the most fundamental discoveries for me was the valuable resources that existed in our set . . . an eye-opener for what exists in other groups.'

It is this emergence of ideas, thoughts and insights when working with others that makes the set so powerful, mused some more philosophically-minded participants. One or two wondered if they could have achieved the same benefits on their own. 'You should be able to "do" action learning on your own,' one of them thought. On the other hand, many drew attention to the fact that the set itself is what triggers off new ways of thinking and new perspectives, 'bringing out things in you that you didn't even know were there'. 'The more you share, the more you get back. You learn from others if you're prepared to share.'

But it's not simply a matter of telling your story and hearing others' in return: 'It's more what they caused me to think about – either because they were asking themselves questions, making comments, describing their experiences – and I'd find myself thinking and asking myself questions . . . I did this particularly when I had the "space" to do so – often after I'd been the focus of attention, and when it was someone else's turn . . . when the spotlight was off me. At times it's difficult in that space to take in fully what has been happening, or what you've been offered by the others.'

Many participants I spoke to said how surprised they were that they learnt as they helped others. 'Hearing your ideas accepted and valued by others meant you began to apply them yourself. But they only emerged because of the others talking about their issues – you'd never have had similar thoughts or ideas about yourself.'

The more pragmatic managers commented on how the sharing – the hearing of others' stories – also made them realize that there are many different styles of management – and that it's necessary to vary your approach sometimes. 'You can't be caring all the time, you have to manage different people in your team differently – but all equally and fairly.'

A 'feminine' process

A number of participants – notably the men – described this sharing as the 'feminization' of work: 'I learnt a great deal from the women in the set – they're better at teamwork and sharing responsibilities with others, and generally using others to help arrive at decisions.' Another man admitted, 'I've never liked – or been – a macho manager. I can now be effective and it all occurs in a manner which is relaxed, informal, collegiate and collective.' And a third manager – this time a woman – recalled how she had for some years felt uneasy at the 'style' of managing that was expected of her. 'It felt unnatural to me – to be authoritarian, a disciplinarian, someone with all the answers.' Her experience of action learning, she said, gave her 'permission' to adopt her own style and, like the previous participant quoted, to be more collective in her approach – though without relinquishing her ultimate responsibility for decisions taken.

A few other participants felt that action learning itself was a 'feminizing' process, because it emphasized sharing and collaboration rather than individualism and competitiveness. 'It's about sensitizing you, making you more "feminine",' said another man, but added forcefully 'but it's not soft, it's not opting for an easy life, and it makes you more self reliant and decision-oriented.' And a senior executive remarked that a good many more senior managers were probably in need of this 'sensitizing' process.

The benefits of increased self-confidence

For most participants this sharing with others – the openness and honesty – revealed that 'we all share the same problems, regardless of organization, function or even project. No matter how we defined what we were working on in this programme, in the end we all landed up with the same fundamental problem – of how to relate to and work with other people.'

One young woman described how she had become more confident: 'I'd been timid and mousey before. I'm not really sure how it happened that I changed. The set were supportive of me, gave me space. But as I saw I was able to help others I realized I couldn't be talking complete rubbish. I heard myself say: "Take your own advice, then, and apply it to yourself." '

The safety of the set offers participants a chance to experiment with new ways of behaving or new approaches back at work. One revealed: 'I'd practise with the set how I would approach my manager, until I felt comfortable and they thought it was fine.'

Support in the set thus legitimizes asking for help, and allows participants to admit to not knowing all the answers or to feeling vulnerable. And the discovery that both activities are 'OK', and nowhere near as fearful and threatening as they

had imagined, can make it possible for them to change the
way they behave at work, to be, as many put it, 'my own
natural self'.

'I now have the confidence to say I don't feel confident,'
said one man. 'I feel it's all right to admit I don't know something,' was a comment many made.

Quite simply, as one manager said, 'you realize that you're
not alone in your worries and concerns, or alone to resolve
them.'

The reluctant salesman

In a set I facilitated, one manager – a deputy branch
manager of a building society – was on the programme
to help him overcome a lack of confidence in himself,
for it was preventing him from gaining his next promotion. It was also stopping him from gaining the sales
experience which he needed for that new post.

In the set he admitted to being shy. During the first
meeting he talked very little except to say that he was
not good at 'small talk' nor at being 'outgoing, like sales-
men need to be'.

There was no point in pushing him or in sending him
on yet another course on how to be a good salesperson.
But as the set began to work, it soon became obvious
that whenever he spoke, the set listened with particular
attention. Everything he said made sense. Slowly he
took on a leadership role. Then he was given feedback
by the set on how they perceived him. At the third
meeting, he agreed with the set that he was feeling more
confident and thought he might try phoning one or two
potential clients whom he knew, and inviting them out
to lunch. He still might not be able to 'sell', but he did
now feel competent to talk to them about their financial
interests in a quiet, business-like way. With the encour-
agement of the set he agreed to 'take a leap'.

When he reported back at the next meeting he was

completely overwhelmed. It had been easier than he had imagined; he had found both men very willing to simply talk about financial matters, and both expressed interest in the services the branch could offer them. Two potential new clients!

He used the next two set meetings to discuss what he could do next, but he was beginning to realize that he could sell simply by being his own natural self – that he could remain in character and didn't have to pretend he was something that he wasn't.

He continued to build up his confidence, and by the end of the programme he could even show financial gains he had made for the branch. His participation in the set meetings was now total, and he was generally considered by the other set members to be the most capable of the group. A few months after the programme he was promoted to branch manager.

Having to take responsibility

Being a group that both supports and shares, a set also has expectations of each and every member:

'The set forces you to take responsibility. They have expectations of you at every meeting . . . On one occasion when I hadn't done what I'd said I would, and came up with some excuses, the set simply told me they were disappointed in me . . .'

'You're made to face up to things because the set asks you and pushes you gently. You're forced to face your weaknesses – maybe it's just giving presentations, and you're avoiding it all the time.'

The discipline of having to report back at every meeting also creates a sense of responsibility: 'You know your turn will come, so it forces you to act, to prepare yourself . . . it's helped me be more prepared now for meetings back at work.'

Members also develop a sense of responsibility for others

– wanting them to work, learn and succeed – and are in earnest about helping them. One woman, newly appointed to a managerial post and unsure about how to work with her boss, hesitated about 'taking action, assertively' and after several meetings her set colleagues decided to frog-march her to his office and force the meeting. Another set – in an academic institution – recalled how they had pushed one member who wasn't making any progress in finding a project: 'It felt uncomfortable at the time, but he later told us he needed that pressure.'

'We're often, in real life, tempted to avoid the heat, to avoid thinking of certain things . . . But the set won't let you. They force you to face things . . . to be angry or sad.'

This is also threatening, as several participants mentioned: 'Your colleagues won't let you hide, they make you confront issues you don't want to. But you don't half feel better once you've talked about them.'

Having themselves experienced the relief of talking, many participants subsequently attempt to adopt a similar openness back at work, trying to persuade their staff to be more open and honest – usually by being so themselves, and so becoming a model.

Taking responsibility, deriving a sense of achievement, gaining in competence and confidence – this heady combination leaves many participants energized and enthused by the end of each meeting:

'I'd come tired and deflated, and at the end of the meetings I was ready to face all the issues that had been worrying me before.'

'I always came away fired with energy and confidence. The next two or three days at work are full of vitality and positive thinking,' was how another experienced it. Others commented that between meetings, or even after the set was no longer meeting, a phone call to another set member could revitalize flagging spirits or confidence.

If only for this result, set meetings seem to be a good thing!

'The set gave me the courage of my convictions. I'd recently become Personnel Director in the financial institution I work for. It was new to me, and there were some fundamental problems that had to be looked into. Mostly to do with changing the culture and profile of the department. But I had a major problem: my predecessor was still there, demoted.

In the set, it was useful to articulate the problem – and be pushed to talk about my real concerns. It feels uncomfortable to be frank about something – we're not encouraged to be frank at work.

It was also really useful to work in a mixed-company and mixed-functional set. We had different perspectives, different values and a different understanding of issues.

Back to my issue: I found I was beginning to adopt the last incumbent's style of managing. But it felt uncomfortable. It was by having the set to go back to and be challenged that I gained the confidence to adopt my own style. I'd wanted to talk to the past director about the uncomfortable situation but couldn't quite decide how to do it. And another thing: I wanted to be called by my first name, and not Mr X, but there was some question about whether this was 'appropriate' for someone in my position, in our company. But I decided it was more important for me to fulfil the role in my own style for a shorter period, than 'play a game' for longer. And the set gave me the confidence to be my own natural self.

I think that without the set I would have come to the same conclusions I did – but this shortened the time considerably, and made working relationships in the department easier sooner. The set gave me the confidence to be honest – because that's what's expected in the set – and I simply approached the previous director and said I wanted to talk out some issues with him because I was feeling uncomfortable. It shook him rigid!

He said he was so pleased I had approached him in this open way. And we resolved the role he was to play in the department.

By being my natural self, and setting this as a 'model' for my staff I lifted a great deal of dormant capacity in the department. I wanted each one of them to be themselves, and to become competent and confident, and work from that basis, and not use their status to achieve things. At meetings I made it OK to express feelings by expressing mine first, and that improved communication considerably.'

Realizing the value of being honest

Being honest with ourselves and others is not, many participants admit, something they are good at. Are any of us? But by working with the same group of people over time, observing the ground rules, being supported in sickness and health – ie in mistakes as well as successes – and in giving and receiving honest feedback: this all helped participants to become more honest, and to value this development.

'The set helped me be more honest with myself – particularly admitting to my emotions and seeing them as a valid part of the picture. So, if I genuinely feel frightened, threatened, hassled, that's part of the equation that needs to be looked at – either alone or with others.'

Another member admitted to being frightened to admit to anger at work: 'There is a code which says you don't show your emotions. So we tried it out in the set: to role play, and help me show anger.'

'I really valued the challenging, the honesty and the feedback – as opposed to the constrained response that you get from colleagues at work,' said a young telecommunications manager.

'It's given me confidence in myself – that I have something to offer. My father always said, "You can do better", and action learning has confirmed that,' said one middle-aged manager.

For many the openness and trust that builds up in the set is 'emotionally releasing. You begin to understand why you react in certain ways, and it helps to control, and not sublimate, those feelings and express them in an appropriate way.'

'I wish we could have an atmosphere like this at work,' sighed another manager. 'I've always wanted – sought – this type of gathering at work but never managed to achieve it – you need to structure it into work.'

Being open and honest does not always come easily. One participant recalled in her reflective document how the set had talked about the need to be open and honest, but 'in reality they weren't – they just said they wanted to be.' Then, during the course of a discussion, she discovered that other set members were not learning much, and her view – which she shared with the set – was that they might if they were prepared to be more open and honest with themselves and each other. Her document continues:

'I was concerned that I had opened up and raised this issue, and that others seemingly didn't share my views about the importance of learning, and how to get there. I felt alone and left the meeting frustrated, and wondering if there was any benefit to continuing on the programme. I felt let down.

I begrudgingly attended the next meeting. Everyone seemed more relaxed, which had the opposite effect on me, and the more I listened, the more I realized I would have to say something about my feelings, otherwise I wouldn't be able to continue. Again, I felt nervous as this was the second time I'd raised the issue of feelings.

The set responded silently and then diffidently . . . but later they admitted that what I'd said had made it easier for them to talk to one another and work constructively, simply because I'd drawn attention to these issues . . . and it had freed them up to admit to some of their feelings.'

Action: Projects and Tasks

The action – be it a project or task – is the ostensible vehicle for learning. I say ostensible, for although it is crucial that every participant undertakes 'action' in some form, it is not the sole means of learning. Learning, as we shall see, occurs from all the elements that make up an action learning programme.

Reg Revans's helpful distinction between puzzles and problems (the former characterized as issues or questions to which there is a single answer, one optimum course of action; the latter as issues and questions which have no one answer or solution, ie there are many possibilities and variations) is a guide to how to choose a project/task to work on. Problems are useful; puzzles are not.

'Pots' Diagram

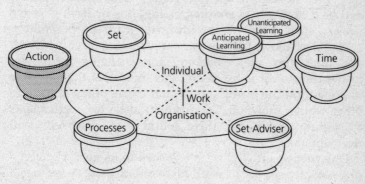

fig. 10

SOME QUESTIONS ANSWERED

Why is it important to have a project?

It is one of the fundamental beliefs of action learning that we learn best by undertaking some action, which we then reflect on and learn from. The main reason for having a project or task is that it gives us something to focus on that is real and important, that means something to us. It creates a 'hook' on which to test out or hang our stored-up knowledge. And it provides a means of measuring how much we really have learnt.

As one manager pointed out: 'the benefit of learning by doing, ie having a project, is that it ties the learning into something relevant. There are a great many things which I learnt as isolated facts, but they only have curiosity value until I can find ways of applying them. Learning by doing takes care of that, and the experience provides a much more indelible memory.'

The main way of learning is by revisiting the action we take. This is how, on an action learning programme, participants are able to monitor progress over a period, witness their own development, learn from mistakes, experiment – and hear how others are progressing. It is by having such a project, such a focus, that participants learn 'purposefully'.

A project allows participants see what they have achieved, and how they are developing and changing themselves in the process. It is by having this focus that they are able to go around the learning cycle and create of it a spiral – in other words, move on. So, a project also gives participants a starting point for their journey of discovery and development.

One participant who wasn't pushed to identify a project – or even other tasks to work on – commented: 'I felt much less involved in what others were saying. I think I learnt less than I would have if I'd had a project.' A female member of a set which addressed just one participant's problem while the other set members acted merely as supports (which I do not believe to be real action learning) said: 'I felt uninvolved, quite bored in fact, and don't think I learnt anything.'

Without a project/task there is thus a danger that the participants will be less committed, and that their learning will have little focus and become merely a string of interesting thoughts. There is also a danger that the set's meetings will start to resemble a discussion group or will veer towards being what some have termed a therapy group. It is the project that keeps the action and the learning focused.

What constitutes 'action', be it a project or task?

The focus for a project/task may be:

- an organizational/departmental issue or need that a participant is working on or is 'given'; this issue can either be new, and hence a challenge, or a perennial difficulty which requires investigating and possibly resolving (for examples of projects see below)
- (for participants in managerial roles) issues, quandaries, responsibilities, irritations, or opportunities with wider ramifications – such as how to resolve a problem of career change, how to deal with a hostile board member, how to cope with a difficult colleague, how to get agreement with team colleagues on an issue, how to manage change, how to create a better relationship with a customer or supplier, how to manage a business, and so on.
- a developmental issue – qualities, competences or behaviours – that a participant wants or needs to develop or improve, such as questions arising from career development or a change of direction.

Reg Revans has postulated four possible types of project (see fig. 11).

For practical reasons, the two most likely to occur are: projects within one's own job in one's own organization; and projects elsewhere in one's own organization.

Types of Projects

	F Setting Un F	
F **Task**	Both familiar	Task familiar Setting unfamiliar
Un F	Task unfamiliar Setting familiar	Both unfamiliar

fig. 11

The essence of a project/task is that it must be something participants:

- can get their teeth into
- will find a challenge: something new that they haven't tackled before
- want to or are able to resolve
- have authority to do something about, ie it must be within their sphere of responsibility, or they must be given the authority
- can report back to the next set meeting on
- will learn from.

A project/task

1 Something realistic, which a participant is:
  - responsible for
  - able to do something about
  - able (ideally) to implement

---

2 Three-part definition of a work-focused project:
   - undertaking 'X'
   - in order that 'Y' occurs
   - which means that I'll learn . . .

3 Three-part definition of a development-focused project:
   - want to develop 'X'
   - will choose 'Y' as a means
   - which means I'll learn . . .

4 Questions which may help in choosing a project:
   - what am I trying to achieve?
   - what's stopping me?
   - what can I do about it?

5 Something which fits into time-frame of the programme (eg six months)

6 Agreed on with client/HRD manager/own manager:
   - after attending assessment centre
   - after a taught course
   - in association with change – of job, work, organizational structures, systems, clients, etc
   - with other identified development needs in mind (eg NVQs)

In other words, not a case-study or research project; and not consultancy – unless this is the specified learning need.

Desk or book research and study into the causes of a problem would not constitute an action learning project, for the simple reason that there is no action. Nor is action learning concerned with finding quick solutions. It aims to go beyond symptoms to fundamental issues and the real problems. Action learning reaches 'those parts that other programmes don't reach' precisely because it doesn't go for the quick fix – instant answers to immediate problems.

Some of the issues addressed in projects:

- managing a particular change
- empowering staff
- introducing new assessment programmes – in an organization or in a school
- implementing Investors in People
- introducing total quality programmes
- improving communications throughout the organization
- streamlining work processes and procedures
- developing middle managers' potential
- modifying a paperwork system to enable managers to spend more time with sales staff
- changing from an autocratic to a facilitative style of managing
- re-organizing a production line
- tackling absenteeism on a night shift
- improving management performance
- increasing the profitability of a small engineering firm
- creating equal opportunities for women or other disadvantaged groups
- creating and building up a new role and defining its responsibilities
- establishing communications system for engineers or sales people on the road

The learning is at least as important as any action undertaken. And evidence of the learning is that something has been created, put in place, or is now being done differently and successfully, and that the participant has gained insights, or developed in some way from the exercise. Knowing that the set will request evidence at the next meeting is a great motivator to everyone. It acts as a goad to do something, and not procrastinate or find excuses. But for many participants what was more important – what made action learning different –

was its discipline: the constant revisiting of an issue to work on it publicly till it was resolved.

'It's the returning to a project, the follow-up of the story at the next meeting of what you did or didn't do, what happened, with what results, and what you may need to do next. That is what makes it so useful and valuable,' said one manager.

Tasks and other short-term issues may thus be resolved over the space of two meetings. Longer-term projects, on the other hand, would normally be chosen to last approximately the length of the programme.

Individual v. group projects:

The other major distinction to bear in mind is that projects may be individual ones, for a single participant; or group ones, where the whole set works on the same project. The choice will be dictated by the purpose of the project. If, for instance, the goal is to create equal opportunities for women or disadvantaged groups within an organization, then the set might tackle the issue as a group. However, even in such group projects, it is important that everyone has their own mini-project to work on.

Those who have experienced both group and individual projects say they gained more from the individual variety because it allowed them to focus on their own learning needs in greater depth. They also felt a greater sense of commitment.

Group projects, however, are an obvious choice if the purpose of the programme is team-building or to improve company-wide performance.

Project: My own development as a manager

A branch manager in a major building society had this aim; his assignment was to work on it by focusing on various everyday managerial tasks. He had been on a

---

number of courses about management, but his performance – and that of his branch – was still proving to be
a worry. 'All the courses I've attended and articles I've
read have given me the theory, but I still don't really
seem to be able to put them into practice effectively.'

One area that he and his 'client'* identified was staff
motivation. He worked on this issue, drawing on the
support and insights generated at the set meetings. This
practical approach resulted in him arriving at the third
set meeting and pronouncing thoughtfully, 'I've realized that the problem isn't about motivating my staff.
It's about motivating myself.'

How is it decided which type of project or task you work on?

The quick and easy answer is: it will depend on the purpose
of the programme, who it is for, and what needs are being
addressed.

One senior manger commented: 'We'd each work on an
issue of the moment that concerned us. Sometimes as you
hear others talk you realize you have a similar issue as well,
and then when your turn comes it tumbles out. It's not always
necessary to come with an issue or have the same one going
forward.'

Another participant alluded to the fact that 'a task/project
doesn't always have to be "a serial" with continuity; it can
be a series of issues where different – or the same – characters
emerge, but you're still the central character.' One manager
commented ruefully, 'You begin to realize that you are often
part of the problem.' (See pp. 277–83 for more information
on senior managers' experiences.)

---

* For a definition of 'client', see p. 139

Programmes for younger participants or those in middle-management roles tend to be project-based. It is felt that they provide a more challenging and focused learning opportunity, thus making the revisiting easier. However, as many pointed out, although they worked initially, and probably for most of the time, on their projects, 'later we also brought our daily problems . . . or we'd talk about other issues that concerned us, like the company culture which discouraged asking questions.'

Others stressed that although initially they saw the action taken on their projects as the most important part of the programme, later on in the programme the learning came to dominate. However, there were also those who admitted to a sense of 'sod the learning, let's get on with the action!'

Who chooses the projects or identifies the tasks?

Ideally, a joint decision will be reached between the participant, his or her manager, the client for the programme, and probably also the personnel/training/development department. Everyone involved must remember, however, that the other main focus is the participant's learning needs.

The choice of project/task will therefore emerge from, or be dictated by:

- An annual assessment that a participant has recently had, and which has pinpointed certain skills that he or she needs to acquire or areas for improvement if they are to progress and develop their career. A project is then identified that will give the participant an opportunity to develop the specified skills or qualities.
- The participant's 'client' may have a project for the participant to work on.
- The participant and his/her manager may identify a project within their department/section that needs working on – and which would provide the learning opportunities for the participant.

- There may be some other obvious issues that the organization needs resolved, and that participants on an action learning programme would benefit from working on. The only danger here – as one programme I investigated for this book discovered – was what the participants saw as the hijacking of their programme by senior managers for their own pet projects, with little attention paid to the participants' learning needs. 'Our project was imposed – and when we didn't seem to be getting results, we began to get negative vibes from managers. But the problem for us was that we were learning, even though visibly we weren't achieving on those projects.'
- If participants are on the programme to work on change – be it within their own work roles or on the wider subject of culture change and introducing new ways of working aimed at involving and valuing staff – then this goal provides an ideal project for each participant on an action learning programme. Thus their focus is to study their own changing role and changing behaviour, as well as ways and means of introducing change that will affect others.

In the last two instances, group projects are a useful means of achieving the desired goal.

One set of young managers was given a choice of projects – in fact a choice of whether to work on a group project or to undertake individual ones. They opted for the former, because one of the aims of the programme was to give them the opportunity of working in a team – something they didn't encounter in their everyday work.

Many of us work pretty much alone in our jobs [in retailing], so it's good to work with others for a change. We also wanted to compare our different styles of managing, and learn more about the business overall. We each work in different segments of our business. There's a feeling in the company that we should all know more about the 'whole' and not just our bits of it. So this was an ideal opportunity.

This group worked as consultants to their marketing director, since gaining consultancy skills was one of the objectives of the programme.

A group project

A set in a local authority which had been brought together to develop teamwork was invited to choose a project which would be of relevance to them all and which they would all feel comfortable working on. Each member suggested a project chosen from their own work environment, and the set then decided which of these they felt was the most appropriate. The project they eventually opted for was concerned with establishing good communications between three geographically separated offices.

At their first meeting, the set decided that the initial challenge would be to identify some of the problems with the current system and to sell the idea to B's (the problem holder's) three offices. Set members then went to B's offices, interviewed his staff, and collected views on problems and possible solutions. Thus, even before the second set meeting, a new telephone procedure – to get around the problem of permanently engaged phones – had been suggested and put in place.

The second challenge – which was discussed at the second set meeting – was how to create more regular and higher quality meetings between B and his scattered staff. 'I wasn't seeing them regularly, so we decided on fixing dates and times for me to see staff. We also decided it would be helpful if I visited locations informally, just to talk to people and hear their problems and their ideas for resolving them.'

Following this meeting, B met with one group of his staff (traffic wardens) who had been 'marginalized' before, and, by adopting an action learning approach to the meeting, he came away with a mass of ideas on how

---

137

to improve communication between the wardens and the community, in particular how to co-operate with senior citizens on their permits and other rules about parking.

'I learnt', said B, 'that there are lots of good ideas out there if you give people a chance to talk! It's helped me to delegate more to my staff.'

The set continued to produce ideas, and at each meeting B reported on progress made to date. For B, the benefit of working with the set as opposed to going it alone ('I don't think I'd have found the time to work on this issue if I'd had to do it alone,' he admitted) was 'the opportunity to talk through my ideas with others, but most importantly to draw on their experiences and what they had been doing in their various, very different departments. I was also concerned about implementing new ideas and how my staff would react. Would this all be seen as a flash in the pan? So talking things through was helpful. I began to appreciate my team back at work much more, and we began to talk more openly, even about feelings! I began to realize how much I was able to affect people. I'd also had a fear of making formal presentations, but having to do one for senior managers on the set's work and what we'd achieved has given me confidence to do so. I gave a presentation to 30 people the other day!'

The other set members also gained:

'It's mind-blowing. I'm in my first managerial job and I'm realizing through this project that people can do so much if you give them the opportunity. I'm soaking things up like a sponge – it's the exposure to others' experiences which is so useful.'

'Hearing others' stories has made me realize there are different styles of management. I've also learnt from the mistakes of others!'

'It's the making of contacts with colleagues – the networking – that's been so valuable. The length of the programme has been crucial: so much better than the short sharp shock of other courses. You realize that you can't achieve things immediately.'

'I chose the role of "chair" of the group deliberately – I know I'm good at that. But what I've learnt is to distinguish between being a manager and a leader – and it's helped me work with my own group back at work.'

All commented that they were now making much greater use of cross-departmental/-sectional/-functional groups to work on new proposals and everyday issues of concern.

Participants' managers need to be involved:

This may seem obvious, but it is worth reiterating why their involvement is crucial:

- A participant's project is likely to be focused on their area of work. The manager may thus be the source of some interesting ideas as to what could constitute the project.
- The manager will be losing the participant and his time while he or she attends set meetings and works on a project.
- Development of staff is one of a manager's prime responsibilities. He or she is the person most likely to be aware of a participant's learning and developmental needs.
- Because the programme is about learning it is likely that a participant may make some 'mistakes'. The manager must realize that making mistakes (not major financial or system mistakes, of course) is part of the learning process.

Why does every project need a 'client'?

A client is a senior manager whom the participant will report to on his/her project and learning. A client is rarely a participant's manager, because a linear relationship can impose other constraints and may not allow both parties to be as open as they need to be about any problems.

Reg Revans has defined a client as someone who 'knows, cares and can' – ie someone who understands the nature of the programme, thinks it is important, and can be influential in making sure that the participants gain access wherever necessary, and that the programme is given high visibility and acceptance. He or she is, in fact, the champion of the programme.

Clients are also indispensable allies for the person – often a training & development manager – who has introduced the programme in the first place.

> 'I came on the programme looking for the answer to a business problem: low profitability. Carrying out the project demonstrated to me that low profitability was not the problem. It was merely a symptom of other problems which have their roots both within me [the MD] as a person, and outside in the market place.
>
> As a result of the research and reflection I have done, I have developed a system model which illustrates just what this business actually does, and how it relates to me, our staff, our customers and society. One result of this is that I am now more aware of the importance of issues external to the firm and I now try to spend time considering what we should be doing and less time monitoring how well we did what we chose to do.'

Is 'implementing' essential in a programme?

Implementing means carrying out ideas and recommendations, ie seeing them through from start to finish. Producing reports and recommendations only to leave it to someone else to work out the implementation phase is the easy option. Being required to implement prevents the set from resembling a think-tank or debating group – for, intellectually stimulating or emotionally releasing as such groups might be, without implementation nothing actually changes. Furthermore, unless a participant puts into effect the developmental projects or tasks they are focusing on, and reports back to this effect, we have no evidence that they can do something differently or better, and therefore no indication of whether any learning or development is taking place.

'The doing triggers off different experiences, thoughts and feelings . . . and so a new learning. If we're to learn to be managers, rather than consultants, we need to handle implementation,' observed one participant. She went on describe how implementation had given her an insight: 'I learnt what was practical, what was bearable and what was acceptable . . . and am more aware that next time I make proposals I need to consider those on the receiving end much more!'

One hospital manager recalled:

> I came up with a proposal of how to involve various managers and consultants in our hospital in a new approach to gaining new business from local GPs. However, it was rejected as being too long – people were not interested. Yet it was crucial to our survival that we act. So, I tried a different tack. I identified a few individuals who were in favour of my plan and informally we began working together. We acquired some new clients and extra business that way, and when it looked as though my idea had some validity, the other managers and consultants began to show interest. So, implementation was crucial for me to gain acceptance of the plan. It's taught me to be flexible and to have various strategies, not just one, for implementing proposals.

On the other hand, many programmes do offer participants a great deal of learning without that final stage. A group of young managers who had set out to 'learn about being consultants' learned from performing that same function for their client. Others in similar positions learnt a great deal about handling people, handling data, negotiating, and a host of other useful skills.

One participant summed up what many others felt: 'Implementing is not necessarily integral. The whole experience is important. and you still learn, even if your project isn't implemented.'

The usual mix of projects in an unusual setting[2]

A large dairy farm – at that time part of the Dartington Trust – was coping with reduced milk quotas and searching for means to improve its profitability. The farm workers, the manager felt, would undoubtedly have some useful ideas.

An action learning programme involving the seven farm workers was therefore run over the winter months. It produced some excellent money-saving ideas including: a costing exercise by the farm mechanic on the farm-owned combine-harvester (which led to the decision to scrap it); a scheme – by the herdsmen – to reduce the milking parlours from three to two; and an investigation of feedstuffs by the relief herdsman (an ex-student from an agricultural college). At the set's request, the farm manager attended the last half hour of every set meeting.

Does a project have to be based on something in a participant's own department or section?

No. Whether it is or not will depend on how the programme is conceived (see fig. 11, above). The main criterion is that it should be something he or she can learn from which is also of relevance to the section or department in question.

Working on another department's problems isn't always the greatest motivator, as one set pointed out. They were workshop-based engineers, and their project involved establishing effective field communications for engineers 'on the road':

> Although we had a lot of useful ideas, we didn't see that *we* would have the benefits, and so we weren't very motivated. Had I been a field engineer with all the frustrations, I would have gained more . . . It would have motivated me to think more.

The aim of this programme was to bring about more in-company teamwork. Allocating to sets projects that are of use to others looks, on the surface, to be an ideal way of achieving this aim. But at another level it may fail to generate sufficient enthusiasm. As a continuation of the programme, the set was subsequently allocated a project within their own section with very different results (see p. 152).

This brings us back to Reg Revans' point: we are most motivated to learn when we are tackling an issue close to our own hearts and work.

How does a participant make sure he or she gets the time to work on their project – that it gets backing, and isn't taken away or stopped during the programme?

If the participant's manager isn't kept fully involved, or at least fully informed, then he or she is – quite rightly – going to feel put out. A well-run programme will have brought participants' managers into preliminary discussions and stressed the importance of the programme.

Where a manager remains unhappy, the participant's client may be able to help, as may the training or management development department – or indeed the instigator of the programme as a whole.

As for giving the participant time off – this becomes less of a problem if the task or project is part of the participant's own work or is something the manager can identify as being important to his/her section or department.

Even so, there may still be problems as pressure at work mounts and everyone takes on more tasks and more responsibilities with only a finite amount of time in which to do them.

Reg Revans coined a very useful catch-phrase to remind people that they are not alone when working on projects – or indeed at any time when attempting to do something. He reminds us to identify some individual or group of people who:

- *know* . . . or are aware of what it is we are trying to do or accomplish
- *care* . . . about what we are undertaking, are concerned it should succeed; and
- *can* . . . do something to help us, ie have some power, influence or authority

Networking, supporting, and influencing are three cornerstones of action learning.

What happens if a participant can't find a project?

This fear is frequently voiced by participants at the outset of a programme. Sometimes it is difficult to pinpoint a project until the participants know more about the nature of the programme – for it is somewhat different from other programmes they might have been on.

A well-run programme will have been set in motion by an organizer who first alerts clients, the personnel department, the participants themselves and their managers, emphasizing to all concerned what such a programme requires of its participants – and in particular the need for a project to work on. Hence the participant is not left alone with this dilemma. To avoid such problems, one company which makes wide use of action learning is considering the setting up of a 'bank' of projects, submitted by managers, on the basis of which suitable participants would be found.

THE VALUE OF PROJECTS AND TASKS

Obviously, the aim of the programme, the choice of projects, whether the project should be tackled on a group or individual basis, all has a bearing on how much participants learn and gain. This is particularly the case where the aim is 'to learn to work in a team'; the learning must be focused up to a point on that aspect of the project.

My research revealed that participants who had individual projects, or mini-projects within larger group projects learnt and gained more in terms of breadth and depth of insights – as witnessed by their comments. A number of participants who had experienced more than one type of programme remarked that 'individual projects allow you to do more personal, deeper learning.'

The quality of the set adviser, and how often the set was reminded that learning was as important as action, also appeared to influence what and how much participants learned. One set, tackling a group project without the benefit of a set adviser, commented: 'We haven't done a lot of conscious learning. Maybe we'll do it at the end.' Another – with a set adviser always present – commented, 'We haven't really stopped to look at how we worked as a team – although we've learnt a lot from the project itself.'

Nevertheless there are many common gains:

1 Participants gain a greater insight and understanding of their own or (in mixed-company sets) other organizations

'Hearing others' projects broadens your horizons, gives you the bigger picture.'

Simply hearing fellow participants describe their projects gives a broader insight into organizational issues and problems – particularly those of people in different functions. 'You begin to understand the constraints people face – for instance, finance and personnel have different issues to grapple with and hence bring different perspectives.'

By examining everyone's projects – particularly on in-company programmes – participants began to see how they and their department were part of a larger entity, began to see how bits of the jigsaw puzzle fitted together. 'I know a great deal more about the company now – and begin to feel much more part of it,' said one young marketing manager.

This cohesion is enhanced when participants discover that people in different departments can help them with their projects – that their insights and questions are useful and make sense. 'I was really amazed at how people from other functions were able to help me – simply by asking intelligent questions which made me stop and think.'

Coupled with this was the realization that, as one engineer put it, 'No matter how we defined our projects and what they were seemingly about, in the end they all came down to the same problems: relationships with others – be they your boss, your colleagues or your staff.'

'The fact that everyone else has problems – not just me – was comforting,' was a frequent comment.

One set of engineers who worked on a project for another engineering section gained the realization that 'we are a "collective" – we now understand better how we are interconnected with the field engineers, and that our overall profitability depends on all of us working together.'

In mixed-company programmes, there is an added dimension of comparing how various organizations tackle different issues – or even the same issue – differently. For one participant this latter experience was, as he put it, 'an eye-opener. I had always assumed that the way things were done in my company was the best and the only way. Now I see this was not necessarily so.'

2 The opening up of networks and inter-departmental contacts

'It was a ticket – a licence to investigate . . . a door-opener to people.' And once the project has opened doors, participants realize that what has lain hidden behind them is not as awesome or frightening as they had imagined. Behind the doors are other human beings!

One young manager was in some dread of visiting the finance director. 'I needed to see him as part of my project. My manager suggested this. I spent 35 minutes with him and he told me not to hesitate if I needed to ask him anything again. I'd somehow not expected such an open approach to me. You begin to see senior managers as approachable human beings.'

'I realized', said another, younger, manager, 'that just a little bit of knowledge and research can give you major insights – and definitely enough to go and talk to others as a basis for discussion. You don't have to be an expert before you go and ask others for something.'

Some discovered that they knew as much as anyone and had equally valid insights. 'I had no need to be in awe of people,' said one research scientist, who continued, 'Before, the marketing department intimidated me. Now no longer. I was amazed at how helpful people were – willing to help and give you their time. I hadn't expected that. I had always thought they would think I was wasting their time. I think people actually like helping you,' she summed up.

Many participants mentioned that the project had done more than teach them the value of using others; it had given them contacts throughout the company which would be of use in other circumstances back at work. Each person contacted knew a host of other people, and this would expand their own network.

'Working on my project with the help of others made me realize that there is always someone I can talk to if I need to. Before, I'd bottle up stress, problems and worries. Not any longer,' was another comment.

One took his experience of such networking – and the help he had received on his project from set members with widely differing backgrounds – a step further: 'In any project team I now have a better mix of people -- with different skills and styles of working. The differences of knowledge and perspective are a strength.'

And where the programme had a high profile within the organization, it gave the participants themselves a high profile – something not to be sneezed at – and a 'licence' to investigate. 'You meet people you'd never have the opportunity to meet. They get to know you, too. It gives you much wider horizons and understanding of the organization – and it gives others a chance to assess you.'

Working on projects had thus legitimized for them the viability of approaching others in the future, whether to ask questions, or simply to go up to people and introduce themselves . . . and in the process to build up their own useful network of contacts for the future.

3 It instils a 'disciplined' way of tackling projects

The discipline that many participants talked about consisted of several elements. Firstly there was the discipline of having to create a plan of action, to work out who could help, and to build up a network of contacts for information or insights. Next came making sure they had the authority to do what they were proposing; then being clear about the final goal. Lastly, building in evaluation stages as the project progressed. These and many other aspects of working in a systematic way on their project they found immensely helpful.

What primarily created this discipline was working under the microscopic gaze of others, who were also able to help formulate the various steps and stages – either from their own past experience, or simply because they were similarly involved in working systematically, and hence could see where the gaps in the project lay.

The other main aspect of discipline was the constant revisiting of each participant's project, at consecutive set meetings, to see what stage it had reached.

As one participant said, 'It gave me some methods and systems . . . a structured approach to any assignment: how and where to look for help and resources, collecting evidence, being clear about the problem; making sure you have criteria for measuring or evaluating what you're doing; having strategies for coping and managing. Before, I'd be running at 90mph and getting nowhere.'

Another ticked off the necessary steps point by point: 'Be clear about the problem – ask questions; establish your criteria for assessing/measuring your work; have strategies for coping and improving; and always collect evidence; and get feedback.'

Another observed: 'Once you have an idea, make it tangible. Have a plan of action, create networks of people who can help you, check out the literature, ensure you have the authority to do what you want to do, hold meetings with others.'

Many alluded to the fact that this discipline was an amalgam of having, in their mind's eye or on paper, a 'learning cycle' – which they adapted into a 'working' cycle. Thus, rather than rushing from idea to action, they built in extra stages, considered more options, worked out different scenarios, and allowed for frequent assessment. Many also talked of building in thinking and reflection time.

Several also commented that they had become aware of the notion of 'task' and 'process' – and the value of stopping to consider the latter. 'Before I'd simply focus on what I wanted to achieve – but *how* I was going to was not something I spent too much time thinking about. I never, for instance, stopped to think about my decision process. Now I set goals, consider options for getting there, flag up issues I need to consider further.'

Thus, for one manager, action learning invited 'a certain caution in what I do. I'm less inclined to give an instant decision or answer. I prepare my ground more, think, go away, come back.'

A number of participants told me that the fact they were working on something visible, that people within the organization – often senior people – knew the scope of it, in itself provided a discipline.

And last but not least was the knowledge that they would be expected to report back to the set, a group who had expectations of them and who would challenge – as well as support – them.

'I now feel much more confident about turning an idea into an action, and accomplishing it. It's given me some basic methods and systems – reminded me to look for help and ideas – to use the resources available.'

'How to work methodically – to be clear about the problems and issues, clear about the means of resolving them, and clear about the reasons for choices and decisions.'

'It's taught me to take a more structured approach now to any assignment I have.'

---

4 It gives participants responsibility for completing a project – and managing all the elements

For many participants this was the first time they had tackled a major project and been asked to claim responsibility for it. It was this feeling of ownership of a project that impressed many: 'Ownership of an issue, the responsibility to carry it out, and the authority to do so, plus real personal commitment to it. You need all three for something to really happen.' It was their experience of what ownership could result in that made many aware that their own staff would also benefit by being given 'ownership'.

One participant commented that his manager's confidence in him had been increased by the way he approached his project. As a result, he was given an increased budgetary control and more responsibility generally.

A young member of a set laughed when she recounted how her manager felt he was learning by listening to her and being party to her thinking as she tackled her project – a small-scale practical one concerned with creating a logging system to ensure that all phone calls to the department were received, dealt with effectively, with the whole process being monitored for its effectiveness.

In another project, a client told the set – who were consulting him on a major marketing project – that he had learned and gained considerably by working with them.

A manager talked of how the project had given him insights into the art of managing: 'In the project you become aware of your responsibility to take control and make judgements and take decisions on what's important, and have the confidence to manage others and not allow emotions to overrule you and intervene . . . a step in the direction of maturity.'

Where implementation was an integral part of projects, and where in addition those projects were based in their own departments, participants felt more commitment. Such factors definitely provide an impetus and sense of energy to set projects. But implementation adds an extra dimension to the sense of responsibility, for the fruits of the project need to be seen as being, as one participant put it, 'practical, usable and bearable'.

'If you don't implement, you have pie-in-the-sky ideas of what you want to do. But you change these if you are responsible for implementing. And it makes you more aware the next time you suggest something be done in a different way.'

For those working on individual projects, implementation was not always built-in. For one participant, however, it was crucial that it should be:

> I came to learn how to communicate better. I'm also a 'theorist', and weak on doing things – I'm not a 'concluder' or a 'producer' So, being forced to produce and conclude was good for me. Our department had a bad reputation, so I set out to improve our communications with other departments through a whole host of initiatives. It's made me very conscious of the need to have good channels of communication in a company.

Many also talked of having to learn to negotiate, to compromise, to take others much more into account. Where implementation was not part of their brief, some participants talked of a sense of frustration at not knowing whether all their hard work would ever see the light of day.

> As part of the company's strategy to build better teamworking, our engineering workshop was put into a 'set' to resolve our own day-to-day problems. Focusing on our own areas of work was a second bite of the cherry – in the first part of this programme we'd worked on problems in other areas of the company. But working on our own work gave us more enthusiasm because it was left up to us. We decided we needed to be more efficient and improve our turnaround time for repairs.
>
> We work on the repairs of a variety of telecommunica-

tion products. We identified what everyone does, what are the problems and where bottlenecks existed. By working together we managed to change the layout, create a system for what happens when a repair job comes in, channel phone calls through one person. We established a system for ordering spare parts and handing work out (before, our manager did this). And we physically re-organized the layout of the workshop to make it more efficient.

What we've achieved is a cycle turnaround that has been reduced from ninety days to five days! Our next step is reduce the five days to two days.

I volunteered to be the 'leader' – because I was interested and saw it as an opportunity to learn and grow. I'd also been one of the people who was always backbiting, so I decided here was an opportunity to do something rather than just complaining. It was a frustrating project at times, and it took much longer than I'd anticipated.

The result of working together is that now people are more willing to co-operate with one another, to share their expertise with one another . . . and to use the phone! Morale has definitely improved. There's more of an understanding that we survive collectively and not individually, and people are more willing to stay on after-hours without claiming overtime. They're also coming up with ideas for what else we could be doing differently – that wouldn't have happened two years ago.

Yes, there are still some cynics who think the whole programme and team-building effort is a great con, but gradually they're coming round. But, one of the lads has for many years been consistently 'sick' three or four times a year, and now the others are realizing that it affects their work load, and have begun to tackle him and point out what he is doing. We're taking more responsibility collectively.

Much of our initiative was made possible by the

attitude of our manager. He's learnt much about the workshop and how it works, he understands our problems and now gives us the opportunity to put things right. I'm not sure we'd have managed to achieve so much without him, with a more autocratic manager.

What it's made me realize is that such a programme is about giving people the power and improving the workplace. And, after all, it's the workpeople who know more about the workplace than their managers. I've learnt to take initiative (not just to gripe!), I've become more assertive, and much freer to be honest and open with managers, and listen to them more. Before, I simply regarded their decisions as being destructive. I just hope that in the future I'll continue to go to managers and explain the impact of any decisions they take.

The Processes in the Set

The processes in a set exist to help members focus on both their actions and on their learning. The processes of a set are very different from processes in other groups. Most participants embarking on an action learning programme certainly have no anticipation of learning anything special by working in the group – other than simply 'helping' other members to achieve their projects. The processes are thus one of the 'eye-opening' elements of a programme and are, for me, one of the main keys to effective action learning.

What is also interesting is that these processes involve some of the basic communication skills that everyone needs to learn if they are to work effectively with others – colleagues, staff or 'bosses', customers or suppliers. Once tried out, they become obvious. 'I was excited by its commonsense,' said more than one participant.

'Pots' Diagram

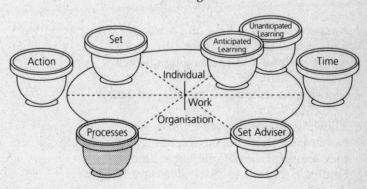

fig. 12

Developing mentoring skills and empowering staff

One of the unanticipated gains from working in a set was learning the skills of mentoring. The combination of working in a support group and using the processes of a set gave many participants insights on how they could change their approach to managing, to working with their staff, to empowering them. One participant said of the set, 'It's like having five mentors!'

SOME QUESTIONS ANSWERED

What happens in a set meeting? What are these 'processes'?

There are a number of fundamental processes that occur and need to be observed (and some avoided) if the set is to gain the real benefits of working with action learning.

The processes are:

1 Airspace: allowing time and space for everyone to work individually and report back
2 Asking helpful and challenging questions
3 Listening 'actively'
4 Focusing on learning as much as on action
5 Reflecting
6 Allowing time and space for silences
7 Not judging or giving advice; not telling anecdotes (unless they are helpful); not offering solutions
8 Finding a formula to share ideas and insights

'What distinguishes the action learning spirit is that it's not simply about answers or solutions to questions or problems, but about questions and space to talk and think. Nor is it about getting advice, finding answers or getting information. It's more to do with responding thoughtfully to questions, and really thinking.'

'For me it's the processes that are crucial to the success of action learning,' commented one manager. 'But it can infuriate action-oriented people and make them impatient!' warned another.

1. Airspace:

This is the time during which one participant tells the other members where he or she has got to since the last meeting. Thus it is the continuation of a 'story' which other members have got to know well, and have become involved in.

If the programme is focusing on specific projects, this story will be an evolving one. And even if participants are focusing less on projects and more on issues with wider ramifications (as happens on programmes for senior managers) there are still ongoing stories, although these may change over the lifetime of the programme.

Time and space for each individual is a key element of action learning. It is an opportunity – rare for most of us – to be listened to with total, undivided attention. For each presenter it is also a chance to stop and reflect, to ask for help and ideas, to be asked questions by the other set members, to have to think things through – in response to requests by other set members – and explain out loud. Often, in the process, they become clear about what has been puzzling them.

'It was my one bit of "luxury",' commented one senior manager. 'A time for myself when I could stop and think.'

Thus, in a set meeting, the 'conch' is passed around to everyone. But such airspace is not a five-minute affair. 'I thought we'd resolved my issue within a few minutes, but when we started working in an action learning way, I realized that we had only scratched the surface,' said one young nurse-manager.

Most participants were surprised at how it usually took at least an hour to get to the bottom of an issue, quandary, or problem – often redefining the nature of the problem in the process – and then work through how to tackle it. 'It really is surprising how long it takes to get to the bottom of an issue . . . that's one of the advantages of airspace . . . that you feel you're not taking up people's time, that it is "legitimate" to work through to the origins of an issue.'

During a participant's airspace it is the task of the rest of the set to help by asking questions that will clarify issues, to 'shine a torch into the corners', and to unfold all the components of the ongoing story – the events and thoughts and feelings and insights.

Airspace is important for the learning: we each need the opportunity to be prompted on, and to reflect on, that learning.

Holding on to this airspace is important, for it means that the set has a 'dialogue' with one person at a time, rather than having a 'discussion', as in other gatherings. A discussion, says David Bohm (see p. 47), is like a ping-pong match, with words and thoughts being tossed around and caught by anyone who is ready. Dialogue focuses on one person.

With the focus on one person, others do not have the opportunity to go off at tangents that interest them, do not hijack the airspace to tell their own stories or shift the set's focus on to them (unless they have asked the presenter if that would be useful), nor do they begin to hold conversations with one another, unless the presenter asks them to (see below).

2. *Questions:*

Helpful and challenging questions are the key to working in a set: by asking questions we hand responsibility back to the 'problem-owner'. Asking questions causes people to think – provided they are asked in the right spirit.

Questions – mostly open ones that cause the presenter to think, reflect and say more – are therefore useful for:

- *clarifying*: 'Are you saying that . . . ?'
- *attempting to understand*: 'Could you explain so-and-so a bit more?'
- *mirroring*: 'So what you're saying is . . . ?'
- *opening up new avenues*: 'Have you explored/thought of . . .'
- *digging deeper*: 'What else was happening?'
- *unpeeling layers*: 'And then what happened?'
- *offering ideas and insights*: 'Have you thought of . . .' or 'Would so-and-so be of any help?'

And, of course, there are the pseudo-questions – those comments and reflections by other set members on what they are hearing – that draw people out further. These can be just as useful, provided they contain no element of censoring or judging the presenter.

'The secret is to get people talking. So saying "I don't understand", "Tell me more", or "You seem to be glossing over . . ." encourages them to say more.'

Questions

- help the presenter
- clarify something for set member
- 'unpack' a statement
- challenge
- offer insights, ideas and suggestions

It is sometimes difficult to resist bombarding the presenter with questions. 'I began to feel I needed to protect myself from all the questions that were being fired at me, with no time to stop and think,' said one participant. As many discovered, asking questions is not that easy: 'I'd never realized how difficult it is to formulate really helpful questions.'

This bombarding is something that tends to happen when

the set is still inexperienced and new to action learning. Again, with time, things change. Set members learn to listen to the questions others are asking, and also to listen to how the presenter is working on them . . . and they learn to wait before asking a question which could take the presenter down a different track.

Bombarding can provide an opportunity for the set adviser to intervene and ask the set to assess what is happening. Such a question makes the set aware of group processes that apply not only to working in a set but in any other group.

Questions can sometimes evoke a defensive response in the presenter. The set can address this either by asking why the presenter is feeling defensive – which in turn may open up an area that needs to be explored further – or, if this defensiveness results from a questioner probing too aggressively, the set will point this out (ie give feedback) to the questioner. If this is pursued, the questioner will in turn learn something about himself.

In this way the processes of the set provide a learning opportunity about interactions for everyone in the set.

I've learnt to 'talk'. I never used to at work, but as a manager this was something I needed to do more of, to get performance out of people . . . and talking to them was a key. By not talking I didn't know what their preconceptions were – they often see situations totally differently.

I also gained confidence in my own opinions – my boss had pointed out my lack of confidence, and others in the set did too. So with the set I worked out a strategy. I'd discuss my opinion on something with them, and rehearse it before going to my manager. They would confirm it sounded sensible, and 'coach' me on how to be assertive. In the process I've learnt that an autocratic boss – like mine – likes you to have an opinion and then argue it out . . . whereas I'd always assumed he wouldn't.

---

3. *Listening actively:*

Listening is one of our least developed skills. Yet it is one of our potentially most important ones.

We think we listen, but often we only hear part of what is said, or we hear at a superficial level; we fail to make connections or see contradictions between what is being said now and what was said a short time ago. Alternatively, we shut out things we don't want to hear; or we become so engrossed with what *we* want to say next that we miss what is being said. Likewise, we don't always 'listen' to the non-verbals signals – the body language, the tone of voice.

When we listen actively to another person, we follow precisely what they are saying. By creating a picture of it in our mind we can literally see the scenario, notice where the gaps and spaces are, where the information is incomplete or puzzling, where something is being glossed over. But listening is not something that most of us are good at!

'I think visually, almost spatially – and I've applied that to my more general thinking – and listening! If I can see issues in a picture form that helps me analyse them. I can now also see myself as part of that picture and where I fit in,' said one participant who worked in the design department of a large company.

It is the responsibility of a presenter to tell other set members if they are misinterpreting what he or she is saying. In this way set members get feedback about their own skills – or lack thereof. The set adviser will probably also comment if non-listening seems to be a trait of one person, or even of the set as a whole. What is valuable about this is that behaviour exhibited in the set is often the same that occurs elsewhere. If set members can learn to listen differently in the set, they are likely to transfer it back to work.

Helpful behaviour by set members[3]

- listen and attend
- learn not to interrupt
- convey empathy
- support
- challenge
- learn to ask good questions
- ask yourself 'Is what I'm about to say helpful to the person with airspace?'
- provide information
- offer advice (at the right time and in the right way)

Effective behaviour by a problem presenter

- prepare for meetings
- structure your time
- be clear what you would like – or would like the set – to focus on
- learn to ask for what you want
- learn how to get an empathetic response
- learn how to receive
- learn to generate action points

Feedback

Many of us are afraid of giving honest feedback. We bite our tongues and hold back, only to gripe later – normally to someone else! We stop ourselves beause we don't know what the reaction will be – will the person be angry or hurt? Feedback may lead to a negative reaction. So, it's a question both of how it's given and received.

Every manager needs to give feedback, and the set

provides an opportunity to learn to give, and also to receive it. So, set members may give feedback to a presenter on how he or she appears, or what they are doing or saying. And the person giving the feedback will in turn get feedback on whether it was done in a helpful manner.

Being given feedback, both positive and negative, may also be difficult. As the receiver, we need to learn to listen to it, think about it, and respond rather than instantly react . . . something that the time and space in the set allow members to start doing.

Feelings of doubt, anxiety or lack of confidence, as well as excitement and energy exist in the sets, particularly at the beginning of a programme, as many participants recalled (see p. 270). They mirror the feelings we have elsewhere but to which we often don't admit. Yet they colour how we are and what we do. They are powerful agents. Recognizing them, and simply admitting to them out loud, often proves not to be as worrying as the idea of doing so, and may loosen the hold they have on us.

Insights and feedback from other set members prove useful. They often share their feelings, which confirms that we are all human after all. This is just one way in which the set can be used as an 'experimental bubble'. The courage gained from such sharing makes it easier to acknowledge, understand and genuinely take such feelings into account back at work.

4. Focusing on learning . . . and changing:

Stopping to think and be aware of what each member is learning is a crucial process. This may take place either as someone is working in their airspace, or at a specifically allotted time.

To help set members become aware of what they are learning when they are away from the set, the set adviser may suggest a moment for reflecting at the beginning of every meeting. Or time may be set aside at the end of the meeting for participants to jot down what they have learnt, to share it with others, or simply to reflect silently.

One of the main roles of the set adviser is in fact to remind the set that they are there to learn, and not simply 'act'. As one set recalled, their set adviser 'used to drip-feed the question "So what have you learnt from that?" ' until it became second nature for them to ask themselves and each other the same question.

Learning is not restricted to the work each person does on their project. It concerns also what is happening in the set – how the group work together. As one young manager remarked, 'You start out with a project, but end up learning so much about yourself.' (See figs 13–15.)

This constant emphasis on becoming aware, learning and changing is probably one of the fundamental ways in which a set differs from other groups: 'It's about change . . . and changing: changing how you see things and interpret them, how you do things . . . and seeing others change. Seeing how you get to this position of "change" through becoming more aware, open and honest . . .' was how one participant described the learning. Others agreed: 'It's about learning to do things differently and becoming sure that what you're doing is effective – through listening to others, telling others, asking yourself and others questions, admitting you're unsure . . . Learning from your interaction with others and their responses, becoming aware of your inner irritations and how they affect what you do or say . . . All of this is open for examination.' (For more on learning, see pp. 228–36.)

Going around a 'learning cycle'

Action learning is built around the idea of a learning cycle: we act, we reflect, we analyse and we plan the next action. But there has to be more to it than this if the cycle is to become a spiral, so that instead of going around in circles we move to a new place in what we do, think and say.

Kolb and Revans Learning Cycles

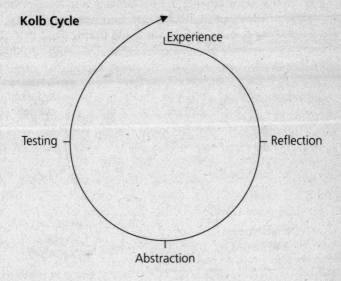

Kolb Cycle

Experience

Testing

Reflection

Abstraction

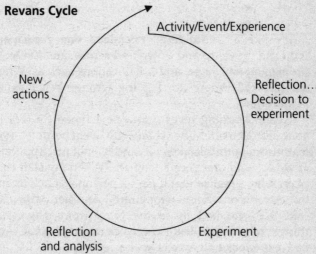

Revans Cycle

Activity/Event/Experience

New actions

Reflection…
Decision to
experiment

Reflection
and analysis

Experiment

fig. 13

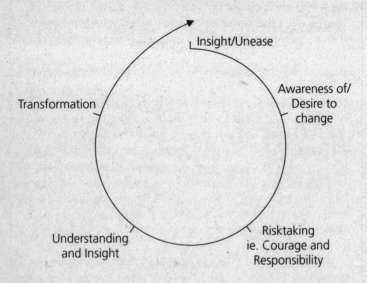

fig. 14

'It's like a 'scaffolding,' explained one participant. 'You can move up and down and across, and "enter" a problem at any stage, and ask questions such as: Where am I stuck? Where am I going wrong? What have I missed out?'

'Action learning gives you a detachment, a tool for analysis. You identify where you went wrong – you learn from your mistakes . . . and it's not just applicable at work,' said one young woman. 'When my staff complain now, I realize that it isn't a personal attack on me, but a result of what is happening.' Another participant said that she had made the jump from magnifying things, to seeing 'a bad experience as simply that – one bad experience. It needs to be reflected on, but not colour your subsequent beliefs or actions.'

If we are to really learn and change, we need to go beyond this purely action cycle to a simultaneous inner cycle which focuses on our feelings as we change. It begins with the sense of unease we may feel, moves to the recognition that this is valid, weighs the risk involved in actually taking some action or doing something differently. Reflecting on each step in the process helps us realize when we have overcome a hurdle and frees us to behave differently – and feel better as a result.

'Often it's the nature of the questions that teases out the real issue. So, a questions such as "What do you feel when you speak to X?" makes you stop and think about how your feelings colour your relationships, and your words and actions. Or, someone may ask you "How would you feel if someone spoke to you like that?" and it brings you up and forces you to think about that . . . and you then have to decide what you're going to do about such instances.'

The 'reflecting' part of the cycle isn't simply something that occurs at one time; it is an activity that takes place at every stage. Reflecting on action, reflecting on analysis, reflecting on new plans . . . and also reflecting on the reflective process itself (see fig. 15).

Going around a cycle – be it an action or inner cycle – thus opens up new avenues to explore and gain insights from.

5. *Reflecting:*

This can mean one of two things. The first is reflecting or mirroring back to the presenter what he or she is saying, or what feelings they are conveying by means of questions such as: 'So you're saying . . .' or 'You sound angry.' This helps the presenter hear what they have said – which may be something other than what they meant to convey – and also gives them the opportunity to say more. Hearing back in this way can be helpful.

167

Reflections at Every Stage

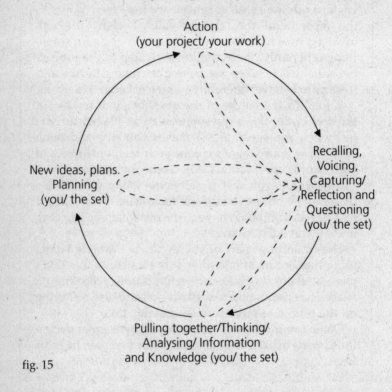

fig. 15

Reflecting also has another, more contemplative meaning. It's something many of us don't do, either because we 'don't have the time' or because 'it isn't in my nature'. In this sense, reflecting is the process of recalling events, feelings, actions and thoughts, and being honest in assessing them – 'shining a torch on them', as one manager described it.

Set members can help one another – and themselves – to understand various ideas and concepts that are talked about but seldom put under a microscope by reflecting in this more contemplative way, perhaps about such issues as 'What *is* the job of a manager?' or 'What exactly does motivation mean?' or 'What do you mean by quality?'

One set recalled reflecting together on issues of commitment, trust and honesty. Another group had reflected on the notion of leadership. The purpose of such reflections is to clarify everyone's thinking, and throw light on why people – or indeed the set members themselves – behave or respond in particular ways.

One could almost claim that without such reflection we don't learn or change; we simply repeat what we have always done. If we are truly to learn and change, we need to reflect on many issues. But simply reflecting on actions – on what we did or others did – isn't sufficient. We need to reflect also on what we thought, said, and felt, as well as the things we didn't do or say. And it may be useful to reflect on what others did and said, or what they didn't do or say – possibly even on what they might have been feeling. In this way we gain a fuller picture and may begin to understand better what actions, interactions and relationships are about.

It is at this stage that reflecting with others becomes a true dialogue with them. This obviously takes time, and there are occasions when it is inappropriate – when decisions have to be taken fast. 'Activists' will particularly feel uneasy about spending time reflecting when they could be doing. But as one participant realized, 'There's more to learning than simply action.' And another said, 'You need to build in an infrastructure of thinking. Action on its own isn't enough – it's merely another project group.'

In an action learning programme the processes allow each participant time to think and question and reflect. The processes virtually demand it. And working in a set with others who have different inclinations, or are good at reflecting, can demonstrate to those who are not so inclined by nature the benefits of reflection.

6. Silence:

This can be – and is – interpreted in differing ways. It may be seen as a person having nothing to say, feeling intimidated, or thinking. It may also simply be allowing oneself the space just to 'be' – to not think for a while, to stop the mad rush of ideas and let some deeper consciousness take over.

Through simply pausing – being still and silent, even without consciously thinking – we find that the insights, answers or whatever we are searching for emerge into our consciousness. 'I'll sleep on that' – a common enough phrase – taps into that other consciousness, that bit of us that 'knows' or remembers but is seldom allowed to emerge. How often do we try to remember something and then say, 'If I stop thinking about it, it'll come to me.'

So, silence can be valuable for many reasons. In fact, one experienced action learner commented that the set she was currently working in – as a member – had a lot of silences. 'The silence is to do with people thinking, puzzling, or simply letting what's been said sink in. I often babble, and one of the set members then asks me, "What do you feel like now? What do you need?".'

'It's disconcerting when you finish saying what you have to say, and there is an expectant silence . . . the group obviously think you have more to say . . . it then forces you to say and reveal more, and say things you've not said before. It forces you to take that extra step . . . simply the expectation of others that there is more to follow,' observed a banker.

But silence can make people feel very uncomfortable and so they try to overcome this by filling the silences. Ways of doing this include making a joke, physically moving, or breaking into it in other ways. And much may depend on how long such a silence lasts; there are comfortable silences and uncomfortable ones. This is another example of an instance where the set adviser might decide to intervene by commenting on the silence, or asking members what they were doing and feeling during it.

7. *No judgement, no advice, no solutions:*

It is vital not to pass judgement if, as we have seen, the set members are to feel comfortable with each other and able to discuss issues that may make them feel vulnerable.

On the other hand, not judging is a far cry from not challenging; nor does it mean agreeing with what is being said. It is the form and the tone of voice adopted that mark the difference.

'Advice', someone once said, 'is profoundly pleasurable to the giver.' This alone should be reason enough for stopping ourselves from giving it. What are our motives? Is it to give help, or to make ourselves look and feel good?

But there are other reasons for not giving advice. Firstly, we are never in a position to do so, for we are not the other person, and cannot ever fully understand them and their set of circumstances, any more than we can know the full extent of the issue they are working on. We often begin a piece of advice with the spoken or silent phrase 'If I were you . . .' to which the only response is 'But you're not me.' And if we were, we might not be in the situation the other person is in.

Furthermore, advice does not require the receiver to work in depth on the issue, whereas having to consider options does.

Not giving solutions touches on a slightly different aspect. We, as helpers, often leap in with solutions before the real problem has been identified. Solutions, like advice, make us, the giver, feel useful and good. But it also creates a 'yes, but . . .' or 'no, because . . .' relationship with the presenter. 'Why don't you do so-and-so?' leads into 'We can't because . . .' – a game of verbal ping-pong.

What's worse, the givers end up feeling angry or resentful that here they are, offering so much, and still the presenters are hesitating. Hesitation, however, may be a clue that the problem presented is not the real issue; deep down the presenters know this, and their hesitance may signal that they are struggling to get to the bottom of things but need help.

Some presenters show no hesitation; instead they sound

very convincing when they come to a set meeting with a clearly defined, well thought out, logical problem. The group may thus be seduced into accepting this, and launching into possible solutions. In fact, even the most confident presenters are sometimes unaware what the real problem is; what they are looking at are either symptoms or second-stage problems which simply disappear once the real problem has been identified and worked on.

As one participant said: 'In action learning we don't seek solutions but rather the real problems. If we solve symptoms, we merely bury the problem.'

'On some occasions I would become convinced that a particular idea of mine was sound, especially if another set member supported it, and if that set member was one I respected and admired. Because of this, at times there may have been a reluctance on my part to be open-minded and to accept another member's point of view. With hindsight I realize that, by dismissing another set member's view, this member may have lost respect for me, and thereby destroyed my effectiveness as a 'change agent' in the set . . .

If I were in this position again, I would put my view forward as a suggestion – as an alternative to the views of others. Once I had more understanding of others, their views and their needs, I would be in a better position to judge how to proceed in order to have a better chance of learning from them and persuading them to be receptive to my ideas.'

8. Finding a formula to share ideas and insights:

Participants come to a programme with a mass of useful insights and experiences. This is one of the strengths of such programmes. Set members also feel they want to help: 'I felt so useless not being able to give X help and solutions' is something participants often say at the beginning of an action learning programme. Most people would admit that supplying a solution makes them feel good. And in many instances – particularly if the presenter has genuinely run out of ideas after trying everything he or she can think of – it is helpful to be offered fresh ideas. On the other hand, it may be that the reason there are no solutions in sight is that the wrong issue is being pursued.

In our efforts to help we so often leap in with solutions to problems and issues we do not fully understand as yet. It's as though solutions are more important than finding out the root of the problem.

The managing director of a small software company on a programme linked to a distance learning MBA came to a set meeting wanting to discuss some issues from a workbook on personal development. He began by focusing on a particular exercise, and the set gleefully followed him into it and began offering advice on how to do it, and what else to read. But this didn't seem to resolve the MD's queries. So he persisted, and eventually, by asking questions rather than offering solutions, the set managed to draw out of him that what lay beneath his questions was a more fundamental dilemma: whether he was the right person to continue running his company. He had created it, built it up, and it was now running well . . . yet he felt that he was the wrong person to be at the helm. He wanted more excitement, uncertainty and risk. In fact, what he probably liked doing most of all was setting up new ventures.

The initially presented issue was therefore not the one that needed exploring. At the end of that meeting he told the set (as has been quoted elsewhere in this book): 'Your advice at the beginning was useless, your anecdotes were boring but your questions really helped me.'

How then can participants' experiences, insights, ideas and suggestions best be shared? There are several formulas. One, as we have already seen, is to rephrase ideas and suggestions as questions, thus giving the presenter the chance to explore, rather than being 'told' to do something (as in advice). 'I think you should do X or Y' is both given – and, more importantly, received – differently from 'Have you thought of doing X or Y?' With the latter there is space for taking something on board and considering it; the former prompts as the first response a list of reasons why you cannot do whatever is being advised. Worse, it doesn't push the person being proffered this advice to think about it in any depth: it is simply something offered on a plate.

Alternatively, a set member may say to the presenter that he or she has had an experience, or done something, which may be helpful . . . and ask whether it would be useful to describe it. Again, this formula gives the presenter the opportunity to accept or refuse (on the grounds that they prefer to use some other process) – thereby taking responsibility for the next stage. They also have the option of stopping the storyteller if they don't consider the story to be helpful in their case.

A third option is for the presenter to ask the set to brainstorm for a few minutes while he or she listens – before returning to the format of airspace.

It may be useful at this point to try and pull these threads together and see the processes that are occurring in a diagrammatic form. In essence there are three simultaneous cycles or spirals: the presenter's action and inner cycles, and the set's processes (not strictly a cycle or spiral) – see fig. 16.

What's so valuable about questions?

The major difference between asking questions in action learning and asking them in most other settings is that, in action learning, questions aren't seeking answers. Rather,

Concentric Learning Cycles

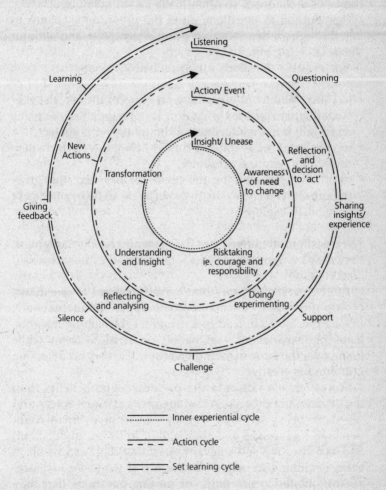

fig. 16

they are seeking to help someone go deeper, to understand, to respond to what is being asked, to give it thought. They are not a quest for solutions. They are an opportunity to explore.

'The value of being asked questions is that they made me think,' is a comment so often made by set members.

Responding to questions gives the presenter a chance to talk through an issue without being interrupted, and without the issue being hijacked by others.

The set asks questions for a number of reasons:

- to clarify points: in explaining an issue to the set, the presenter either confirms what is or is not happening, or gains an insight into their feelings or thoughts on the subject;
- to check out an avenue of thought they have which they think may help the presenter.
- to follow up something the presenter has said: this gives the presenter a chance to go down avenues he or she hasn't previously explored.

The questions are often ones the presenter hasn't thought of, or perhaps doesn't want to ask – questions they may be afraid of asking.

As the presenter hears him/herself respond to questions, certain inconsistencies may become apparent; alternatively, talking out loud can lead to a presenter developing insights, ideas or explanations that hadn't occurred to them while going over the issue in their own mind. The very act of talking out aloud is creative.

Moreover, it's not only the presenter who benefits from the questioning process. As set members ask questions – and see them being seriously considered – it gives them confidence in themselves and their ability to listen, understand, and ask effective and relevant questions. This can result in them beginning to behave differently at work; for instance, raising queries in meetings, or putting questions that they have previously been too nervous to ask to their boss. When a question of theirs helps someone else, it can make them think, 'That was a good question – I ought to ask myself that question, too.'

Choosing helpful questions:

Helpful questions are those that open doors in the mind. They are designed to get the presenter to think more deeply, to test their beliefs and assumptions, to really explain what they mean, to explore why they do things – and what stops them.

Open questions are more helpful than closed ones. Questions that encourage the presenter to consider the 'how' and 'what' rather than the 'why'. 'Why did you do X?' is thus a closed question; examples of more helpful open questions would be 'What did you hope to achieve by doing X?' or 'What prompted X?' or 'How did you think X would help . . . ?'

Examples of helpful questions

The purpose of all questions is to help the presenter (and also the set members) to understand an issue more clearly. To this end, the best questions are:

- those that begin with 'how', 'what', 'where', and 'when' rather than 'why'.
- precision questions:
     'What exactly?' or 'How exactly?'
     'Bigger than . . . ?' or 'More than . . . ?'
     'Everyone?' 'Always?'
- powerful questions (when a presenter says 'I can't'):
     'What's stopping you . . . ?'
     'What would happen if you . . . ?'
- reflective questions (mirror back what presenter seems to be saying):
     'So you're saying . . .'

'You seem . . .'
'idea' questions (without spelling out the details!):
'Would so-and-so be of any use?'
'Have you thought of . . . ?'

So, questions uncover what we don't know. Only then do we realize what we need to pursue in order to further our knowledge. As one hospital manager said, 'Identifying what you don't know is a first step to beginning to learn.' This echoes Reg Revans, who has said on so many occasions: 'We only begin to learn when we become aware of what we don't know.'

This jolt – this realization that asking questions is the key to beginning to think, to doing different things, and to doing things differently and learning – is something many participants comment on, but as one young IT manager complained: 'The trouble is that I now realize the value of stopping to think, but there is no space allocated for "thinking time" on our work sheets.'

In some organizational cultures, asking questions can create difficulties. One set voiced unanimous concern at this, for the culture in their organization was one of 'don't ask, just do as I tell you'. On the other hand, some of these beliefs may be based on fear of what happens when you do ask questions – as one participant recounted: 'I've learnt to question my managers and they don't – as I'd assumed – bite your head off. In fact they treat me with more respect.'

Echoes of Socratic dialogue:

This questioning device has its origins – for the Western world – in Socratic dialogue. But, unlike this older form, action learning questioning is softened because it takes place within a set where there are ground rules which exclude judgement; which preclude questioners vying to show how clever they are and how much they know; and which stress being supportive and challenging at the same time.

The primary intention is to help and indeed *make* the other person think, not to arrive at a truth or to develop an intellectual debate – regardless of how stimulating that might be. That can take place in the bar after the meeting!

Other helpful questions:

1. Individual and the project/task
   - What is your position?
   - What's your issue/question? Would drawing it help you 'see it' more clearly?
   - What problems does that cause? In what way is that a problem?
   - What isn't happening now?
   - What do you want to be different?
   - How would you like X to respond?
   - How do you think that Y needs to be changed/altered?
   - What would you like to do – ideally?
   - How do you feel about that?
   - Can you tell us more about that?
   - Who have you consulted/talked to?
   - Who else might you talk to?
   - How does the other person/department see the issue?
   - Have you thought of . . .
   - What's stopping you?
   - What would happen if you did X/did the opposite/did nothing?
   - How will you go about it?
   - In what way will that help?
   - Who else can you involve/get to back you?
   - What else would you find helpful?

2. Individual and the set
   - What response would you like from the set?
   - How can we help you?
   - Can you tell us a bit more about that?
   - I don't follow what you are saying?
   - I don't understand that?

- Are we getting away from your question?
- Do you want to tell us more?
- What's at the back of your mind?
- You sound . . .
- Is this helpful?
- How do you feel?
- Have we helped you?
- Are you being honest with yourself?

3. General process questions and statements
   - What is happening here now?
   - What are we doing at the moment?
   - Is it helpful/productive/getting us anywhere?
   - Why haven't we tackled . . . ?
   - What have we learnt?
   - I feel uncomfortable/confused/angry/helpless
   - You are stopping me from working
   - Please don't interrupt me

Can't you reflect and learn on your own? Why is it necessary to do it in the set meetings?

Yes, you can reflect on your own. The advantage of doing it with the set is that we are forced to do so, and can't escape by claiming we have no time, or feel it might be more comfortable next time. Or maybe it wouldn't be all that useful, anyway.

We can reflect on our own, but the value of doing it with others is that none of us has a monopoly on good or helpful questions, insights and perspectives. Working with others therefore increases the scope of our reflection and learning.

Participants recognize that ultimately they must learn to work on issues without the help of the set, but this is not to deny the benefit of coming back to the set for an injection of others' insights and perspectives.

Undertaking this reflection and learning on one's own also means we do so silently – yet many participants said that having to express things out loud caused them to say things that had never occurred to them before.

In the process of carrying out the research for this book, and in writing it, I found that although I did not meet with a set, I talked to my word-processor! The very act of writing down a stream of consciousness so often resulted in ideas and insights emerging that I had not had while thinking about what I was going to write.

Thus, writing – the equivalent of speaking – had the same effect of bringing into the open new ideas and insights, ie an element of creativity.

Perhaps it has something to do with emptying the brain of one mass of data to enable it to create more. Maybe the producing of words – on screen or out loud – is akin to an artist or musician learning by trial and error, creating something that is then modified, added to, and so on. The idea of pots to represent the five elements of action learning emerged as I played with words (created) and came up with the notion of spin-offs, which in turn developed into the metaphor of the potter's wheel spinning.

Why is it so important for set members to report at a subsequent meeting what they have done, or what has happened since the last set meeting?

Reporting back creates a rigour. It means that everyone is expected to achieve something between meetings – and the expectations of others are a strong goad. But the rhythm of having to act and report back is also important. It creates momentum.

Reporting back is also a way of assessing the evidence of what you've done and learnt. It's also a means of seeing –

and getting others to give you feedback on – how you're developing and changing, what you're doing differently, and what you have yet to master. It's a form of benchmarking.

'It makes you think – and act,' and 'It makes you reflect on what you've done, what you've achieved, what you're going to do next. It keep up a momentum,' were just two comments from participants on the usefulness of reporting back.

One participant remarked on the benefits of 'the discipline of that hour, and needing to do my homework – either some action, or plan, and report on what I'd done. The expectation of others focuses the mind!'

To another set, it was the creation of a thread in the story that was critical. One manager said that for him reporting back was the key to action learning: it made the difference between action learning and any other form of talking, sharing or discussing.

Do you keep notes or some other form of documentation?

Programmes differ. Some have a requirement – or strongly encourage participants – that some form of reflective notes or a diary be kept as an aid to learning.

Since one of the key elements of action learning is to go around the learning cycle – in the sense of recalling what has happened since the last meeting, reflecting on it, being asked questions, beginning to understand better, and making plans for how to go forward – it is often helpful to keep notes about actions, thoughts, feelings and insights. Not only do they jog the memory for the next meeting, they are also a story in themselves of the journey of achievements and development that participants experience. We may think our memories will not let us down, but they do – and it is only in keeping a diary or some other form of reflective document that we realize how much we tend to forget.

Using a diary or learning log in this way – to see where we've been and where we are now – helps when we again face similar situations. It tells us what we did or didn't do last time, and gives us a wider repertoire of possibilities with which to progress in the future, as well as reminding us of what we should try and avoid.

Diaries/Logs

These thoughts can be applied to projects, as well as any encounter with others, and with the set.

- What I planned to do
- How I went about it
- What took place
- Outcomes/What happened?
- Was it what I'd anticipated?
    if yes, what went well?
    if not, what could have been done/said differently?
    my reflections on it:
    what was I thinking?
    what was I feeling?
    did I do/say what I'd planned?
    if not, what was stopping me?
- What have I learnt/observed?
- What do I want to focus on next time/in future?
- Thoughts on how my learning is occurring

If participants are encouraged to keep a note in their diaries not only of what they've learnt but of how that learning came about – then it becomes a learning log, a record of how that participant learns, which may be a useful reminder and guide in the future. The log might reveal to a participant that he or she learns best by plunging into action first and then reflecting; or by talking things through first; or by working with others on their issues and asking them questions; or by being asked questions, and so on. All of these insights are useful since throughout life we need to learn, adapt and develop. Knowing how to make such transitions easier and more effective is obviously to our advantage.

Some programmes require participants to write a learning document at the end in which they assess what they have learned and gained from the programme. This is now standard practice on programmes with an academic slant, such as universities' management programmes based on action learning, and even some in-company ones.

'I found keeping a diary the most useful part of the programme,' said the young branch manager of a building society. A finance officer found that the learning log was the key for her – the insights and learning recorded therein would, she felt, be of more use to her later than a string of actions successfully accomplished. Some participants, on other hand, have found it difficult. A form helps people who feel stuck when facing a blank piece of paper!

Are there any taught elements?

Some programmes include taught input, others don't. The taught elements will be either directly related to the programme and the learning that participants are hoping to gain, or they will be mini-inputs which enable participants to gain the most from action learning. 'We had short inputs on transactional analysis*, information gathering and the Kolb learning cycle – which were very helpful,' said one group of young graduates for whom action learning was part of their induction programme. Others sets mentioned mind maps, SWOT, and force-field analysis†. Participants will often ask the set

---

* A way of showing how our ways of addressing and treating people affects their responses and vice versa.

† SWOT: listing the Strengths, Weaknesses, Opportunities and Threats in any given situation

Mind maps: a diagrammatic way of creating a 'list', or developing an idea, which also allows you to draw connections between items

Force-field analysis: listing, in two columns, the forces in favour of or supporting an idea, decision or plan of action, and those forces opposed to it

adviser to organize mini-inputs which relate directly to their work.

Some programmes, depending on their objectives, also incorporate other taught elements related to teamworking (including outdoor programmes) and communication; or more functional inputs linked to business strategy, marketing and finance. There are also subjects which lend themselves to having action learning incorporated with them, eg project management.

Several participants who had attended a previous week-long management development programme said they couldn't imagine attending an action learning programme 'cold', without that previous input.

A number of programmes are in fact built on previous courses and are seen as a consolidation of them – a chance to try out, to see which of the taught elements is useful, and where or when it is applicable – offering a unique opportunity to share experiences and insights and ask further questions.

Increasingly, action learning is being incorporated into management courses offered at universities, and in distance learning programmes. Participants gain knowledge from lectures or workbooks (in the latter instance) and meet for action learning days, where the emphasis is on applying the learning to real-life instances/projects. Sets work like any other non-academic set. (For a list of management courses using action learning as an integral part of their programmes see p. 327.)

A brief introduction to action learning:

At the beginning of every programme there is always an introduction to action learning. Some introductions may last just a few hours; others a day; some feature a couple of days spent on a team-building exercise. Those who experienced the latter said it was most useful in helping the set to gel.

A few participants, however, felt that 'there was too much theory at the beginning – all about change and projects and the philosophy of action learning.'

There are several ways of overcoming the paradox of lecturing on action learning. One way that participants find helpful is by actually trying it out: either in a fishbowl, or in threes (see below).

Two practical exercises

The fishbowl: five or six of those present form a 'set' and, sitting in a circle, they work with a set adviser while everyone else sits around the circle and observes the process. An empty chair is left in the inner circle; anyone from the outer circle wishing to participate on a point may join the inner circle by sitting in the empty chair. At the conclusion of the exercise, the set and the presenter are asked to comment on their experience, and then the discussion is open to everyone.

Triad exercise:[4] Divide participants into threes or fours, and ask one member of each group to 'present' an issue – a quandary, challenge, or irritation – but nothing too large.

Ask the presenter to hold on to their airspace for 15–20 minutes. Meanwhile the others should try to focus on asking questions, giving feedback, reflecting, and turning ideas or suggestions into questions.

When the time is up, ask each group to discuss the experience, beginning with the views of the presenter. Then bring everyone back into the larger group and discuss. First, ask the presenters what it was like to be the focus. Then ask the others how they experienced their role.

These practical exercises can prove interesting. 'You realize how difficult it is to ask questions – in particular good questions. I kept falling into asking leading questions!' Others remarked how difficult it was to resist giving advice, or telling of your own experiences. Those who presented problems commented how being asked questions helped them focus, and how they began to uncover aspects they had not looked at while on their own.

One group, who had previously tackled an issue as an ordinary discussion group, felt that they had 'resolved' the presenter's issues within ten minutes, and were taken aback when they discovered – through keeping to action learning processes – that they had only scratched the surface of the issue, and had not in fact been very helpful! It took them nearly an hour to really get to the bottom of the presenter's issue – and they were left reflecting on the comparative value of discussion group tactics v. the action learning way of working.

THE VALUE OF THE PROCESSES

From initially assuming the set would simply be the group in which to foregather and help each other learn, participants began to value the processes as one of the most important elements of action learning – and a high point in their own learning. Moreover, it was learning that could be instantly applied back at work.

The benefits of having airspace

Having their own time and space was something most participants said they had seldom experienced before. Normally there are interruptions, the hijacking of your issue and space by others who are noisier or better with words. With a discipline imposed, however, it created a sense of confidence in those being listened to. With the help of thoughtful and probing questions they were able to resolve their own issues. And, what surprised most participants, was that in listening to the presenter and confronting his/her problems they were able to learn 'at least as much as from working on my own issues'.

At the outset, though, several participants said they feared that their issue/story/problem/quandary wouldn't be of sufficient interest to the rest of the set. 'And then the realization that what you have to say is of interest, of relevance to others . . . that they are learning from the "interaction", makes you feel good and gives you confidence.'

'I didn't realize how powerful – but also how unnerving – it was to be the focus of everyone's attention, to have their undivided attention. It felt wonderful!'

Hearing themselves talk out loud was also a novelty:

> As you talk you resolve your own problems – if you're honest about what you say, and the set will extract that from you, anyway. Someone will detect a cover-up if you're being economical with the truth.
>
> If you only consider 'internally', in your own thoughts, your mind can lead you down all sorts of pathways. But somehow as you speak, your voice can give you away. And others are listening, and can spot the flaws, where the gaps are, and will pursue you down the alleys you are following. Eventually the trick is to learn to do this yourself. Though having others listen will always add an extra dimension.
>
> As you explain things to the set, you hear your own inconsistencies, the missing elements, the illogicalities. But you need to do it out loud.
>
> If you rely exclusively on your own thoughts and assumptions, you'll come a cropper. I've so often failed to spot other people's agendas – but someone in the set usually will.

Invariably, set members were amazed that it was possible to learn so much by focusing on others' stories. 'You learn from others. You hear and see what they do, and you see yourself often doing the same thing! So you begin to resolve both your own and others' issues simultaneously.'

Many made the jump from realizing how much they had

gained personally – by being given the time and space to talk and by hearing others do the same – to the relevance such a process could have if applied back at work. 'After all, those doing the jobs know most about them. We ignore them and their ideas at our peril.'

For others, the ability to share was emotionally very releasing. 'You begin to understand why you react in certain ways, and it helps to control (not sublimate) those feelings and express them in an appropriate way.'

Hearing others' perspectives – particularly those from other disciplines, departments, even organizations – was, for many participants, like seeing their story through a new pair of eyes.

Almost all commented on the fact that initially, as they told their own stories, they found themselves using 'we', 'you' or 'one' to generalize their experiences. 'What I learnt', said one participant (though this was almost universal), 'was to *own* my statements. To talk only of "I" and not say "one usually . . ." or "you always" – distancing myself from what I was saying.' Others began to realize how often they generalized and talked of what others thought, felt or did.

Learning to listen – and having others listen to me

So as one person tells their story or voices their quandaries, others listen.

'You learn to listen, not simply to hear,' was one verdict. 'And in listening, you begin to notice a whole lot more than the words.' Mused another: 'Listening is the most important management skill.'

'It's taught me to listen, and not just to hear,' was a common response. 'I now really talk to others – I watch, listen and I ask questions. It's made me more professional at work . . . I take it more seriously.'

'I've learnt to listen to others, and through listening to ask myself why I don't think of doing something, or ask myself

189

certain questions which can give me insights into myself.'

Thus communication skills are improved by the simple device of listening.

Pragmatists soon realize that it's possible to learn from others' mistakes. 'It's by listening to others that I began to ask myself questions about what I was doing and thinking.'

But listening has other lessons, too: 'It was in listening to others that I began to ask myself – almost challenge myself – why I didn't do so and so, or why I hadn't asked myself a question they were considering.'

Hearing her questions being given careful consideration, led another young woman to realize 'that I made sense, that I had some good points to make' – which then led her to ask herself these same questions. It marked a major step in gaining self-esteem and confidence in herself which had been lacking before. 'Much more beneficial than an assertiveness course,' she laughed.

However, as several pointed out, listening is not an easy task – though we assume it is. 'Listening is a task that requires a lot of practice. Complete listening is about comprehension, not just recall . . . and comprehension is also about empathy, and being non-judgemental . . . and trying to understand, and burying your biases . . .'

Listening brings awareness that 'there are good ideas out there'. Action learning's emphasis on listening also has some interesting knock-on effects: 'I've realized we're not all singing from the same hymn sheet – it's useful for a manager to know that!' said one young woman. And many remarked on the experience of being listened to – how it improved not only communication, but also confidence. 'Being listened to builds up your self-esteem and confidence.'

One participant who said 'I like to listen – and do a lot of it,' nevertheless found himself asking half-way through the programme: 'Was my preference for listening a cop-out or true? Was I avoiding something by listening so much?'

'Using action learning in the sets has been dramatic. I am beginning to change my whole approach to interactions. Even at home! I have recognized why in the past I have found others, particularly friends and partners, so frustrating when I've asked to discuss a problem: they give me their solutions! I have not necessarily found asking questions easy, however, and I realize how demanding the level of concentration required in the sets can be. The difference doing this differently is making is that, although I am taking it more slowly with people, they are coming to a conclusion faster. Somehow I am becoming more patient, too. I have tried to get one group of sales managers to use action learning questioning techniques, and six out of eight found it almost impossible – mainly due to their 'need' to push people in a certain direction.'

Empowering:

Definitions of empowering and becoming empowered refer to individuals gaining in confidence, feeling they have something to offer, knowing how to put across ideas, how to ask questions, how to take responsibility . . . as well as being given – or taking – the opportunity to become more active and involved.

Action learning provides some useful models which, if followed, are the stepping stones to both being empowered and to empowering – and hence managing – others. For managers, this can mean removing the blocks that prevent staff from carrying out their jobs effectively.

In the end, however, it is impossible to empower someone who does not wish it. It has to come from within the individual. Others can merely create an environment in which becoming empowered is made possible. Thus a manager's greatest contribution to the empowerment of his or her staff might be the removal of structures or systems that block development, or the modification of his or her own behaviour towards staff.

The set and its processes illustrate types of behaviour conducive to empowerment:

- airspace gives people a chance to talk and be listened to, and builds in them the confidence to speak up elsewhere
- the discipline of asking questions; learning to ask effective and helpful ones; gaining the confidence to ask simple ones
- sharing and being helpful – all part of helping people to empower themselves and others
- undertaking an 'action' and being expected – as well as encouraged – to complete it, and receiving constructive and honest feedback

So the democratic processes of action learning give people a sense of their own worth. But transferring the sense of empowerment achieved during a programme back to the workplace isn't always easy. It can be all too easy to fall back into old habits: 'I can't do X, my manager won't let me'; 'That's not the way we do things around here'; 'I haven't got the time', and so on.

One young woman was quite open and honest:

One of the men in our set was very domineering. I felt able – after some time – to tell him that I didn't like what he was doing and that it was difficult to work with him. At the time I felt I had been rude to him – simply pointing this out! But he acknowledged what I said. So I felt pleased that I'd plucked up the courage to tell him because in fact it changed the way we worked in the set from then on, and we became much more conscious of processes. But I still find it difficult to say something like that back in the 'real' world. But at least I've begun to sometimes say what I feel about a person's behaviour. I've begun to separate out process from 'content'.

Another manager talked of 'the problems of transferring some of the "me" in the set to the "me" back at work. It'll take time. I've established a personal style over the past 20 years, and it's difficult to change that. What'll others say? How will they react? They still see the old me and expect me to do certain things in certain ways . . .'

'Maybe we need reminding,' said several participants. 'Maybe we need regular "injections" of being in a set . . .'

The power and discipline of asking/being asked questions, and not giving or getting advice

Asking – and being asked – 'different questions than the ones I normally asked or ever asked, or wanted to ask, myself'; checking on assumptions and understanding; clarifying points; turning advice and suggestions into questions – none of this was easy, as many participants found. But it proved to be valuable, once they had begun to master the art.

'Good questions tease out the real issues. They get you to think. They're often questions you haven't thought of, or ones you wouldn't dream – or want – to ask yourself.'

One participant gave an example of some of the questions the set adviser had asked her when she revealed that she was having problems working with a colleague. 'He asked me questions such as "When you speak to X, what do you think her views are?' and 'How did she respond?', or, when I told of an exchange we'd had, 'How would feel if she had said that to you?' and so on. Questions like these expose you to a different level of thinking, a different slant altogether.'

'At the beginning, when it was my airspace, I kept asking the others questions – then I realized that the answers are in myself – only they need to be brought out. That's where the set helps you, and lets you go back out into the world again feeling stronger. It changes the way you are back at work, and how you approach tasks.'

'I'd been told by our set adviser not to give advice but to turn everything into questions – but avoiding the obvious leading questions such as "Have you thought of doing X, Y and Z, so that . . . ?" That's obviously the same as giving advice . . . Sticking to just asking questions sounded a bit strange to me, a bit "forced". But then when I was on the receiving end of being asked questions – ones that really probed – I realized how much more useful it was than being given advice or told of others' experiences. The advice is usually impractical and I get frustrated hearing too much about others' experiences . . . but it's also useful to hear some of them. It's about getting the balance right.'

'Asking questions has helped me both in my professional and personal development' said another participant. 'It's sharpened my thinking.'

Yet although some find it 'very refreshing' to have questions fired at them, there is a danger that the presenter might feel 'put on the spot' or bombarded: 'I didn't have time to think . . . and I felt they wanted me to give answers.'

'Asking questions is much more difficult that I had imagined,' was another set member's response to this comment. 'You're dying to give advice, tell the person what to do,' laughed another. 'You somehow feel that that is "helping" them – we feel we've offered something concrete by suggesting a solution.'

The skill is to learn to ask helpful questions – questions that will help both you and the presenter to understand, and that will enable the presenter to form a clearer picture of the issue than they had before.

Mastering the technique of asking questions can in itself bring unexpected insights. One participant said he structured the sequence of his questions: he would lead with the 'what' and 'who' questions, to begin to form a picture, followed by the 'whys', to clarify the story; only then would he progress to the 'what and how' questions, directed at what actions or interventions were possible or appropriate.

Almost every participant I spoke to said something along the lines of: 'It's extraordinary, how what you think is the problem often isn't – the questioning reveals the real one!'

'I learnt the power of asking questions – very different ones from those I'd asked before. But that added to my frustration because I gradually realized that managers didn't always have the answers – and that they wouldn't listen to me.'

The skill of asking effective questions – and in the process letting the other person know what you are trying to get at – eliminates the danger of leading someone down a particular path or making them struggle to following the questioner's drift.

Whereas in the past they might have been afraid to ask questions, participants found that action learning changed their perceptions: ' "Ignorance" is OK. I'm allowed to not know things. We're often so afraid of asking questions in case people think us stupid.' The new-found freedom to say 'I don't know' without feeling guilty about it gave many participants the courage to be honest back at work, too. 'Why pretend?' some of them said. 'Asking questions isn't a sign of stupidity.' Instead, questioning was seen as a constructive action when they didn't know or understand something.

Moreover, several participants alluded to the value of questions in 'exchanging' or sharing information: 'You can learn from others if you're prepared to share. The more you share, the more you get back from others.'

Learning to tackle difficult people and situations

Although not everyone had encountered problems with difficult set members, those who did have to tackle such problems felt they had made significant progress and gained in self-confidence as a result. The reason there were few opportunities for this was probably due to the self-selection that most programmes operate (in fact, one of the criticisms that some participants levelled at their programmes was that they did not help them to work with the politics of an organization, including certain categories of difficult people).

One set I spoke to did have the opportunity, and learnt from it. But the person who probably learned most was the young man in question. Very bright and aggressive in manner, he kept his set in thrall for just one set meeting. He interrupted, talked most and loudest, always had a comment or observation, and turned every discussion around to what he was doing or what he thought. The set adviser decided at the first meeting not to interfere with what was happening but to wait and see if the set would respond.

During the second meeting, one young woman took the initiative. She told him she found it impossible to work with him in the group, and itemized what she found disruptive in his behaviour. One other woman added her comments, too. The man thus confronted began to explain and justify his behaviour, but failed to modify it to any great degree. However, at the next meeting there was a sufficient change in his behaviour for the set to be able to work well and constructively on everyone's projects. His 'airspace', however, continued to be taken up with how bright he was, followed by disparaging remarks about all around him at work.

At the fourth meeting he was unusually silent, which others commented on. He responded by saying he had thought about the previous meeting, felt he had learnt a lot by working with the set, and would like to share this with them at the following meeting. At the fifth meeting he told the set how he felt he had changed, and that he was now a much happier person. He felt his behaviour sprang from a sense of insecurity, and – for all his noise – a lack of confidence. He was aware of how his behaviour caused problems and was disruptive both at work and at home. He'd done a lot of thinking, had talked to his manager, and was moving to a new

job which they both felt he would be better suited to –
dealing more with ideas and concepts and less with the
practical day-to-day issues which brought him face to
face with people all the time.

Stopping to think and reflect, and becoming more aware

Many managers are action-oriented; indeed, most roles
emphasize action to the point that stopping to think and
reflect is seen in some quarters as not working. Many participants remarked on this, particularly after they had experienced the 'time for thinking and reflecting' that the set offers.

'I've learnt that action isn't the only way of learning. You
can learn when there is little action,' laughed one active manager. Another said, 'At work we're achievers of activity. Here
you can legitimately look at the reverse of this: the thinking
that is needed for any activity to be ultimately effective.'

The questioning approach is for many a first step in the
direction of reflecting. Questions often raise issues they
haven't considered. Or feedback for set members may prompt
a looking inwards. 'The set gets you to try and look objectively at what you're doing or thinking . . . and you often
find that you are part of the problem you have described . . .
We're all so good at blaming others.'

Becoming more aware – aware of everything – was something most participants alluded to: awareness of people's
behaviour and what it might mean; sensitivity to what people
were really saying; awareness of undercurrents; awareness
of their own impact on others and vice-versa; listening and
not simply hearing; and acknowledging the existence and
validity of feelings. And an awareness that openness and
honesty produce results whereas closed-mindedness and
game-playing are ultimately destructive. Many struggled to
put these insights into coherent sentences and phrases. 'I'm

just more aware – conscious – of what goes on around me,' said one man. Others talked of acknowledging feelings, being honest, being conscious of having insights, picking up on people's unease.

And this awareness also related to learning: 'I've learned that there is learning to be done and that it's dynamic. Back at work, when staff say "I'm learning" I automatically ask "What are you learning?" ' Another participant had realized that 'everything is data from which I can learn'. Others remarked how it was now second-nature to them to stop and reflect on what they were learning, ie going around a learning cycle in their minds.

'I'm very self-confident and also competitive. I'm also a high contributor, I suppose in a way because I feel responsibility for a group I'm working in. So, I gave my 'all' to the set. But I'm also quite perceptive about processes – so I was able to tell the set that I usually do babble and talk. One day I joked that the set gave me the 'licence' to talk. At the next meeting the joke back-fired on me, when someone commented 'jokingly' about how much I talked . . . and they laughed – but more at me than with me. I sat and said nothing for the whole afternoon, part self-pity, part tantrum. Nor did anyone say anything to me. I didn't help the person with 'air-space', and wrote, after that meeting, in my diary: 'Am I being over-precious? Have I joked at others? Do I talk too much?

At the next meeting one of the people who'd laughed commented that she felt she'd contributed to the meeting last time because I'd given her the space to do so.

So my question to myself then was: 'Is silence the most I have to offer?' I felt odd for a while, and then realized that I could sit silently, and that would be OK. I just made one or two quiet points to the person whose airspace it was, and some time later he told me that my comments had changed the way he tackled his project,

---

ie it was my quiet, reflective insights that had been more helpful than my talkative self.

What I also learned was that by being too polished in telling them about how my project was going, I was leaving nothing for them to explore with me, which left them feeling inadequate. I decided for the next meeting I would be casual, and I purposefully experimented with being less prepared than I was comfortable with. I apologized for not being prepared – and I felt really uncomfortable and inadequate. But the set told me later that they felt more able to help me, and in fact we all felt that we had jointly worked very well together to help me reach some decisions. And they felt the working together was brilliant and they gained from it.

What I learned was that if I was too polished I inhibited others – and that could apply at work, and not only in a set. And it was quite painful learning for me, for I was contemplating – inside myself – issues of pride, arrogance and a questioning of my motives.'

Having the opportunity to study a group working productively

Working in the set gave participants a taste of what it might be like to work in such productive groups back at work. They also welcomed the opportunity to study the group and its processes – all part of the emphasis on learning.

'I've learned several transferable skills by working in the set: how to listen and focus on questions, how to facilitate and act as a mentor, and how to present – you find you're presenting to the set in a mini way all the time.'

'You learn the value of good, productive communication that occurs in a set . . . and want to transfer it back to work. It's the contribution that everyone makes that is so noticeable.'

'Asking for and giving constructive feedback . . . Why can't this happen more back at work?' Another added wishfully that 'the ideal would be if the action learning spirit could be carried over into working groups – so that they become a set . . . and hence some of the honesty of the set would begin to emerge at work.'

A number mentioned how productive it was to have an opportunity to challenge and not be met with resistance, anger or defensiveness.

Several managers were planning to transfer some of the set's ways of working back to their work environment. One admitted, 'I've never liked – or been – a macho manager. I realize I can now be effective and can manage in a relaxed, informal, collegiate and collective way.' And two or three were planning to turn their staff 'teams' into sets. 'After all,' said one of them, 'each of my staff is an expert in her own field. I can hardly play the autocratic manager with them!'

'You realize that by changing behaviour you can change a culture,' pondered another manager.

'The processes have given me a template of how people can work together effectively. You sense the atmosphere when a group is working well – and I don't mean agreeing with one another. They're listening to each other, and you know because you see how what they say relates to what the previous person said. Silences are OK, and the body language tells you a lot. And, importantly, disagreements are approached constructively.'

Many felt they were now more effective at meetings in their workplace, and one even remarked: 'I feel it's legitimate to comment on the processes in meetings – and not simply address comments to the chair on the agenda!'

One woman observed, 'The ground rules we have in the set have made me realize that we assume we have common ground rules back at work – when we don't.'

I tend to be quiet – the set had told me to be more forthcoming, more assertive. I now remember that, like a drip-feed. I found that before the programme I'd justify not keeping in touch with other managers because there was no particular issue. But what it's taught me is that just a quick point of contact keeps the lines open, it maintains good relations with others, which is important.

It's also made me more effective in applying the technical knowledge I have because I deal better with colleagues and staff, and feel happier with them. I'd always had good ideas, but I threw them in, so to speak, and they never got noticed. Now I repeat, or say things more forcibly.

I also didn't know how to react when people said 'no' to me, or disagreed. I now have a wider repertoire of responses. What had happened in the set was that someone pointed out 'You've already made that suggestion three times and no one's reacted. Why don't you follow it up – support it further – ask for a response – own it as an idea?' So, many more of my ideas are now being taken up and it gives me a sense of achievement and success. The doors are open, if only you'll walk through!

For instance, I suggested that two of our offices who rarely meet but have to work together on the phone, should have a weekend away – somewhere to just get to know each other. There was an enthusiastic response – people said it was the first time in five years that they'd had the chance to sit down in one room together. There was also another problem: that we in the London office were always seen as 'driving the ideas'. So, the suggestion was floated, not imposed; I set no agenda, but got everyone together, and on the first morning we settled jointly on issues we would talk about. I also 'modelled' behaviours I felt would be helpful, and admitted to my feelings on several occasions – which seemed to free others up, too.

> The weekend went really well, and the following week there were some congratulatory phone calls saying how useful the meeting had been. It certainly seems to have broken down the barriers.

Keeping a diary or log – or simply keeping notes

Very few participants kept diaries or wrote reflective documents. One programme required them to, but more for the participant's own use than as a form of assessment. The academic programmes were slightly more insistent.

One person commented that he hadn't kept a diary because he wasn't sure what to put in it. 'I'm not a scribbler,' he added.

Those who did keep diaries, however, found them beneficial. They acted as a memory – a way of stepping back into the event – part of the reflective element of action learning. It reminded them of what they'd done and felt, and what they'd thought, and what progress they were making. 'I always kept it. For me it was interesting to see what I did, and what I now do differently. You can see your own learning and progress. You begin to feel you're achieving something, getting somewhere. It shows up your journey.' Another diary-keeper remarked, 'It was helpful in retrospect to see my feelings, both the successes and the moments of pain, and which ones were triggered off by what. I could then look to see if there was a pattern!'

One woman said that the actual writing had given her an insight: 'I found I couldn't write when I felt low – so I learned that I don't learn at the moment when I'm low, I do so later, when I'm able to reflect. But I could write when I felt good – and so could reflect and learn more quickly.'

A group of trainers/developers, on a distance learning programme, found it very helpful to keep 'learning logs' which chronicled their own learning and their discomforts at certain stages. This, they saw, gave them helpful insights into how those they 'trained and developed' back at work might feel – so that they would in future be more aware and more sensitive to the emotions being expressed.

For one participant, keeping the diary was 'an extension of the set, another way of "talking".' And an action learning 'old-timer' said, 'I keep notebooks with insights, questions, ideas, fragments, reflections and "bubbles" . . . You might call it a learning log, but it's really more notes.'

A production manager – who prided himself on being a fire-fighter, able to think on the move, no time to plan, stumbling from crisis to crisis and coping regardless – commented how the first entry in his learning log was: ' "Reflect and be planned" – a corruption of print and be damned. Not the best of entries, too vague, no actions, no review date, but when acted on was one of the most valuable learning experiences.'

Another manager noted that one entry in his diary went as follows: 'Lessons learnt: Stand firm, don't wilt under pressure. Senior managers, who on the whole are "bright", can have significant weaknesses. Extremes of emotion destroy relationships, credibility and respect in a business environment. Never forget the other person's point of view. Do not be vindictive; it casts a shadow over future dealings with others.'

Taking notes at meetings and then turning them into something more coherent was something that many participants did. These notes were either for their own benefit or, in some programmes, formed the basis of reflective documents required at the end of a programme. Such documents are not submitted for any real assessment, rather they are intended as an exercise in reflection and learning.

Participants who kept diaries found they moved on from initially simply registering events to thinking about their reactions to them, what significance they had. One woman found the exercise to be an interesting experience: 'As time went on, my diary changed from being an Adrian Mole diary to one more like Anne Frank's.'

'Maybe the word diary is the wrong word to use,' mused

another participant, 'It's more of a daily portfolio of reflections – not so much of events and timing'.

To help these reflective moments, some sets would take time at the end of their meetings to reflect, write, and in some cases to share with others. They also noted their future action plans. Doing such reflection on the spot – at least of what they had learnt at the meeting – was, many found, the best way to keep track.

At the end of every meeting we filled in 'action forms' – what we planned to do and how. I found I was approaching and tackling my project totally differently from any previous work project. I was doing very little hands-on. Implementing the project [a communication one] was always uppermost in my mind. I found I could change my mind – I gained the confidence to do so. I made mistakes (which I documented), nothing too critical or life-threatening. I noted that I was no longer fobbed off by my manager. I considered lots of options before deciding. And I asked for feedback and ideas. I was making my own staff more accountable, and asking them 'What have you done and what will you do . . . and how?' Before it was me who told them.

I also wrote down questions going round in my mind, for instance: 'Can I say "I don't know" and not feel inferior?' And I'd keep track of what I was thinking and feeling. If I made mistakes I'd go back to the point where things began to go wrong, and see what I could have done differently.

The Set Adviser

The set adviser – the facilitator to a set, who helps the participants with their learning – was not a role envisaged by Reg Revans. Nevertheless, it is an important role, but one that differs in many respects from that of tutor or counsellor.

It is crucial that this role is played competently and professionally. For most programmes and participants, the set adviser provides the key to awareness of the learning. A good set adviser will make sure that participants stop, reflect, and consider their learning. A less competent one will merely focus on actions.

So, the task of the set adviser – together with set members as they gain more confidence – is to keep a balance between the project and the learning; but also to remind members to keep a balance between actions and self-development at work, ie not to lose their awareness of the learning possibilities when caught up in daily affairs.

'Pots' Diagram

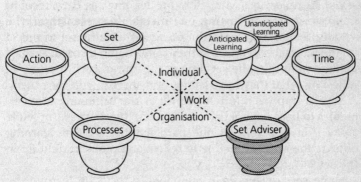

fig. 17

SOME QUESTIONS ANSWERED

What is the role and task of the set adviser?

The main task of a set adviser is to encourage the set – and each individual within it – to look, listen, question, understand, and learn. In this sense the set adviser is part of the set.

Thus the set adviser works with the set to help each participant focus on what they are achieving, what they are finding difficult, what they are gaining and learning from the programme, and what they find they are doing differently. As far as the set as a whole is concerned, the set adviser helps it to focus on the processes it is employing as it works – and on the learning from them, ie identifying which processes are helpful and which are not, and the implications of this.

A set adviser will keep a finger on the pulse of what is happening, and will intervene when he or she feels that there is an issue – someone's learning, or the set's processes – that is worth focusing on and analysing. For instance, if one member is talking so much that no one else can get a word in edgeways, the set adviser may comment skilfully on this (if no one within the set has yet done so).

The set adviser uses a variety of means to remind members of the importance of learning. Either participants will be asked to reflect on what they are learning as they recount their stories; or, following one member's presentation, the set adviser may ask both the presenter and the set to reflect on the interaction and what they noticed and learned. A third method is to give the set time at the end of each meeting to reflect on what they have learnt, and share it with the others. A similar approach (often helpful at the beginning of meetings) is to help members focus on what they have learnt while away from the set. As one participant said, 'The learning outside the set is often due to reflection points brought up in the set.'

Some set advisers help members to focus on learning by asking them, say after three meetings, to think about what they are doing differently back at work, and what difference that is making. Asking them to describe something to others forces everyone to be explicit. As one participant put it: 'Working within the set forces you to exercise your brain.'

A further task of the set adviser is to acknowledge and legitimize the fact that there are emotions bubbling around. Some participants may feel that it is inappropriate to voice emotions. By voicing his or her own first – modelling – the set adviser begins to free them of inhibitions, though of course this won't necessarily release them from the fear of what might happen when they express their emotions.

The set adviser will also use his or her judgement about how – and how far – to push a set member, or the set as a whole, to learn. Is a gentle and understanding approach the most beneficial? Or will the learning be greater through harsher confrontation?

A good set adviser will encourage participants to become aware of their learning on a number of scores:

- gaining new knowledge and information
- reasoning differently
- behaving differently
- becoming more aware
- gaining greater understanding of their motives
- altering beliefs and values
- acknowledging feelings and their impact

Finally, the set adviser is responsible for creating an environment conducive to learning – comfortable surroundings, coffee and tea breaks laid on – in which participants are unencumbered by other problems such as deadlines, telephone interruptions, and meetings.

'It took me a while to realize the set adviser was not going to teach us anything', commented one participant, echoing what many others said. This, inevitably, causes frustration,

207

at times anger, in some participants. For others it was liberating!

What the set adviser is not

- a tutor
- a lecturer
- a chairman
- a group leader
- an assessor/evaluator of set members

A set adviser's role is to facilitate a learning set, not a talkshop.

Do you need to have a set adviser?

Most people who have participated in action learning programmes find the presence of a set adviser helpful, for some of the reasons already outlined above. 'You definitely need one in the early stages,' was the general consensus, 'to help, to guide, to remind you of the processes. But later, as the set learn how to work effectively, and to focus on the learning as well as their actions – a set adviser may be less necessary. Maybe you can invite them in for particular meetings.'

A set adviser is, in a sense, a non-involved, external, objective voice, able to see what is happening, able to intervene when he or she deems it necessary, able to bring the set back on track. It's helpful for the set to be reminded that one of their main tasks is to learn, to help each other learn, and not simply to focus on their actions.

As the outsider the set adviser can also ask the simple 'idiot' questions that set members may not think of – or want to – ask. These often test beliefs and assumptions.

The role of the set adviser is to judge – perhaps 'sense' is the better word – how best to help participants to learn. Will they, for instance, learn best when pushed, or when cradled? Will the stick bring results, or is a gentler, more supportive approach more likely to see development and change? Each individual reacts to different goads: a set adviser has to make sensitive assessments.

It is elements such as this that set members will also become aware of. Such an assessment is indispensable to anyone who is a manager, for it relates directly to the question of: how to 'motivate' staff. This is just another example of how working in an action-learning set has obvious benefits for relationships back at work.

The set adviser will also take decisions on whether and when to intervene if he/she feels that emotions, values, beliefs and other fundamental issues are being glossed over. Often a good adviser will act almost intuitively, picking up vital clues, listening intently, or becoming aware of body language. A set adviser's unease may very well be the same as that being felt by set members, who do not want, or do not know how, to confront it.[5]

One set recalled, 'When we complained that we were stuck and weren't getting anything out of the set, the set adviser asked us to list how we felt about that, and what we thought was causing it. That opened us out, and we began to work better. On another occasion, when again we felt our learning had stopped, he got us to draw a graph to express how we saw our learning up to that point, and note down how we had been learning. That again released us and moved us on.'

Others talked of their set advisers 'keeping us on track, pulling us back when we went off at tangents, or became involved in wider discussions.'

'If the set adviser isn't good, or isn't present,' remarked a participant who had experience of such an adviser, 'the temptation is to concentrate on the tasks (the projects) and forget about watching our processes and our learning. That then misses entirely the point of action learning.'

One set was of the opinion that it had worked well on the group project and had learnt a great deal about the issue worked on. They were, however, less sure of their learning where the 'ostensible' purpose of the programme was concerned: teamworking. 'You can operate without a set adviser, but I don't think we necessarily challenged each other enough when we were alone. Maybe we need that catalyst. We found ourselves falling into suggestion/advisory roles . . . and anger was not expressed.'

But the task of every good set adviser is to work themselves out of a job, as set members gain similar expertise. Frequently set advisers will contract with a set that after three or four meetings they will review their role. Where a programme has been arranged to run for, say, six months, the set adviser will continue for this time. But if a programme is subsequently continued, the set may not need the set adviser any more, or may ask them to attend at intervals.

Sets I interviewed which had worked without set advisers were in two minds. One, a mature set consisting of experienced action learners, felt a set adviser was unnecessary. But two other sets who had worked without set advisers were both of the opinion that they would have gained – and learned – more with one.

To summarize: the role of the adviser is akin to that of mentor and facilitator. It should not be confused with roles such as tutor, lecturer, chairperson, or group leader.

Interestingly, my research showed that the role played by the set adviser caused a number of managers to rethink their roles as managers (see p. 217).

Is the adviser a specialist or expert in any particular field?

Yes, the best set advisers are skilled in observing and highlighting 'processes' – including the process of learning. They observe how a group is working together, listen, see, and sense what is happening, and then express this to the set – frequently in the form of a question! What they are thus doing is distinguishing clearly between tasks and processes. Their other main focus is on helping participants to learn, and become aware of how that learning is taking place.

One participant, whose set adviser turned out to be knowledgeable in the field of marketing but less so in facilitating, said: 'I would have preferred a set adviser who understood more about processes . . . I'd have learnt more. There was little distinction between him and a tutor.'

In demonstrating helpful processes, set advisers model particular behaviours that they judge to be useful and effective. Simultaneously they are adopting the action learning practice of handing back to the set responsibility for what they are doing, and giving them the 'power' to do something about it. So, when asked direct questions by the set, a set adviser may decide that giving a direct answer isn't, in fact, helpful. Instead they may suggest that the set should work on the question.

Many participants admitted that initially there was confusion – even anger – over the role that the set adviser adopted. As one member stated: 'The set adviser didn't direct or tell us what to do, he sat there . . . I found it all very disturbing. You're used to having tutors who point you in a direction . . . and here was something different that I didn't understand . . . Until I realized what she was doing . . . getting us to take responsibility and "power" and learn by doing so.'

What is *not* a set adviser's role or task?

'Expertise in a subject is the kiss of death in action learning,' was the conclusion of one participant. The minute the set adviser feels he or she has specific 'functional' knowledge, and the set picks up on this, there is a danger of the set adviser becoming a tutor to the set, reverting to semi-teaching role, and doing work on the set's behalf.

Other sets recounted how their line managers had been appointed as set advisers: 'They didn't distinguish between being chairmen/group leaders and "facilitating" – two very different roles.' Some managers had in fact only had a couple of hours' training in this new role – not very satisfactory!

By being a chairman or group leader, the set adviser is again removing both responsibility and 'power' from the set – a paradoxical situation in an action learning programme!

It thus takes time and requires some form of training to develop the skills of an effective set adviser. Some people take to the role naturally; others find it more difficult. As a role, however, it has close affinity with the role of a mentor. It also has many parallels with the role of a good manager who enables and empowers his or her staff, giving them responsibility and allowing them to develop.

How much does a set adviser intervene?

At the beginning of a programme, as set members become accustomed to working in what is to them a novel way of doing things, a set adviser may intervene quite a lot: to remind the set what their task is, ie to help each individual learn – even when the programme is about teamworking.

But as a set gains more experience and learns about the processes of action learning, including how to behave in a supportive, challenging yet non-judgemental way, the set adviser will probably intervene less.

The set adviser is also a member of the set in the sense that he or she will participate – when appropriate (ie without taking over from the set!) – in the asking of questions. But at the same time the set adviser should keep a watching eye on what is happening.

Some sets had different experiences – not always, in their view, productive. One set which had two set advisers over the period of the programme compared them: 'One became quite involved with us. He knew a lot about our task [a set project] and our work environment and got us to ask questions we'd never thought of asking. He checked also how we felt we were doing as a team. But he tackled individual issues outside the set in private. The second adviser, by contrast, kept a distance – even sat outside the group – and commented only on processes.' Neither was entirely satisfactory, in the view of the set members.

In another set, participants were concerned that their adviser had become too involved with them – almost part of the set – and thus less helpful because 'he tended to agree too much with us', and 'he talked too much.'

One of the traps new set advisers sometimes fall into is not distinguishing sufficiently between individual learning and group learning, and emphasizing the latter at the cost of the former. Both are important, but the idea of 'airspace' for work means focusing primarily on one person's learning at a time. This may of course involve looking at how the set helped or hindered the process – a learning opportunity for the set or certain individuals within it.

Such group learning may be left to the end of a person's airspace, or until the end of the set meeting. Some sets pause at the end of a meeting to reflect on their learning and share with each other what they observed, felt, or learnt.

So what do you do if you have a 'bad' set adviser?

The best response to this question is: 'Use it as a learning opportunity.' This, however, would require courage and skill (and is something that sets working with a good set adviser would learn to do naturally!)

Unfortunately it can and does happen that set advisers are not helpful. This may be because of a lack of understanding about what action learning is, or because they have had no training or experience in this form of facilitation – which is very different from being a tutor or running a seminar.

To gain the full benefit of action learning, participants need – and deserve – to have a good set adviser. The programme organizer is responsible for choosing set advisers, and it is to them that participants unhappy with their set adviser should turn. But participants need to be clear what exactly it is they are unhappy about. If they want the set adviser to hold their hand, and the latter refuses, this may not be sufficient grounds for changing a set adviser – especially since he or she may have the set's best interests at heart.

For instance, one participant recalled a set member who talked non-stop, 'hogging the time'. 'The set adviser did nothing. We weren't sure how to tackle this man – was it OK to tell him what he was doing? Eventually two of us did. I'm pleased I took the risk – it helped us work better as a set, and I learned that giving that sort of feedback isn't as terrifying as I'd thought.' Thus she learned a lesson she might not have if the set adviser had taken up the issue first.

There are also, sadly, instances of unprofessional behaviour by set advisers – such as being judgemental, picking on individual members, and being abrasive and dismissive. One set talked of their set adviser standing by idly while 'screaming matches took place in the set, he didn't intervene, he did nothing . . . And we also felt powerless to react . . . all very confusing.'

Yet another had experienced a set adviser who was 'critical, condescending and aggressive. We didn't trust him at all. We lost one member because of him, and another withdrew and didn't attend regularly. He picked on us, and we became victims. It puts you off learning.' No one in this set tackled the set adviser, either. They did not feel able to do so, did not feel they had skills to do so; it never occurred to them that they could do something – or even that it was their responsibility (if only to themselves!) to do something about it: a situation remarkably similar to that many people find back at work and feel equally powerless to resolve. A common case of actual or perceived powerlessness!

One set talked of a set adviser who did not observe the confidentiality ground rule, thus limiting the work done in that set.

Relationships with set advisers can be difficult territory to negotiate, and any unhappiness, complaints and queries should be raised first with the set adviser in question, and then with the programme organizer. Whichever course of action is taken, it is a learning opportunity for the set and for the set adviser.

THE VALUE OF WORKING WITH A SET ADVISER

Making us aware of helpful processes

'Our set adviser "taught" me to listen and analyse, to question and encourage others to say more, to help them – and the others – understand . . . She did this by modelling that approach.'

Another participant described how the set adviser 'steered the dialogue, in the sense of seeing the positives of the differences between people, because differences make you look at your own and other people's assumptions.'

'The set adviser', remarked another, 'would often pull us up if we began to blame others for what was happening. We'd be reminded that we also had a choice – to go along with something or not. To do something or not. To respond or keep quiet.'

215

A member of a different set remembered how 'the set adviser pushed us but rarely gave us answers, just went on asking questions – to get us, of course, to reflect and find our own answers. Even our own behaviour in the set. He'd ask "What's happening here now?' – which throws you at first, then you learn to look at the processes: who's angry, who's dominating, who's listening, who's running away . . . It makes you so much more aware of what happens back at work, in meetings or teams.'

Building on this, one young woman said she now felt freer to comment on what was in fact happening in groups or meetings she went to – something she would certainly not have done before.

'Action learning promotes a different way of thinking and behaving, which our set adviser promoted as much through her own behaviour as through what she told us about action learning. It makes participation in any discussion elsewhere – at work – a skilful matter, as you learn to really listen, to ask questions that are helpful to the speaker and not designed to show off your own knowledge or point of view . . . You become sensitive to what people say and how they say it . . . And you learn to 'own' your statements: no 'people always . . .' or 'we', just 'I'. So no generalizations or platitudes. Your statements then become more precise, you become more personally engaged and your level of energy remains high.'

Made us aware of learning – anywhere, anytime

'Our set adviser drip fed the question to us all the time: "So what have you learnt from that?" It became like an ever-present echo.' This was the view of one set. They then went on to say that each of them now asked themselves that question almost subconsciously, no matter what they were doing or what was happening.

Others said it was their set adviser who got them to 'plumb the depths' either by his comments or questions.

Not all sets are so lucky.

A role model for 'managing'

A number of participants also commented on the role of the set adviser as a model for managers to follow. 'Coaching and mentoring is part of every manager's job. By learning to work as an effective set member by using a good set adviser as a model, you're learning the processes you need for mentoring and coaching as a line manager,' was the realization of one participant.

Others went further, beyond coaching and mentoring, to everyday managing:

> I used the set adviser and his way of 'managing' us, the set, as a model for managing. The format of the set with a set adviser has given me a new way of working. I see my role as being a 'set adviser' to my team, wanting them to achieve their potential, and not feeling threatened by it . . . I try and adopt the way our set adviser worked, using questions in a quiet way, and dropping in the occasional 'pearls of wisdom'.

Another participant had similar thoughts. 'Our set adviser kept us to our learning agendas . . . he didn't teach, but he'd ask us what we'd learnt from various things we mentioned or talked about. I've tried it with my staff and find I'm increasingly using the set adviser as a model.'

One participant made the connection that, for her, 'facilitating – something we as set members learned to do – is in fact the best form of consulting.'

'Our set adviser could have so easily have taken over and directed us when we were floundering, or been judgemental, or simply not known how to cope. Instead he allowed us to empower ourselves.' The lesson in being empowered was not lost on some managers, who back at work were now following a similar model with their own staff.

Time

An action learning programme takes longer than most other programmes or courses – except for academically-based courses. Why is this? Could it take place in a shorter time-frame? Time is money: can employers really be expected to release people from their everyday work for so long?

SOME QUESTIONS ANSWERED

Why does a programme take so long?

One reason for programmes taking long is that learning takes time. We may assimilate ideas or new skills quite quickly, but consolidating them – making sure we really have understood and mastered them – takes longer. We only know this by testing things out in a process of trial and error, and by

'Pots' Diagram

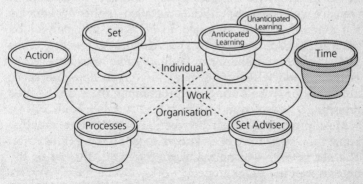

fig. 18

revisiting the errors to learn from them, and revisiting successes to learn equally from them. If it's behaviour or attitude change that is being looked for, these develop over time, not overnight.

The other reason why programmes take longer is because they are project-based. To work on a real project and manage it through its various stages takes time. Nothing in organizations is done instantly. And to gain the full benefit of action learning, each participant needs to go around a learning cycle more than once, ie they need to report back at least two or three times in order to feel they are moving forward with their learning, let alone their actions.

Is there an ideal length?

There is no ideal length. However, if a programme is too short the learning will be more superficial. Less than three months is probably not useful, because this limits the number of times that the set can meet.

The frequency and length of meetings is crucial. Ideally, sets should meet for a full day once a month. A programme lasting three months allows for only three meetings, so that there may not be enough time for everyone to revisit their actions and their learning. This will be exacerbated if the set meets for only two or three hours, because the amount of airspace will have to be radically curtailed – either by reducing the amount of time allocated to each set member, or by limiting airspace to one or two participants per meeting. Thus in a short programme it can be impossible to explore issues in depth, and where participants are given time and space only once or twice during the programme there can be little revisiting . . . which in turn may lead to less learning.

Most programmes last between six and twelve months. Some, however, have been known to go on for several years. The set adviser will normally contract with the set or the organizer of the programme to work with the set for, say, six meetings. Thereafter, the contract can be renegotiated.

Those sets that continue for longer usually do so from the participants' choice. Those most likely to last that long are made up of very senior personnel – chief executives and managing directors. They, in turn, are less likely to be able to meet once a month, because of pressure of work and responsibilities. Instead, such groups tend to meet every two or three months, often for an evening plus the following day.

Continuing with a set – which, as many point out, is the only time they have for themselves, and the only place where they can drop their masks and share their questions and anxieties with others – is invaluable.

One managing director who has in fact been a member of a set for some ten years – although some of the members have changed over that period – said it provided him with the mirror he needed to help him reflect on decisions he was facing, issues he was dealing with, and was a time to tap into the accumulated knowledge and experience of other very senior managers with no axe to grind.

How do you persuade or convince your manager to let you have so much time off?

As discussed in the section on **Action** (see p. 139), participants' managers need to be involved very early on, and should indeed be party to the selection of a task or project. If that project is focused on a work-related issue, or is of relevance to the employee's job or the section/department they work in, the manager is more likely to be willing to allow them time off.

The way to convince an employer or manager is to explain why it takes so long and, perhaps more importantly, to point out the benefits and the tangible results.

It is essential that the programme has the support and backing of a senior manager (the 'client'), because this will ease any tension with a participant's immediate boss. Once the importance of the programme to the organization has been stressed, participants should have fewer problems with their managers.

Having suffered at the hands of their managers, a number of participants felt very strongly about the need for managers and clients to be involved in the early stages of any programme. 'You must have the commitment from managers to the programme – otherwise you risk being hassled by them. The day [of] a set meeting my manager would, almost like clockwork, come up with an important meeting that I had to attend, or other things that I had to do that day. It made things very difficult for me.'

'You need energy, motivation and commitment to persist with action learning. Don't give up early – even if you're dubious and feel it's of limited value. Time is crucial. You become like a sponge – gradually saturated – and then you need more time before it begins to drip out, and you realize what's been happening, and what you're learning.'

THE VALUE OF TIME

'Action learning sows seeds that take time to germinate,' as one action learning old-timer put it.

Reflection takes time

Many participants commented on their realization that the act of reflection was not something instantaneous. It was something that happened over time. Ideas take time to take root – in many cases insights would come at times seemingly unconnected with what was happening in the programme.

'Time and reflection go hand in hand,' observed one participant. 'Reflection isn't the instant thoughts you have. It's a longer, deeper process, and insights may occur at times which have nothing ostensibly to do with the set or programme.' Another added: 'Action learning makes you think – but that doesn't happen quickly either. It takes time. The questions often dam up old routes of thinking, and it takes time to go down the new ones.'

Learning takes time

Referring to the benefits of an action learning programme over and above, or following on from book-learning or taught-learning, one participant on an academically-based programme commented: 'I came to accept the concepts [of action learning] early on but it took time to see the real benefits, and to know how to do it. Much of that was because, at first, I kept wanting books and experts to be around, and it takes time to get used to doing all the questioning and learning yourself!'

As a corollary to this, many remarked that action learning programmes are particularly useful when participants are trying to 'consolidate' knowledge acquired on more traditional, taught courses, where the subject matter – eg management – has to be applied back at work. Built onto a more traditional programme (thereby lengthening it) action learning gives participants the opportunity to test out and determine what is useful and what is less useful, what they have forgotten, or what they may have misunderstood. It is, after all, what many professions and craft-based skills still require.

> You learn on various courses about relating, communicating, motivating, being assertive, and about management styles . . . but you have to practise and practise to overcome years of doing things differently. And that's the value of action learning – the repetition and the constant building on what you've tried out once, to get it better.

Time therefore allows each participant to reflect on changes in themselves, and how those changes had come about – ie how they learnt. The value of this is that, once participants know how they best learn, they can recreate those conditions in the future.

Six months was not long enough for one participant: 'I became a great deal more aware. For me it was all too short, I was just beginning to open out, learning, gaining the confidence to talk. I'm an introvert and I'd just begun to come out of my shell . . .' His set members gave him – in my presence – some feedback on how he was now talking and participating much more than at the outset. He said this was being mirrored back in his department where he was now talking to colleagues and feeling much more relaxed. He was also talking more about work issues – and in greater depth – than before. He felt the quality of his work had improved as a result.

Others associated time with anchoring the learning. 'The length of the whole programme – nine months – was important. The opposite of the short sharp shock soon forgotten . . . And the longer you are there, the more committed you become.'

Many participants underlined quite emphatically the fact that 'It takes time . . . you must give it time . . . Giving up after one or two meetings when you feel not much is happening isn't giving it a chance. I'd say to anyone: give it time, hang in, don't be dismissive.'

Action learning processes – including going around the learning cycle – take time

Time is one of the keys to action learning, because you need, as one participant put it, to go around a learning cycle, and that doesn't happen in a day, or even a week. We not only have to learn to do new things; we must first unlearn old things. And then we need to test out the new ways. There's no quick and easy way to learn: 'You need to spend a year doing it – a week full-time isn't the same.'

Time is also tied in with continuity – the repetition of sets and set meetings and the same sort of questions lends a sense of continuity to the discipline of thinking, planning and doing, reflecting and coming back to thinking again. 'Going around the learning cycle once isn't sufficient', said one participant thoughtfully. It takes time for the results to become apparent: 'We meet monthly and feel – and can see – that we've matured over time.'

The time occupied by each meeting is also crucial: it must be long enough to allow for airspace – ie the time that each individual has for continuing their 'journey' – about one hour per person, ideally. 'You think you've solved a problem in five minutes, but if you spend more time, you realize you haven't. You've only scratched the surface. After an hour and a half we began to feel we were really getting somewhere.'

Mutual support and trust – as well as individual self-confidence – develop with time

It takes time for participants to get to know each other and to trust one another (usually). Only when set members have confidence in one another and feel safe enough to be honest can the set really begin to work.

The continuity of having the same set members (most of the sets I met had had the same members throughout the programme) helped enable participants to be honest and admit to emotions, or to not knowing. The observation that 'it takes time to develop the trust you need in the set to allow you to work really well,' was echoed frequently by participants, as was the sense that 'Real honesty was a long time coming, but when it did the progress was incredible.'

Time showed them that: 'Confidence is a moveable feast. As you get to know people, you see that they may feel confident about one thing, but not about another. Or their confidence came and went with different moods.'

'The value of the set is that you can work on these moods and emotions as and when they occur. This in turn helps you to respond to them in others, rather than react.'

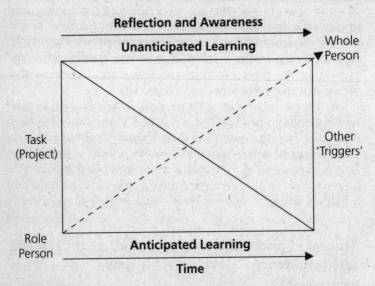

Time and Its Value   fig. 19

The passage of time enabled participants to see how various people participated: some earlier, others later, and some when they felt they had some relevant skill or knowledge to offer. For example, in one set, a relatively silent member came into his own when the set began preparing their final report for the client, because he was a designer and used to presenting material visually and professionally. It's worth noting, however, that this was also a set which did not work with a set adviser, who might have brought this silent member in sooner.

'I realized everyone had something to offer, given time. If you dismiss them early on you may be losing a valuable resource . . . It makes you realize that your preconceived notions of others are wrong – it makes you much more open in other settings. You cease to judge others instantly.'

It is only through time that participants recognize how impressions change; that first impressions are not necessarily ones that last or should be built on. This applies particularly to action learning: many participants commented how anxious they were at the beginning, and how initially they behaved 'out of character' – or rather, they acted as they do in other new groups. But this time they had the opportunity of studying their own behaviour!

'First impressions are often very wrong. That's the advantage of working with a set for a long time on lots of issues. You see people from different angles, and how over time they present all the different sides of their character.'

So, what was valuable in having more time was the opportunity to study these issues, and discuss them and learn from them. In a more hurried programme there would be less time for such learning (see fig. 19).

Time is an ally

From recognizing the value of time on the programme it was an easy step for participants to see time as valuable in other circumstances. Many described how they began to view time in a different way: not as something to battle against, or something which they 'lost'.

The metaphors – and hence the way people viewed time – changed. Time came to be seen as an opportunity for 'investment' of ideas and reflection on them. 'I gained the confidence to work with time . . . to look at the long-term and marry it with the short-term. To acknowledge that we need more time, and need to stop constantly rushing, finding the quickest way forward.'

Another participant remarked, 'I see time as an ally – it gives me a sense of perspective. It's no longer a foe or enemy. Instead of "I must" or "I should" I now find myself saying "I will" which has a longer-term and more thought-out ring to it.'

Where time is equated solely with money, however, there may be little time for action learning methods. As one participant commented: 'You need time at work to talk as we did in the set, but work pressures don't allow this.' Where learning – as opposed to assimilation of information or knowledge – is valued, time is normally found. We always have the time; we simply choose to use it in different ways. It depends on what we value.

The Learning

The learning on action learning programmes is very individual, and although much of it follows the path of the learning agreements made (see p. 107) a great deal of it cannot be anticipated. For as participants become increasingly aware of the notion of learning from everything, so they begin to gain insights which they could not have predicted.

Much of the awareness of learning begins in the set, often prompted by the set adviser asking the question, 'so what did you learn from that?'. It also emerges as participants begin, initially consciously, to use a learning spiral, and consider how they learn, while observing how other set members learn. Keeping logs (see p. 183) also helps to recall and reflect on what they are doing, thinking, feeling and noticing.

'Pots' Diagram

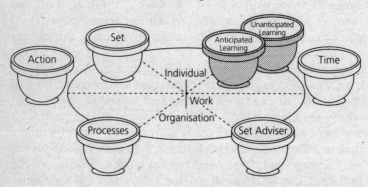

fig. 20

Preferred learning styles

- Activists, who prefer immediate action and maybe stop to consider later
- Reflectors – who prefer to stop and think and tend to be cautious
- Theorists who integrate what they have seen or done into rational schemes
- Pragmatists who are keen on trying out ideas, theories or techniques

Different approaches to learning

- Incidental learners, who learn when shocked or jolted into realization
- Intuitive learners, who somehow learn but aren't quite sure how
- Retrospective learners, who learn by recalling and reflecting
- Prospective learners, who plan to learn
- Opportunistic learners, who learn from every opportunity and both plan and review

Becoming aware, the first step to learning, gradually begins to take place outside the set as well. Many participants commented, though, that this shift of learning from the set to everyday situations took a bit of time.

ANTICIPATED LEARNING

Action learning programmes, like any other, have outcomes they hope to achieve. The various programmes described in this book had various projected outcomes, and these formed the basis of 'anticipated' learning for participants. (For a reminder of unanticipated learning gains, see p. 257.)

Where organizations specified programme outcomes, they were:

- teamworking;
- introducing a new management culture;
- engaging senior managers in management problems;
- recommending new business strategies;
- encouraging managers to take responsibility and decisions, and to question; to be more energetic and proactive; to coach and counsel their staff; to encourage leadership and initiative.

Where the anticipated learning outcomes involved participants' own personal and managerial development, they talked of hoping to:

- challenge myself intellectually;
- compare and try out new methods of working and managing;
- learn how to motivate my staff;
- learn about leadership;
- become a better team member;
- grow as an individual.

In some instances, individuals also sought to gain specific skills associated with communicating, implementing quality programmes, creating human resource development programmes, liaising with clients, implementing IT programmes, and so on.

Before moving on to participants' own words, a brief word about assessing action learning. This is a perennial question.

What, many participants ask, will they need to do for an assessment? Is there a 'pass' or 'fail'? Will they have to produce written material – and how and by whom will it be judged? And is it the project or the learning that will be evaluated?

What is assessed in an action learning programme?

The answer to this will be decided by each organization running such a programme. If the organization has an action-oriented culture, the measurable and visible results are what will be probably be assessed primarily. In development-oriented organizations, personal development may be viewed as at least equally important to any achieved 'actions'. Thus certain outcomes or criteria for success will have been mapped out, and participants may have some form of a learning contract.

Areas for assessment might include whether someone now reasons differently, behaves differently, has a greater understanding of his/her motives, has altered some beliefs and values, and is able to acknowledge his/her feelings and their impact.

Participants remarked on the fact that assessing the action was easier: action could be observed – a task performed, a report prepared – and (as we've seen) clients and managers often become aware of, and are impressed by, participants as they work on a project.

For many participants, however, their learning was the most important element, and the one on which they preferred to be assessed. In other words, how they have changed and developed as a result of their learning, and what they are now doing differently – which inevitably has a knock-on effect on their day-to-day work and relationships.

How do you learn?

- by talking things through
- by taking a risk
- by reflecting
- by listening to others
- by helping others
- by practising and repeating
- by analysing and understanding
- by trying something out
- by reviewing successes . . . and mistakes
- by being asked questions
- by reading
- by hearing myself think aloud
- by getting feedback
- by writing
- by drawing/creating a picture

How we learn depends to an extent on 'what' we are attempting to learn (see learning agreements on p. 107).

When do you learn?

- when I'm given the time and space
- when there is a sense of urgency
- when I can see an end-use: results and benefits
- when I am allowed to make mistakes
- when I am encouraged and supported
- when I'm 'kicked'
- when I'm appreciated
- when I feel confident – and competent
- when I am interested
- when I want to achieve something for my own satisfaction

Being aware of responses to these questions is useful, for it highlights, for the future, the circumstances and conditions in which you will best learn.

How is an action learning programme – and participants' achievements – assessed?

There are a number of ways of assessing both an action learning programme and what participants have learnt:

- By asking participants to assess themselves and other set members, evaluating achievements and even mistakes – ie self and peer evaluation.
- By asking participants' colleagues and managers; those brave enough could ask participants' staff. The client will also have some insights about both.
- By asking the personnel and training/development department for their observations, and using the next assessment centre to evaluate the change in the participant.
- By asking the participants to write a report and/or a reflective document. The former would describe the actual achievements of the project; the latter would describe the journey of learning.
- By asking participants to give a presentation to clients and other interested parties, including senior managers. Such presentations might cover both 'action' achievements and learning.

If participants are on a qualifications-related programme, they will of course need to write a dissertation or some other 'academic' paper

The important thing is to decide what form of assessment – if any – is going to be used, and to make sure that all participants are clear about it at the beginning of the programme.

One set described in some detail their unhappiness at the lack of clarity over their assessment:

> We weren't told what exactly was going to be evaluated, nor who was interested in hearing it. All we knew was that we had to make a presentation of some sort. So we decided that, for us, our learning and development had been the key part of the programme. Our individual presentations covered our actual tangible project

233

achievements, and then we began to get on to the learning part of the programme, but were stopped, and told that the managers had no interest in this!

As a result, the set were left feeling disillusioned with their managers – and the company – for being so disinterested in individual growth and change.

An interesting exercise is for participants to go back to what they hoped to learn (see learning agreements on p. 106) and compare this with what they are, in fact, learning.

There will be visible, tangible benefits, won't there?

The tangible benefits will be many and varied. If the participant's aim was to develop managerial and personal skills, these will be visible. If the participant aimed to achieve something more tangible – introduce a training programme, create a new system or process, introduce new ways of communicating, build up a new client base, resolve a production problem – then the results will also be clear to all.

In terms of wider development, it is impossible to specify what each individual will take away from such a programme – but the preceding sections of this book provide a survey of the breadth and depth of the potential learning gains to be had.

Failure to achieve tangible results may not be the fault of the participant. It could – and often is – a consequence of problems within the organization that preclude the hoped-for tangible results: amalgamation of departments, staff redundancies, major restructuring, and so on. But the *unanticipated* benefits of action learning remain.

How action learning is assessed

- By the client
    on the basis of a written report, a presentation, or having a meeting
- By the Human Resource Development/Training Manager, or participants' own managers
    on the evidence of behaviour and attitude changes
    visible results, 'bottom line' or other achievements
- By set members (with the individual present)
    assessing changes in each other
- By colleagues at work (with the individual present)
    assessing changes in him/her
- Self-assessment
    in written form
    verbal (to all or any of the above categories)

How do you keep track of your achievements – particularly the learning?

In many instances, to ensure that individual and set learning was not lost, participants were required to produce written reports or short reflective documents (intended more for themselves than for a formal assessment). See p. 186 for more on diary and log-keeping.

Sets differ in their approach to assessment. One set which was highly successful in tackling a project as part of a team-building programme, when asked about how and when they assessed their learning, said they might put a few hours aside at the end of the programme for evaluation. Others assessed the learning as they went along. The set adviser might, for instance, ask participants at the end of a meeting to note down their observations, reflections, what they have learnt from the day, and share this with other members. This also provides an opportunity for members to give each other feedback – a very useful commodity when learning!

But there is more to learning than learning:

To paraphrase Dwight Eisenhower: 'To have learnt is nothing; learning is everything.' Learning is a process in which the final achievement is but a by-product. How we achieve is as important as what we achieve. We need to know what enabled us to learn, what happened to give us that insight. When we say 'I've learnt', what do we now do differently to justify that claim?

Some, but not all of the programmes I studied concentrated on the 'how' of the learning as much as on the end-product. 'I've learnt to listen,' was a frequent response, as were: 'I found that asking others questions made me think more about the issue and gave me insights' and 'Listening to others grappling with problems helped me resolve some of my own.' These are just a few instances of 'how' participants learned. Having made such discoveries about their learning process, those participants now have some ideas on how to recreate situations which help them learn.

For others it was having to take a risk – do something they'd never done before – that provided insights. Action learning enabled them to come to terms with their fear, and recognize it as a sign of a learning opportunity ahead.

The six skills participants whom I interviewed most commonly anticipated learning were: how to achieve better teamworking; how to effect a 'culture' change; how to be a more effective manager; how to take on more responsibility and a more active role at work; how to challenge myself intellectually; and how to consult and facilitate. On the following pages, participants describe in their own words the action learning approach to mastering these skills.

How to achieve better teamworking

This was the stated outcome for three in-company programmes, although individuals on other programmes also hoped to achieve this. The reason why action learning was chosen, as opposed to a more traditional team-building programme, was that the organizations in question felt that working on a real project and having the benefit of working in sets would add more depth to the learning – primarily because of the simultaneous emphasis on action and learning.

Nevertheless, participants could have improved their team-working skills on other programmes. What they said they gained through action learning, however, was applying themselves to real-life, work-centred projects, which in two cases involved implementing their jointly agreed plans and ideas. They also valued the time they could spend on it, the discipline of action learning processes such as airspace and questioning, the time for reflecting and the emphasis on their learning.

At the outset of the three programmes, participants had been introduced to Belbin's model[6] (see box below for main team roles and their characteristics). Most had completed the questionnaire, and had been 'labelled'.

Belbin's nine team roles

1 *Innovators/Plants* – original thinkers who provide new ideas;
2 *Resource investigators* – bring in ideas from contacts outside;
3 *Co-ordinators* – social leaders of the group, guiding it towards its objectives;
4 *Shapers* – provide the energy and drive to implement ideas or projects;
5 *Evaluators* – appraise proposals, monitor progress;
6 *Team workers* – provide and maintain contact away from team/meetings;

> 7 *Implementers* – translate plans into manageable tasks that team can get on with;
> 8 *Finishers* – make sure the team delivers;
> 9 *Specialists** – those with specialist knowledge
>
> Each person will probably fulfil at least two roles.

Many participants were also familiar with the four learning styles defined by Honey and Mumford – activists, pragmatists, reflectors and theorists – and had completed the 'learning styles' questionnaire. This had helped them understand their own approach to learning, and to accept those of others, so that they might value and learn to work with them. They found these useful as reference points, and when they talked of how they had changed, a number mentioned learning how to work with and 'use' people whom they now recognized as having complementary skills. Other participants talked of trying to develop different styles, eg becoming more reflective or more active. 'I've learnt', said one manager, 'that there's more to learning than just being active.'

Participants in the three team-development programmes worked on group projects. In one instance they selected a project to improve communications in one member's workplace, and each member focused on an issue related to this. In the second programme, the set themselves chose to work on a group project; in this case, a 'consultancy' project (ie it did not have an implementing stage). In the third programme, there were two variants. In one, each set focused on a single set member's issues and acted merely as 'support' to that member. The outcomes here were not entirely successful, because the other set members felt uninvolved. In the second variant, one work section became a set, charged with reorganizing their own work area – a shopfloor. This was a highly successful experience (see pp. 152–4).

* A category added later.

In the first two programmes, the participants had never worked together before, nor were they accustomed to working as cross-functional teams; their only experience of team working was with their own staff.

To summarize participants' experiences, they claimed to have learnt the following:

To work better with others, and be more understanding and patient:

'I listen far more, and am more than ever now committed to team work. I'm a "shaper", so naturally I have a clear view of what I want, and am often tempted to impose it on others. Now I appreciate more where others are coming from, and can read their reactions better.'

'I'm now more aware that some team members' skills are more useful at the end of a project than at the beginning, and I've ceased to judge people in other teams I work with for not participating early on in the work.'

'I've learnt that my first impressions are often very wrong. That's the advantage of working in a set for a long time on lots of issues. You see people from many different angles, and you realize how wrong you can be, and how, if you act this out at work, you are likely to lose someone valuable.'

'During our joint project activities I developed set ideas on who had worked hard, who had contributed most – because they'd talked most! But then at some stage everyone pulled their weight. I remember one member who had said virtually nothing, and I was ready to condemn him, when he suddenly offered some really useful insights on what we, as a team, were doing which wasn't leading us anywhere.'

Others noted how 'leaders emerge during team activities, and leadership swapped for different activities because of the different skills we needed at different stages of the project.'

A greater awareness of what happens in teams – and meetings:

'It taught me to be more aware and to concentrate on what was happening, particularly in meetings, or when I am with others. Before, I'd concentrate only on what was being said. Now I'm more aware of body language and silences. The "task" isn't the sole important thing.'

How to let go of control:

'I'm normally frustrated when I'm not in control in a group. I've learnt that I don't have to "own" and control everything. I'm more tolerant of others and they are then better able to work with me. I'm also more aware, more able to stop and see myself. Being a perfectionist is a problem!'

For many participants, the opportunity to observe, over time, various roles – and the behaviours and communication patterns that went with them – anchored the knowledge and theories they already had (mostly gained on taught courses) in real life.

It also helped one manager who was, in her own words, an 'activist' to become more pragmatic and, as she herself was the first to admit, probably an easier person to work with. It was this young woman who, almost in the same breath, added that as a result of this teamworking experience she had come to realize that being a manager was more than knowing all about her speciality (surveying) and talking loudly! This was something she had not anticipated. 'Mind-blowing,' was how she described her experiences. 'This is my first managerial job. I've been given responsibility for making money in my department – a surveyor's department. In action learning I've realized that managing is much more than being good at the work of my department – and simply talking loudly. I have so much more to learn – and it isn't to do with the "tasks" we tackle, but with the processes we adopt when we work together.'

The Learning

This 'jump' in thinking and awareness is just one of the typical outcomes of an action learning programme.

How to delegate and give staff more opportunities:

One woman said she was giving her staff 'more opportunity to "give". I'm delegating more to them and they're enjoying it. I've learnt that there are good ideas out there . . . even someone you've mentally dismissed has them.'

The art of delegation was also an 'unanticipated' gain for a young manager in retailing. She found that the programme was taking up so much of her time that she simply had to delegate! As she put it:

> This was not one of my learning objectives. I was learning how to work in a team. But I simply didn't have time to do everything at work once we started to work on the project. I didn't know how to delegate. So we – my staff and I – learnt together. An offshoot, so to speak of what I was doing on the programme!
>
> I didn't initially give my staff enough background or guidance on what they were to do. And they didn't at first ask me either – they were afraid of my reaction. So I'd phone and give them detailed instructions on what to do, and then phone to check how they'd managed. But then, as they began to cope better, I created a tape of tasks they need to carry out, but not how. And they managed. Soon I found that all I was doing was phoning to reassure them, praise them and tell them what a great job they were doing. They are so pleased, since it's given them much more responsibility – and they've proved they can do it.

Another manager commented on how he had become aware of the difference between managing and leadership: 'In the latter you set standards and lead from the front, take on board conflicts with others, don't retreat; they're challenges, and as you resolve them you feel a sense of achievement.'

'I appreciate my staff much more and take on board their

suggestions as well as their feelings. And I'm more aware of the effect I have on people.'

How best to re-organize teams back at work:

One of the more senior members in one set described how he was now using cross-disciplinary teams to work on departmental issues, thereby getting a wider range of perspectives and achieving greater cohesion within the department. He went on to say: 'The best people for solving problems are not necessarily the most senior people . . . the action learning programme encouraged me to re-organize my department and introduce a management team which isn't drawn solely from senior people. Involving people in a more consultative way can be uncomfortable, but it's worth it for the results.'

A marketing manager was excited about working in a totally different way:

> I run several projects at once. I now talk to as many people as possible. Before, my department had a bad reputation: we were told we never communicated. One of my current projects needs – to be successful – to involve operations, sales, marketing and finance people. I've decided to draw in people from various locations around the country and have them all work together, in the same building, for the duration of the project – more of a matrix-type of organization. Before, I'd have made assumptions about what each of these departments would say, or want, and how they'd view my suggestions. Now they have a direct input into any plans. I also work at a much 'deeper' level – mostly through questioning. It's important to overcome physical barriers to communication, as well as the 'psychological' ones, ie the beliefs and assumptions we have, bred by silence and distance. I'm really pleased because one of my main objectives in going on the programme was to improve my own and my department's communication.

Another participant remarked, 'I used to dread departmental meetings or team meetings I chaired. I've changed my style – modelling meetings much more on our set processes – and now everyone is contributing more freely. I've used the SWOT analysis as a tool, and I feel the team going with me. Even the doubters are beginning to participate and value the different way of working.'

And yet another described how her team 'is now running as a set, because they're all experts. How can I go around telling them what to do? The way our set adviser used questions, and how he "managed" us in a quiet way, has now become more my style of managing.'

One young banker had moved since the programme to a new job as a quality manager. 'I've moved the teams away from having a "structured" approach to their meetings, and working, to a more action learning approach. So although we go through what has been achieved (for an agenda and report to be written) we give everyone "airspace" and we use questions rather more than a general discussion.'

'As a result of working on the team project during the programme I've changed my approach to the planning process. Everyone on my work team is now involved. Before, I did it alone. I've realized it's a common cause.

I'm also doing a lot of cross-grouping – putting people from different sections together to build up a team and get greater harmony. Before, people would meet in corridors and have conversations, or they met behind closed doors.

I can see that my staff are more involved – and they're talking to me more – and talking more openly. I really think that rank and status are beginning to break down. I'm sure that's what motivates success.'

How to effect a 'culture' change

Two company-run programmes specified 'culture' change as their anticipated outcome. What they meant by this was 'creating a more energetic, proactive, responsive environment' and 'building a strong teamworking culture' to increase team performance. But neither detailed what different behaviours they hoped to see, nor did they anticipate the fact that changes would have to be made in structures, systems and procedures if the desired culture change was to have a chance of occurring.

Of the two, the first company appeared to succeed, at least in part. It had introduced an action learning programme at each of its sites with the stated aim of improving team performance across the company. This arose out of a realization that communication within the company was sadly lacking and was resulting in poor communication with customers.

To paraphrase one senior manager's view, the company was run by natural fire-fighters rather than good planners. No deadlines were set and there was little monitoring. As a result, staff were beginning to lose confidence and respect for management. 'What they wanted was strong managers who took decisions . . . without discussion. But we're a US company, where teamworking is important. So, we selected teams to work on issues, and by using action learning we were saying to our staff: If you have a good idea, go ahead and tell me and do it. At first there was a lot of cynicism that this was a new gimmick that wouldn't last . . . a waste of time. But what we did was, rather than span the gap instantly, we began to build small pack bridges.'

Another manager said he noticed a definite difference in how his staff were working after the programme:

My staff are more aware of what is happening both inside and outside our own group. It's made it easier for me to let go and give them the tasks to work on, because I've seen that they're able to do it. Before, I'd be telling them what to do; now I involve them in decisions. And they're asking me more questions – that's part of the improved communication: more listening and more talking. It's the process of action learning that has helped. Before, we would fire from the hip, now we stop and take stock.

The second company which set out to effect a culture change was less successful, largely because the programme was too much of a 'drop in the ocean', involving only a handful of people. So, although those on the programme changed their way of thinking and acting, the rest of the company – not only the staff, but all the systems and procedures – remained unchanged. In such circumstances, little if any real change in the culture was likely. Those who had participated in the programme were left wondering what was the use of changing the behaviour of one small group. They also felt that it was crucial for action learning to start at the top: had senior management set about initiating culture change by themselves attending a pilot programme, the outcome would have been far more successful.

As an IT manager observed, for a culture change programme to succeed, not only does the programme need to be an in-company one; it also needs senior managers' commitment and active involvement. Without that, the participants can only hope to drip-feed changes.

How to be a more effective manager . . . and individual

Participants on every kind of action learning programme, whether in-company, mixed-company, or academic, were eager to improve their effectiveness as managers. What they had in mind were the normal managerial needs: to create better relations with my staff, to motivate staff, to communicate more effectively, to learn to delegate.

Organizational terminology usually states such projected outcomes in terms of 'creating more responsive and energetic managers', and 'learning to empower staff'.

Participants' comments showed that they had achieved in no small measure what they had set out to learn.

More understanding of what managing is about:

'A manager's role is to manage the business, and not carry out the tasks. It's really made me think about prioritizing my time.'

'People – your staff – respond more to what you do and how you do it than what you say. By changing your behaviour you begin to change the culture.'

'If you don't have authority to do something, get it! Get senior managers to help you make things happen . . . don't sit around, or moan, or behave like an ostrich.'

More skill in relating to my staff:

'I have a better understanding of my people – I don't walk all over them, and people respond more favourably to me . . . I'm more aware of my staff.'

'I've realized', said one departmental head in a university, 'that I don't feel threatened by having my staff ask me questions and give me their opinions. Before, I feared I'd find that threatening, so resorted to being autocratic, and not being my natural self which wants others to share and be motivated. So, I've learnt to motivate others, while simultaneously having to take tough decisions about resources or people.'

'To involve people more, ask their opinions. Before, I was quite dogmatic. Now I realize I was often wrong – the problem of having power! Now I listen more.'

One young woman commented, 'I've learned not to jump in so quickly with responses and ideas, suggestions, comments or criticisms.'

'I've learnt the need to challenge – which is not the same as confronting. At work, challenge is often interpreted as confrontation, and the person so "challenged" often gets defensive or angry rather than considering what has been pointed out, or asked.'

Another spoke at length of how she had become aware of assumptions she made about others' behaviour, and the origins of such behaviour, which on further investigation had proved to be unfounded. She talked particularly of people being aggressive, negative and cynical, and how she had taken 'evasive' action where she thought someone might react this way. In other words, she was adapting her behaviour to fit with assumptions she was making. And if she was behaving this way, perhaps others were too. She summed up these experiences, and her increased understanding of her own behaviour, by saying, 'I have begun to practise a more open-minded approach . . . I have also learnt by my own personal behaviour that a positive attitude is infectious.'

One participant's view on the programme she took part in

I was very negative at the beginning – felt it was a total waste of time, all too vague. I had come for 'career development'. I was disillusioned and bored with my job and was looking for a challenge. But, I was the only person from my function, so I felt out on a limb because I was seen as a technical boffin, and I was the token female. Everyone else had a sponsor, and I didn't; everyone else had a project, and I didn't – and my manager wasn't being very supportive. But I decided I wouldn't be 'ground down' and would get what I wanted.

While I was trying to identify a project, and was still having problems with my manager, someone in the set – as they were trying to help me – asked me if perhaps he was scared of me. I'd never thought of that. On my way home I began to wonder what motivated me (I wanted to get on) and what motivated him . . . and that was helpful to try and understand our relationship.

After our second set meeting I was really enthusiastic – people were listening to me! Someone was interested in what I had to say. I went back to work feeling buoyant, and began asking questions – questions I'd not asked before. I eventually identified a project with my manager's manager: improving communication in a sales team – something quite new to me. Two other projects I looked at were out (one was too 'political', the other wasn't challenging enough).

The third meeting was for me more of an exploration of issues like motivation – was it money or position? – and getting some insights with the help of the set on sales issues and questions I needed to investigate. I went away feeling motivated and full of energy.

By the fourth meeting, though, although I seemed to have done a lot I wasn't sure where I was going. 'You're too action-oriented,' someone in the set suggested. 'You need to develop another style – you need to stop and think more. Design your strategy.' So, someone had read me correctly. That's always been my problem. But the set said they felt disappointed in me, because I'd not done what I said I would – ie be more thoughtful and methodical. That was a turning point for me: the understanding that the set really wanted me to achieve something, and believed I could!

For the next meeting I decided I wanted to brainstorm my strategy with the set, look at other options and decide. I learnt from doing that I had tenacity. But I also was finding that I was able to help others – I was able to explain technical issues to them, and was really surprised at how little they knew and understood about IT. Someone said, 'You're a goldmine of information.'

Something else that was commented on was my honesty! My own confidence was growing. I began to believe I could do anything, even if I made mistakes. I was no longer being fobbed off by my manager, particularly when I'd done my homework. I began to think a lot more, and to ask for help and feedback. I have also stopped spoon-feeding my staff. Before I used to say, 'We'll do X'; now I tend to say, 'Why don't you think about what you could do, and come back and we'll talk about it.' And I now remember my successes, and I've begun to take life less seriously, too.

I've also got a new job – as quality manager in charge of our quality programme, and I plan to combine quality circles with action learning.

Empowering my staff and achieving a more open relationship with them:

'I give my staff more positive feedback because I feel more confident,' said one participant. 'A manager's skill should be to listen. I've certainly learnt to do this better,' commented another.

A young manager pondered: 'Before, if my staff asked me how to do something, I'd have told them. Now I say "What do you think?" But I'm aware that asking a question isn't always the best way. Making a statement may be better, or showing them what I think is best, and then next time asking them to generate ideas.'

'I wanted to learn how to manage – and I've achieved it, or at least begun to understand. Before, I would "mother" my staff and tell them what to do. Now I give them more rope. I ask them what they've done, how they think something should be done . . . If they're puzzled, we work it out together.'

'At the end of the programme I sat down with my staff and said, 'Let's start doing things differently. Let's try and be more open, and give feedback, and use mistakes to learn from . . . And then I started doing it. Staff found it a bit uncomfortable – it's often comfortable to remain passive. And this way of working can also be frustrating, because every-thing takes longer to accomplish – but what we do is better.'

'I'm more tolerant of my staff. I have a tendency to be pedantic. Action learning has made me reflect more, and allowed me to allow my staff to make mistakes, with me as a support to see where they went wrong, and what to do differently next time – learning from the last time. It's the learning cycle again: reflect, evaluate what you've done, and think what you could have done differently – and why you did what you did in the first place.'

Another manager had achieved a greater appreciation of his staff's different styles at work: 'I now respect those differ-ences. But I'm also more able and confident to do so because I've acquired a wider repertoire of skills and "interventions" – in particular, how to ask good questions.'

An older manager, who had been rather timid, found it had made him 'much less hesitant . . . I find if I sound convinced, people take me more seriously! I'm delegating more to my staff and they are "enjoying" me more – I get invited out to drinks and lunch. If they do something wrong, I work through it with them, encourage them, and act more as a consultant and guide than as a reprimanding manager. And the more confidence I have in them, the better they do things. It's also improved my relationship with my daughter at home. I get her to suggest things – before I would make all the suggestions!'

A manager whose entire company was undergoing a pro-gramme, his staff included, spoke of having more visible com-munication with his staff: 'I'm more aware of them coming to talk to me, and they're asking me more thoughtful questions. They're more aware generally.'

Becoming more organized

Participants listed the following:
'Being more organized, writing lists, structuring what I'm doing. Before, I was pretty chaotic.'

'Managing and organizing my time. It's been vastly more

useful than the time-management course I recently went on!'

'I've created an open style office to go with the more open style of management I've introduced into the department.'

'We're a very traditional company, but I now have ideas on what we can be doing differently. I was in a set with four people from different companies, and you hear them talk, and you get ideas. I'm hoping to free people up in my department, to get them to take initiative rather than blindly follow rules.'

'Since the programme I've had to do a major re-seating of people – in terms of computers and phones. I spent hours thinking, talking, working out how various schemes would work. Before, I'd have piled in and made mistakes as I went along – at some considerable cost and with lots of aggro. I was a pragmatist! Now, I've become a "reflector" as well. The problem is, there is no thinking time allowed on our time sheets! So, I still at times feel guilty when I'm sitting and thinking, and not rushing around and "doing".'

There are times when fast decisive action is needed. It would be inappropriate for a fireman to ask a house owner which side of the house to start dousing first. However, where there is no need for instant action, discussions will generate options that one person alone would not have thought of.

How to take on responsibility and a more active role at work

This was another category of learning that participants and their organizations hoped to gain from action learning – with a view to creating a more energetic, proactive and responsible climate.

Again, judging from participants' comments, they managed to achieve a great deal:

'The processes of the set have helped me intervene more effectively in other meetings – and run them better. I now feel it's legitimate to comment on the processes I see happening, and not simply work on the "task".'

'It's generally heightened my sensitivity back at work. Everything is data: memos, interviews, group discussions. I begin to recognize what is happening, and it helps my responses and reactions.'

'I spot more opportunities, and I'm less inhibited. Action learning could be a really powerful way to get cross-functional groups working together, and understanding each other's point of view.'

'I now respond rather than react,' said one manager, and went on to describe how he now tended to stop and think – and thus respond – rather than jump in fast, which he saw as a reaction. In a similar vein, another participant said, 'I know I don't have to blindly accept what I'm told to do, and that I can go back and redefine the issues.' A third commented, 'I'm no longer the passive recipient of information to regurgitate.'

'It's made me stand on my own two feet, take responsibility for myself and my work much more, analyse my problems rather than run for guidance. And I help others do the same – using the well-worn action learning technique of asking questions!'

Said one young woman: 'I'll now ask my managers why they're proposing to do something in a certain way. They don't, as I'd thought before, bite your head off. In fact, some now treat me with more respect, probably because I do ask, in a constructive way, not aggressively. You need to say things, and ask, in the right way.'

However, another participant offered a different angle on this: 'I behave with greater confidence with senior managers, though at the same time I have less respect for them. They've lost their aura. I realize they don't always know, or have the answers . . . but neither are they prepared to listen to my thoughts.'

A number said they were trying to introduce an action

learning way of working with those around them, but it wasn't always proving easy. 'It's become a way of life for me, but at first it created difficulties because my staff – and others – expected instant answers. In fact, I infuriated them, because I kept asking questions and pushing and challenging them to find their own answers. I know, though, that you have to be aware of not going to the other extreme and having no opinions and no responses.'

A training manager related how he couldn't get the notion of action learning accepted by his company, so he was introducing 'action projects' to his other programmes and leading participants to a realization of what they were learning from such projects.

How to challenge myself intellectually

Interestingly, the meanings of 'challenging' and 'confronting' were frequently compared by participants, who made clear distinctions between the two. The former was seen to describe a non-judgemental approach, the latter implied criticism. The former was an action learning approach, whereas the latter was what participants talked of encountering all the time at work.

'Challenging can be developmental – both as you challenge others and they challenge you. It brings you up face to face with your assumptions and prejudices . . . and if you're pushed you have to explain them, not justify them. That's much harder.'

'I'm better now at challenging myself, asking those awkward questions.'

'I've learnt to think more laterally and see the broader picture in everything I do.'

'I found I enjoyed the intellectual challenge of some of the issues that arose – the depth of thinking that was required to really penetrate to the crux of the matter . . . something we don't do enough of.'

And back at work? Participants experienced a lack of

challenging input: 'Exposure to constructive criticism in the set makes you aware of its absence at work. I seek it though, and encourage it, and try to give it myself.'

'Questioning and challenging has become a way of life for me, but at first it created difficulties with my staff and others because they expected instant answers – usually from me.'

'Why don't we have more challenging – rather than confronting – back at work?' exclaimed several participants

Another participant, the MD of a small engineering company, had expected the programme he attended to 'sharpen up' his thinking, but it had done that and more: in fact, it had completely changed his way of thinking. 'I now appreciate the complex symbiosis between me and the business. I realize that business growth requires other skills besides analytical ability, and that building relationships is very important.'

Learning to consult and facilitate

This outcome was specified in only two programmes – in one instance with sets of young managers identified as 'blue-eyed boys'; in the other with bright young managers who had little or no 'consulting' experience. In both instances the learning vehicles were group projects which required them to act as 'consultants', so their task was not to implement their recommendations but to present them to the client. In 'purist' action learning terms, implementing proposals is an important element. Interestingly, one of the sets did, almost by accident, have the opportunity to implement one of their recommendations, and this provided a major insight: when you have the responsibility of implementing, you are more realistic and thoughtful over your recommendations.

They felt that they had learnt:

'How to look at issues in a more strategic way. How to gain people's confidence when you're suggesting change.'

'Learning to cope with a manager's non-availability when we're consulting him but also needing to get information from him in order to help him . . . We learned to keep him involved and updated on what we were finding, we scheduled regular meetings with specific agendas and questions. Our client even told us that he was learning from the project and the process!'

'I've just been coaching a sales team back at work and I got them to consider more options, look at what might stop them achieving what they set out to, and think about how best to approach the issue – by having a contract with one another, and working as a team with individual responsibilities . . .'

None of the participants talked of what they were doing differently back at work in terms of 'consulting'. They had all returned to their managerial roles, where 'consulting' – as normally interpreted – played no role. But they had gained insights on teamworking, their own styles of managing and working with others, and they had learned to delegate to their staff – mostly by default, and from necessity, since the programme had made more demands on them, and kept them away from work longer, than they had anticipated.

However, one participant on an 'academic' programme, who was in the process of changing jobs to become a consultant, related how she was using the processes of action learning in her project, which was simultaneously a 'consultancy' for a real client: 'My consultancy project and how I work with my client is mirroring my working and learning on the programme.'

A Dutch set, which began after a residential programme, ran for several months without a set adviser. At the end of their programme, they listed the following thoughts on what they had gained and learnt:[7]

- It enables me to hold up a mirror and see what I am doing.
- I have to order the case (project report) in order to explain it, which is good for me as it helps me to see things more clearly.

- Questions! The questions are fantastic and really help us to think things out. Quite often these are questions we would not have thought of ourselves.
- When we don't see the forest for the trees, explaining the case to someone else, together with their questions, helps us to regain perspective again.
- We all have different experiences which we can share.
- It gives me freedom to think, to be inspired.
- It's a wonderful mental game.
- You come out stronger than when you went in.
- All the wonderful hints we get from one another!
- Our self-confidence and self-esteem increases after each session.
- We role-play different scenarios so that when the day comes, the right scenario gets played out.
- Support from all the group members. This is not just that we are friends. We call each other regularly to check progress, and if someone is having a difficult time we will make sure one of the others speaks to him/her at least once a week.
- This is a group of people who really listen to what I have to say.
- It gives an opportunity to look into other companies and other sectors, a sort of benchmarking.
- Friendship.
- Learning both from one another and together in a synergy where we learn quicker and better.
- We define concrete 'truths' which can be used again and again.
- We can distil a lot out of the notes we took at previous meetings; they are still relevant, even several years later. Still right on the mark.
- Core competences.
- Shared learning experiences.
- It gives the ability to look at a case as an outsider, objectively.
- We all read different things, so we keep each other informed about interesting developments in manage-

ment and such.
- We create more effective processes.
- We always discuss learning points, both individually and as a group.

And some tangible results

In addition to the learning and development experienced by participants, there were also some real success stories with tangible and visible results: departments restructured to take account of client liaison, participative communication systems introduced, new marketing strategies put into place, cost-cutting exercises implemented, consultative projects implemented, a workshop reorganized, a personnel department given a new lease of life, an improvement in levels of staff involvement and motivation in many departments, and so on.

There were no instances of projects being shelved. All were found to be useful – even though in a few instances implementation took time (to many participants' frustration).

UNANTICIPATED LEARNING

In addition to the anticipated learning gains, participants reported numerous and valuable unanticipated benefits. This will come as no surprise to people who have participated in or managed action learning programmes. This 'unanticipated' learning is a shift away from the learning focused on skills, behaviours and knowledge, into learning based around values, beliefs and awareness. This in itself is an interesting 'learning' for participants, for it indicates how when we think of learning we so often focus initially on those more concrete items.

Of these unanticipated learnings, four in particular stand out in that a majority of participants referred to them:

- gaining greater self-confidence
- gaining greater self-awareness
- learning to network
- learning how to communicate more effectively

Much of this learning emerged from the way the sets worked, and from the participants' increased ability to apply the same methods elsewhere. When asked, 'How did you learn?' many responded: 'by being pushed by the set', 'by overcoming my fear', 'by taking a plunge', 'by being asked questions I was avoiding', and 'by stopping to reflect more'.

Some found that helping others in the set was a major step towards their own learning. As was simply listening to others working hard on their own issues, and using the spaces and silences to think and reflect.

Often this unanticipated learning – which is powerful and is where much of the 'change' through learning occurs – is left undocumented except in personal diaries, or learning reports (if the programme asks for them). It will in part, of course, be also captured by colleagues and managers who notice a change, and by set members who see the personal transformations as they occur. It is worth reiterating comments that participants made.

Improved self confidence

Almost everyone mentioned this. The range of 'confidence' that grew and emerged is quite startling. For some it might be as simple as giving a presentation and offering their own ideas; for others it was taking on new tasks and having the confidence to disagree. Thus confidence is a variable commodity (see fig. 21).

Participants talked of developing the confidence to be themselves, to admit to feelings, to have, as one of them put it: '. . . the confidence to say I don't feel confident.'

Others talked of confidence in their own views and opinions, and thus to feel able to challenge what they were

fig. 21   *Spectrum of Confidence*

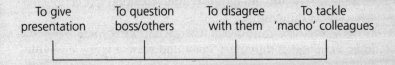

| To give presentation | To question boss/others | To disagree with them | To tackle 'macho' colleagues |

told. 'I'm prepared to be controversial,' said one. 'I know I don't have to accept blindly what I'm told to do – I can and do go back and redefine issues . . .' said another.

'I'm more forthright. I'm not afraid of saying what I think, even to my manager. It's given me the confidence to disagree constructively, and as he gets louder so I just quietly repeat my disagreements.'

'Not to accept blindly what I'm told but think about it and question it – and go back with a different/better suggestion. Managers don't bite your head off. You have to do it in the right way, though.'

'I'm crisper, more forthright; less amenable, more challenging – and my manager and colleagues have remarked on this. Before, when my manager suggested something which I thought was ludicrous or outrageous, I wasn't able to respond – through fear and doubts. That's gone.'

'I'm more confident, and my boss has more confidence in me. He's delegated a larger budget to me, and asked me to prepare a report for him – for the Board.'

Others felt relieved that they could admit to not knowing all the answers, to having gaps in their knowledge, to not having instant solutions . . . even to having made mistakes!

'I don't feel I always have to be good at something – or even everything. I can say I don't know – and that's OK. I know I'm good at certain things.'

'I can now admit to having made a mistake – to be honest, in fact. That's what's required in the set. From that I also learned the confidence not be overly diplomatic, conciliatory or accepting.'

And another participant talked of 'listening to my own inner voice more – call it gut or intuition, but I know what should be done or said because I have an inner voice that tells me . . . Before, I'd ignore it until someone else confirmed what I was thinking.'

With this new confidence often went what many referred to as a change in thinking: 'The mind set changes – and your thinking becomes more positive.'

'It increased my confidence that I could tackle and resolve any problem I was presented with. Before, I'd have shied away and thought "Oh no!" Now I feel positive.'

'If I'm faced with a problem I say, "Right, I'll take it away and consider it." Before, my reaction was "Help!", and negative. So it's a subtle change but actually a very powerful one. It's to do with "I may choose not to do X, but I know I can do X." '

Others remarked on the new-found confidence to ask colleagues for their help – and feedback: 'Exposure to constructive criticism in the set makes you aware of its absence at work. I'm seeking it, though, and encouraging others to give it.'

'I now discuss real work issues with colleagues. Before, I bottled them up and had merely superficial chats or discussions about them – even if they were work-related issues. Or I'd sit with a problem . . . or avoid it.'

And then there were more elusive examples of growing confidence: 'I can cope with silences. I no longer have to fill them,' said one. Another felt she had acquired 'the confidence to work with time – not to always be rushing.' And a third remarked, 'I don't readily accept others' accusations, or feel guilty if something doesn't work out or isn't successful or has failed.'

'I always had good ideas, and would mention them to others, or at meetings, but they were never noticed. Now I repeat or say things more forcibly. I also didn't know how to react when people said no to me, or disagreed. I now have a wider repertoire of responses . . . the set helped me with that.'

An older manager grinned: 'I've learnt more in the past 18 months on the programme than in the last 20 years. I participate more in meetings, I stand my ground, and my manager is now giving me much more responsibility.'

Of peaks and mountains

We started as though we were a group of mountaineers setting out on an expedition. We all worked in the same place and knew each other . . . vaguely. When we arrived at 'base camp' on the first day we had to sort out our baggage and the necessary kit for the expedition which had just been dumped in a pile, and that took some time to sort out. By evening we'd organized it, struck up camp, and sat around the fire socializing and making new friends.

The next day we were shown the map of the expedition, but wondered if it was the right map . . . it wasn't as detailed as we'd anticipated, and we felt this could make the expedition somewhat dangerous. But also we weren't even sure which peak we were meant to be climbing.

The range of experiences and abilities in our group meant that different sub-groups formed to tackle different routes. One group decided to go for the really high, awesome peaks because they liked the challenge that the route would provide. Another group tackled the same peak, but by a more scenic nature trail. They wanted to enjoy the views but weren't interested in taking the risks of the first group. The final group – an intermediate group – said they didn't mind the odd dangerous climb but would also take the scenic route at other times.

Throughout the expedition various peaks were scaled, walked around, or simply admired. Once or twice, when a group or even an individual was half-way up a peak, a sudden squall would blow up and the climbers returned to camp.

Tales of their achievements abounded. For some this was the first ever expedition of this sort, and there was a great sense of excitement. Others had been somewhere similar, and had already had their first views of nesting ospreys, and a few simply sat and admired the views.

So, some returned exhilarated, physically tired, emotionally elated and intellectually challenged. Others merely commented that it had been a pleasant enough break, and they'd enjoyed it.

The mountains are the learning. Some slopes are steeper than others, some have plateaus where you can stop and rest. It isn't getting to the top that really matters, but how you tackle the experience and what you gain from each bit of the walk.

People have different reasons for their actions and behaviours. It is sometimes difficult not to judge others by our own standards. So climbers may think walkers are wimps, whereas the walker thinks the climber is rash and foolish. People's hidden agendas, motivations, call them what you will, mean that they approach the same environment equipped differently. Their individual achievement is in how they feel they have done and what they will take with them into the future.

What the programme did for me was to learn from others where some of the paths up the mountain were, and how you can get the right kit to ascend safely, and know where to rest in a squall. Experience shows that taking risks pays dividends, but you may end up bruised if you take the wrong route or ignore the weather conditions. The confidence I've gained means that I'll scale mountains where I'd have chosen the nature trail before . . . and I know I may stumble a few times.

An increased awareness about myself . . . and how I learn

This aspect of learning, probably more than any other, came as a result of the amount of emphasis that was placed during the programme on reflecting and learning – and not simply on actions. Reflecting, in this instance, is, as one participant put it, 'making an honest assessment'.

The source for this emphasis was usually the set adviser – at least initially. Once sets became more accustomed to stopping to check on what they were learning, such awareness began to emerge as part of each participant's 'story'. For some it became the main focus.

Thus for one participant, 'The light bulbs went on.' Another observed, 'It brings you conscious awareness. It makes your brain work at a different level and speed.' A third commented, 'It's taught me to be honest with myself, and see my emotions as part – a valid part – of the picture. So, if I'm genuinely feeling frightened, threatened, hassled or uneasy . . . that's part of the equation and needs to be looked at, as well as what's causing the feelings.'

Others became aware of how and when they learn: 'I've learnt that I learn best when I'm challenged by others. I have a tendency to dismiss things quickly.' Another spoke of the realization that 'learning is evolutionary. I now expect to learn from every situation I'm in.'

Several remarked that '. . . challenging others can be developmental – both for them and you.' And one or two found that '. . . only when you admit you're stuck can others help you.'

Some saw awareness as linked to the benefits of 'being my natural self', not playing games and not pretending – or, as one or two put it, 'wearing a mask'.

'I've learnt to be my natural self – to be direct, friendly, blunt when necessary . . .' said one participant. Another commented: 'It's created a radical change in how I operate – it was very personally challenging. The onus is on you as a person, rather than you as a role player, and it resonates with how you want to be.' One of the set members remarked, 'It's taken away my naïveté.'

Some became more pragmatic as a result: 'A bad experience is simply that – just one bad experience. It needs to be reflected on, but not colour one's subsequent actions or beliefs.'

'I have discovered that I learn best in a social environment where others are willing to share their learning experiences . . . Sharing in this way adds a richness to the learning by hearing others' views and making the experiences more memorable . . . I have also learnt that by allocating serious thinking time to reflection on action and all that is involved has made me more aware. In particular I have seen patterns in my own behaviour. This has made me better equipped to question my behaviour, and to adjust it if necessary.'

'We all carry baggage around with us – baggage from previous experiences, feelings and thoughts. Part of my baggage was a fear of speaking in front of a group of people, giving presentations, talking to people I don't know, and having responsibility for others' work . . . During the programme I've had to deal with internal and external contacts of differing levels, and with different personalities, some of whom intimidated me considerably during the early stages of the programme. This led to bungled meetings with insufficient or wrong information being presented. But during the programme I learnt a great deal about communicating in general, and now I find I make fewer assumptions, I have greater self-confidence, and have almost lost my fear of asking questions in case I appear to be stupid.'

Networking: learning to use others as a valuable resource

Learning how to network was a major breakthrough for most participants. Many had not considered doing so before, for a variety of reasons – the most commonly stated of which were fear, scepticism as to the value, and 'never thought of it'. Thus, experiencing the value of working closely with others, in the set, often from different functions than themselves, proved to be an eye-opener for most participants. The support of the set also encouraged those who were nervous of the idea of networking to try it out!

Furthermore, participants gained a better understanding of each other's work, and of the work of the organization as a whole. And they were able to provide each other with access to even wider networks through their own contacts.

As a result, many discovered a new confidence about networking:

> I lost my fear of approaching people. I may still be apprehensive but I know that if I'm clear about what I want it'll be fine. I had to go to talk to senior managers as part of my project. It forced me to network, particularly with those senior people, as well as with the marketing department, which I'd always been a bit scared of (I'm only a scientific researcher)! But I realized I had as much knowledge as them, and as much ability as others, and it gave me a great sense of my own 'power'.

> I've realized how much help others can – and are willing to – give you. I'd always feared people would be dismissive or would find excuses.

Networking also gave participants a wider picture of their company (particularly if they were participating on an in-company programme) and helped them understand 'how things hang together'. The majority felt more committed as a result, simply because they understood better.

'Networking broadens your perspective, widens your horizons and gives you the bigger picture. I think more laterally now.'

'In our set we've had people from different departments, and you see them grappling with different problems, and you begin to have much more understanding of them and their problems. Also, communication is bad in our company so the set is making up for it. We can now pick up the phone to so many people in different parts of the company – and they can give us contacts beyond – so its tentacles are spreading out further.'

Another participant was more philosophical: 'Managers, on the whole, are somehow meant to know, to be aware of what's happening elsewhere in the company, only there's often no mechanism for this to happen, merely informal contacts and lots of "technology", as if the existence of this technology means that thing happen differently. But after action learning, and when you know other people, maybe the technological wires will hum more.'

A means to personal development

- improved relationships at work
- self-awareness
- an enquiring, questioning mind
- mentoring skills
- empowering others
- networking

Communicating more effectively

On the whole, what stuck participants was how valuable it was to simply listen and relate questions to what the speaker was trying to do rather than cutting across or going off at tangents. In other words, having a genuine dialogue with another person.

'It's taught me to listen, and not just to hear,' was a comment almost everyone made in one way or another. 'I now really talk to others,' was something many also remarked on. 'Action learning forced me to talk in a way I had never talked before.'

Often participants described how difficult it was to really listen, and understand, and ask for clarification.

Responding to questions, rather than answering them – ie not feeling the need to give reasons or justifications, but rather using questions as an invitation to reflect – this was another major learning gain that many participants commented on.

And then there was the giving and receiving of feedback – and seeing that as useful, rather than as criticism. As several participants said wishfully, they would welcome such openness at work.

One phrase which seemed to sum up much of what participants had to say about the value of better communication was: 'The more you share the more you learn.'

One participant's lasting impressions of action learning

- being challenged by questions to honestly review situations as they are;
- listening to other people's experiences;
- sharing knowledge and techniques and examples of their implementations (practical solutions);
- the caring and support of the set, which helped me through difficult situations.

He went on to say: 'The process is less disruptive than a course as it allows you to actively work on issues and reflect during the process, and does not deflect your attention as on some course where action planning and reflection only happened on your return to work.

'The key learning from the programme for me was:

- managing myself is as key as managing resources
- development is all about taking actions, not just understanding theories
- sharing problems and concerns allows you to better visualize situations and plan/develop appropriate actions
- good facilitation is key to effective group work
- reflection is one of the key tools to development

'I am looking to use action learning within the new organization I will be joining soon. Its first use will be within the development programme for first-line supervisors, where I see it supporting a current education programme.'

DISCOVERY AND DEVELOPMENT

So, if we look at the learning, both anticipated and unanticipated, we see that participants were discovering how to work differently while at the same time developing themselves.

Their discoveries included:

- The way you 'instinctively' want to manage, but in which you may have been thwarted, can still be possible, even acceptable;
- You have the ability to redesign a workplace even if you are only a member of the workshop staff;

- If you're a manager, you have the ability, by using your own behaviour as an example, to give your department a 'facelift';
- You don't have to become a different person from who you are to 'sell';
- Others are a helpful resource, a network to be used and developed;
- By behaving less competitively and working 'constructively' with others you can achieve more;
- You can – even if you have little responsibility – contribute directly to strategic decisions;
- You're not alone with your quandaries and dilemmas, or your doubts and fears;
- The most common problem that everyone faces is relationships with others;
- Communicating is more than talking and arguing;
- Managing means managing yourself as well as others;
- You can achieve more and be more effective by being 'yourself'.

But participants also discovered that their goals and ambitions were not always instantly achievable; that some organizations – and people – may be unable or unwilling to accommodate their 'new' way of thinking, working and being.

When it came to their own development, individual participants felt it was taking the form of:

- Beginning to achieve their objectives;
- Realizing that they had choices;
- Gaining the confidence they needed to accomplish their goals;
- Taking initiative and responsibility and asking, 'What can I do about X?' rather than waiting to be told or asked;
- Helping others to develop;
- Giving their staff (in the case of managers) the space, time, opportunity and support to develop and grow;
- Acquiring skills that permit real communication to take place between them and those they worked with;

- Beginning to know and understand themselves – and others;
- Knowing that preserving their own integrity and being honest with themselves was crucial;
- Realizing that being open and honest was less stressful than playing games or covering up.

But learning doesn't necessarily come easily

This may all sound like a smooth passage. Yet for many it can be difficult and traumatic. Some feel like quitting after the first session because the lack of structure upsets them; the expectation of being open and honest frightens others; while some get anxious – even scared – about the prospect of having to complete a project.

'It felt like hell on the first day. A total culture shock, both in relation to work, and any other form of learning or education I'd experienced before.'

Others feel daunted and nervous: 'How will we know when we're working in an action learning way?' was a question several participants asked themselves at the beginning.

Participants – all of whom lasted the 'course' – were very honest and open about what they had learnt. They were equally prepared to admit that much of the learning had not been easy – in some cases, it was a real struggle. Others had to overcome their fear of taking risks, or force themselves to talk about issues they'd prefer not to think about or admit to.

For some, these emotions were strongest at the beginning of the programme, for others they continued until well into it. Several thought the hardest part was taking the plunge and admitting that an issue was troubling or puzzling them and they needed to discuss it.

'It's threatening because you can't hide – your colleagues won't let you . . . they make you confront issues you didn't want to. But you don't half feel better once you've talked about them.' (The issue in this instance was how to 'energize' a management buy-out which was losing momentum, and facing up to what were the other managers' hidden agendas.)

Others talked of being nervous at the outset, not so much of the people but, as one put it, '. . . of disclosing issues I wanted to work on. Would the others be interested in it or would they be bored? But I grew to be fascinated by it, by the process. And in the end, the time went all too quickly, and the others seemed genuinely interested.'

'At times it was really nerve-racking – like taking a driving test,' smiled one participant.

So at the beginning, participants had mixed feelings, and in many instances felt lost and confused.

'I nearly didn't come after the first set meeting, it was nothing but talk for an hour, but then something popped out of the woodwork, the set starting asking questions, and I realized that something very useful was happening,' – this comment came from a participant who now uses action learning in all his work.

'I was on my guard at the beginning – I didn't feel positive – and this wasn't helped by my missing the introductory day,' said one young bank manager.

Others spoke of feeling 'daunted', and a few admitted to feeling 'cynical'. One had asked himself whether action learning was 'just another fancy name for something very obvious. Now I think it's something very special.' Another participant said that in his set, 'We began by calling it "therapy", then we realized it wasn't – it was considerably more than that.'

For a few there was concern, at the outset, about whether they were doing it the right way, and whether they would eventually gain something. A young scientist recalled, 'It was just a lot of questions at the beginning – and I wondered how I would ever know if I was learning anything. Would there be something tangible at the end?' Someone else described the experience as, 'dark at first, then grey – then, at last, it dawned.'

On the other hand, there were those who felt elated at the beginning: 'I started on a high – this was something new, sounded interesting, and I'd been selected. Then, my spirits flagged as I started work on my project and got bogged down. But my energy and enthusiasm rose again as I began to see results and began to learn.'

So, with time, the emotions became more entangled. 'For me it was a great mixture – of hard work, excitement, tiredness, frustration, energy, fear!'

A participant who admitted to feeling 'freaked' by the first meeting nevertheless was adamant: 'You must persist. It's later that the penny begins to drop.'

One set reminisced: 'We went up and down through the year – from excitement at the beginning, to frustration somewhere soon after – mostly at not being able to focus on a project – followed by more frustration at the rush, and not having enough time to concentrate properly on everything, followed by friction at the support that some members were getting back at work – and which others weren't.' A couple of participants remembered how 'it was a "battle" all the time, with our managers always fixing meetings for the day the set was meeting, and we were determined to come to the set meeting.'

My first feelings were ones of shock and horror. 'I'm not going to express my doubts and my feelings to someone I don't know.' It was all slow and tedious, and I saw the set adviser as being 'manipulative', constantly asking questions, prying. When he worked skilfully with one other set member, my worries went up one notch further. I didn't want to hear what I might have to say about my feelings. But then, gradually, as others took the risk, I began to think, 'It might be OK. After all, I've nothing particular to discuss, no issue of any concern. Why would I, and what I do, be of any interest to others?' Then suddenly it was my 'airspace'. I began to talk about the issue I'd decided to bring . . . and next thing I knew an hour and a half had gone by. Others were saying, 'That was interesting', and I began to feel valued. They'd given me their attention, but no judgements. That was a revelation to me – to say what you want to say, and not be judged.

But at the end of the first meeting I decided I didn't want anything to do with it. I heard myself being sarcastic – which is a sign, I now recognize, of my fear. That evening I wanted to go to the pub and two of us went off to discuss our discomfort at what we called 'middle-class head banging'. It was all too gentle for us hardened Eastenders. Nothing to do with the cut and thrust of managing.

Slowly, though, I recognized that part of my fear was my lack of skill at it – I didn't know how to ask helpful questions, so I didn't feel I could participate fully. Yet something in me chose to continue. The real breakthrough for me came when I challenged something the set adviser said! But it took four meetings before I plucked up the courage. And it was OK. That's when my 'apprenticeship' began, for I'd been a telecommunications engineer all my life until then.

Now I sit fairly and squarely in management development, and use the action learning approach in all my work. I'm now convinced that when people work with real issues – the stresses, the delegating, the motivating and the decisions – they're learning and doing something about them simultaneously. That's the power of action learning: it works on the 'inside'. So it may be my attitude to a problem that is the problem, and not the stated problem.

An older manager admitted that he came 'in fear and trepidation, convinced I'd be out of my depth. I'd spent 20 years in the building trade with little formal education.' But he soon found out it was about experience and common sense and that he could easily hold his own with the other members of the set – all from different organizations. And at the end he was proposing to introduce action learning back into his company, in support of an Investors in People initiative.

Others talked of their frustration at the apparent lack of 'structure' in a programme with no milestones or goalposts, no timetables to follow, and no lectures. There were, they said, no obvious, stated measures of success or failure. Indeed, was there even such a concept as failure? And there was no homework, either – except your next actions.

This novel approach to learning puzzled a number of participants at first. 'I asked myself, "What am I doing here? The facilitator gives me no answers – is this a waste of time?" I felt frustrated and was convinced people there wouldn't be able to help me.'

Faced with a group of 'non-experts', one participant asked himself 'Was it the blind leading the blind – how can we learn from one another? But that's not the case – the blind leading the blind, I mean. You don't have to have the answers; you need to know what questions to ask – which isn't always easy – and help others pinpoint who may be able to help them.'

'No books, no lectures; you have to find things out for yourself,' was how another summed up his first impressions. 'But then you begin to realize that the answers are in yourself, and you begin to bring them out with the help of others. It changes the way you work and approach tasks.'

'I wondered how I would know if I was learning anything at all,' was a common concern, echoed by many first-timers. 'There were just lots of questions at the outset – and nothing being "taught". Would there be anything tangible to hold onto?'

One participant felt unable to participate fully, she said, because one of the fundamentals – confidentiality – was not being observed by set members or, worse still, the set adviser. This participant – a new lecturer at a university – was very unhappy with the entire programme. Another participant was also upset by the behaviour and attitude of her set adviser, as were her fellow set members: 'The set adviser was arrogant, abrupt and condescending.' She knew advisers to other sets were nothing like this, and merely regretted she'd had the 'bad luck' to be in that particular set. (See pp. 206–15 for more on the role of the set adviser.)

In spite of these initial doubts and fears, by the time they'd reached the halfway point, most participants were feeling much more confident, and were beginning to see the fruits of their work.

The advice of even those who had expressed ambivalence, fear or disappointment at the outset, was: 'Hang in, don't give up after the first one or two sessions.' 'The longer you're there, the greater the benefits,' was another comment.

Being thrown in at the deep end

All programmes begin with 'an introduction to action learning' (see pp. 185–6). And many participants commented on how important it was to participate in this introductory day, and any other exercises planned.

The arrival of a newcomer can prove disruptive for a group which has begun to work together on the introductory day, because it means starting from the beginning again. But, as one participant pointed out, 'Although it does disrupt a bit, it's also a good insight into how groups and teams react to new members!' Everything that happens should be turned into 'a learning opportunity' – another essential aspect of action learning. Everything is data to be learnt from.

Some participants complained that they were not reminded, once the programme was underway, about the important elements of action learning – which happened particularly where the set adviser lacked experience – so that the group turned into 'just another talking shop, with little or no emphasis on the learning.'

Others were simply bemused. 'We're so used to plunging in with suggestions and advice, and thinking that is the way to help someone. I felt useless and helpless just asking questions,' was how one manager described his feelings after an introductory exercise lasting just half an hour. The presenter, however, remarked to him how useful it was to have space to talk through his issue and not get suggestions and advice!

Participants who felt they had gained nothing

Of those I interviewed, five individuals said they had learnt nothing; they were unhappy, disillusioned, and felt the entire exercise had been a waste of time. Three others were slightly non-committal. Two of these admitted they had come on the programme to investigate whether action learning had any use back in their companies. Although both had gained, they were unsure about its value for their organizations.

The five who were unhappy identified the reasons as follows:

- no confidentiality in the set
- lack of interest and 'empathy' with the action learning process, in particular with the set
- incompetent and unhelpful set advising
- irrelevance of the 'group' project to the individual's work
- unhelpful set members
- 'my own emotional state'
- the nature of the project

The three who were unsure identified various sources of their disquiet: it was too vague; it might be more useful in a set where everyone was from the same function; the project chosen by one participant had focused on an issue in which she alone was powerless to influence the company (these last two individuals were in mixed-company sets, and I couldn't help wondering if their views would have been different if they had been on in-company ones).

In addition to the few instances just mentioned, there were other participants who had confronted aspects – or experiences – in their programmes that they didn't like or weren't happy about. (For more on participants' reservations, see pp. 284–7.)

VERY SENIOR MANAGERS' EXPERIENCES

There is one group of participants – the more senior managers and managing directors – who deserve a separate mention. The reason for this is that the programmes they attend are focused slightly differently, in that such senior people do not work on defined projects in the way that the majority of participants tend to. Rather, their responsibilities for the organizations they manage become their 'projects'. So, each comes with the anticipation of discussing issues of strategies, decisions, relationships – and any attendant questions, dilemmas, worries, etc.

Because such senior managers have few if any 'peers' in the organizations they manage, they normally participate in mixed-company sets. This is the only feasible – and safe – way they feel able to discuss their problems and gain from their 'cumulative wisdom', as one put it. In the process, many talked of their 'loneliness'. For, as another chief executive admitted, 'Many of us have got these senior positions by convincing others we can walk on water!'

One such MD remarked, 'Action learning is a management development process. The issues you bring are ones of the moment, and usually inter-personal ones. The people you might have been able to discuss issues with "back home" are often precisely the ones you are having difficulties with.'

A time to be 'me' and 'human' – to step out of role

Many talked of the pressures of being at the top and not being able to be 'human':

'It's an opportunity to meet on human terms – not in a role. At work I sometimes forget I'm human, too!' laughed one senior woman executive.

'There is a perceived image of people at the top being totally confident,' said another. 'But we're full of doubt'. The set allows these doubts to be voiced and explored. 'I was comforted, and surprised, that all these other managing directors and chief executives are not super-human.' The set had given one chief executive the opportunity to see beyond his preconception that other very senior people were 'all brilliantly successful, and only me struggling . . . I've discovered that's not the case.'

The job of a chief executive is very lonely . . . It's invaluable to rehearse some of the problems and situations with others who may have similar experiences. It's also helpful to unload and contemplate . . . I have great confidence in questions, in the process of probing, because questions help clarify what I think the problem is. It's particularly helpful when people have similar experiences . . . and I feel secure because any stupidity of mine won't go beyond the set.

Sometimes work and private problems are very interrelated. On normal courses you never go into private matters, but in the set you can bring personal issues onto the agenda. Our reaction at work often depends on what is happening at home, so it's relevant to bring them into the open.

I have confidence in sharing with others, because they are not judgemental.

A few weeks ago, I had a very difficult working relationship with one of my senior managers, and so being asked questions about how I felt, how she might have felt, how she responded, what I said – putting things like this under the microscope – helps understand what is happening in the relationship. At other times I bring along an issue I've been thinking about and want to explore.

As a senior person in an organization, you have to keep so much of yourself back, and be careful with information you impart. I also have to appear quite sure and crystal clear . . . often when I'm feeling neither. I'm not allowed to express uncertainty. So, I need a sounding

---

board. I've also found I learn by listening to others. I gain insights, think, 'That's an interesting way to approach that particular problem, maybe I can use it . . . Why didn't I think of it!' We all share, and I feel privileged when someone shares their vulnerability with us, and helps me learn by doing so.

The set is my one luxury – I almost feel self-indulgent – it's almost the only time in my life when I say 'this time is for me'.

I'm still learning about myself . . . that I'm stronger than I thought and have greater tenacity, but I need to be reminded of that. And I enjoy the intellectual challenge of the set.

I've also used the set adviser as a model, and I think, 'How would he deal with this situation, or deal with this person?'

It takes time to develop a way of working that is helpful, and you do need empathy with the others in the set. But I always come away refreshed and invigorated and feel a great burst of energy the next day, even if I've made a prat of myself in front of the set.

I'm not sure it's a programme for everyone, though. You need to give it time to realize what it's about, and not be dismissive. Someone who is selfish and won't listen to others will also have problems, but the set might change that . . .

So what did very senior people gain from such programmes?

Asked what they had gained and learnt, and what they were now doing differently back at work, they talked of benefiting from working openly with a forum of peers, valuing time to take stock – a time for themselves, a place to admit to doubts, a place to be challenged, and a place to share and to hear others.

The brief accounts below give some flavour of the insights and learning gained, although as always there were some dissenting voices. One managing director felt that the set was too polite. She described how, in 'this gathering of competitive, high-achievers', she was concerned that at one meeting she had, as she put it, 'let myself down by talking about a particular issue that concerns me.' She went on to ponder whether this emphasis on sharing, useful though it was, didn't in fact encourage a slight veneer of civilization. 'We rarely go for each other's jugular. Much as I appreciate people who are prepared to reveal themselves in this setting, I still sometimes think I might not like them in other situations. Is something "real" missing from sets?'

Key learning for one managing director

- managing yourself is as key as managing others
- development is all about taking actions, and not just understanding theories
- sharing problems and concerns allows you to better visualize situations and plan/develop appropriate actions
- good facilitation is key to effective group work
- reflection is one of the key tools in development

A senior manager's response to the question: 'What aspects of action learning do you value in particular?'

'One aspect is that the reporting back to the set can be quite searching if the set is doing its job and being challenging (a very big *if*). You ought not to be able to get away with doing a snow job, and the weakness of your position – if it is weak – should become apparent and give you the opportunity to rethink. Better to be exposed among friends than when you go public!

'The second aspect is the insights you get while working on someone else's problem. It is almost as if when you are the focus of the slot, you are so busy giving and receiving information, responding to questions and "defending" your position that there is no opportunity to reflect. However, I get some of my most creative insights when it is someone else's slot and I find there is time to reflect during the comparative eddies and back currents surrounding the work on someone else's problem. I frequently scribble things down which I pick up on later.'

Taking action learning back into the organization:

'The set was fascinating – a great mix of people including the contrast of an army guy who did everything by numbers and a psychiatrist who was very reflective.

'We discussed mainly professional issues – although the psychiatrist did once bring up the issue of having only seen his wife three times in the past 14 days.

'For me it was interesting because it brought so many different perspectives to each issue. There were some crunch points on which I was stuck and looking for guidance. We spent 90 minutes at one meeting on my issue and it was really helpful. I began to find myself saying, "I want to discuss such-and-such an issue with my set." It helped me particularly with group work – as a senior manager so much of my work is group-based, with me chairing. I know I gained confidence from seeing that everyone else was in the same confusion and muddle as me. But I feel that less senior people on the teams are now more responsive than they used to be.

'And the luxury – and benefit – of having one problem on the table at a time, with the space to tackle! I've introduced this idea back into our organizations. I'm getting people to work in small groups and run our projects on action learning lines. The time and the rigours of action learning are particularly useful. More thought and effort now goes into our initial exploration of questions, into the preparation; things are more focused, better designed, and commitment to our projects is greater, because it's given people more opportunity to go into more depth.

'We've extracted, and use, some core elements: an initial question is floated in, the group looks at it and reshapes it, then we design our next steps . . . an action learning approach.'

Gaining and learning from others' experiences and perspectives:

'I'm a one-company man with no experience of other companies or other industries. What I've learnt is that the more you talk to others, the more you realize there are the same basic threads and themes . . . which comes as a great comfort! You realize you're not after all working for the worst company!

'The other set members ask you searching questions that colleagues might never find the guts to ask you, or aren't able to because of my seniority and the fear of how I might react. So, I have a chance to explore, and exchange experiences and get second opinions. The decisions are still mine, but I've not damaged people in the process. I have little to lose by such an opportunity, and much to gain. I know I've come to decisions differently.

'The programme also forms part of my time for me – to step back from everyday things that drive me, and take stock. I can use the set to experiment and try things out . . . without crossing boundaries with people I work with everyday . . . and then I can walk away from the set. But at the next meeting I update them – which is important, because that way we learn from everyone, not just our own stories.

'However, for this to work you do need a professional facilitator, knowledgeable about processes and sensitive as well.

'I'm now watching people more carefully, and listening to what's being said, and don't assume that everyone is agreeing with me. When you're the boss you can sometimes think they're nodding like dogs – but now I know they're not. I look for signals over and above the words. I'm more aware of my effect on people, especially as I'm very task-oriented, and can tend to forget others.'

*

A codicil

The term action learning is now applied to many other programmes which have some of the characteristics described in this book.

It is not necessary, obviously, to define any programme incorporating all these ingredients as an action learning programme. Some, in fact, find the name is a hindrance – too vague and not sufficiently focused on outcomes. They therefore call their programmes by some more eye-catching name, while ensuring that the component parts are retained.

What *is* misleading, however, is when programmes call themselves action learning and are but poor imitations. They will be deluding all who are involved, and depriving participants of the potential benefits of a well understood, well managed and well delivered programme.

Part 4 of this book gives some pointers to ensure that a programme is understood, well-managed and has the 'right' ingredients. (And on p. 324 there is a list of further reading which will take any interested reader beyond the scope of this book and into much greater detail – both theoretical and practical.)

A Summing Up

PARTICIPANTS' RESERVATIONS OVER ACTION LEARNING

Not everyone, however, was enamoured of action learning, nor did they think it was the solution to all their problems.

Some participants who did not find it useful, or had decided not to try out 'action learning' approaches at work, or who had other reservations, raised the following issues:

'It's too time consuming' (ie project work)

This will often be the case when the project or task is not directly related to a participant's work. Where it is, it becomes a part of their everyday responsibility.

'It seems to advocate a matrix-type of organization, but most organizations – ours included – are hierarchical.'

This is true! But it offers skills to deal better with hierarchical impedimenta.

'It's too nice and cosy – not challenging enough. This company is largely run by macho managers. Our department seems to be different, but we're not typical.'

A good set adviser will ensure there is challenge, even if set members try to avoid it. Many participants do not see action learning as insufficiently challenging. If anything, it challenges them in ways that they have not been challenged before. But there is some truth in this, in that if participants are self-selecting, more macho and aggressive people are less likely to put themselves forward.

'It's too vague for money-minded managers. Its benefits are not concrete enough – too hit and miss, not specific enough.'

Action merely to create action, regardless, is something that action learning tries to redress. And using money as the sole or even the most important criterion by which to judge actions is a journey on the road to disaster – in the long term. However, it is precisely concerns such as these which have led many who introduce action learning to focus mainly on the 'action'. The real question is: are these true action learning programmes?

*'It needs some **P** [taught inputs] to really catch on.'*

Many programmes do include some, but only where it is strictly relevant, and ensuring that it does not 'take over' the programme.

'It claims to change culture, and it would do, but you'd have to involve everyone – senior managers in particular. But they back away.'

True. But small changes can occur among staff, and filter upwards.

'It doesn't seem to help with the politics that infest most organizations.'

It does and it doesn't. It can't remove them, because where there are people, there will usually be politics. But it does give participants a greater understanding of them, and some tools for working around them. For a start, set members can form a network and create their own 'political' grouping of those who want to change things!

'It advocates sharing, but doesn't address the other individualistic and competitive aspects in most organizations: the reward system, primarily.'

It will do if these issues are addressed by participants. Such programmes are for participants to explore whatever they wish and subsequently take action.

'The problem is, we've created a working environment in the set, and we've worked on projects – been given responsibility – but when we get back to work, it won't be like that.'

285

This is undoubtedly true. But a well-managed programme will have made clear to employers that they will not get back the 'same' people as they sent on the course. Indeed, many participants get promotion after such programmes – either through their own initiative or because their bosses see they are now ready to tackle new challenges. Organizations which fail to recognize the changes that have occurred will probably sooner or later lose valuable employees.

What can go wrong?

From all that has been written so far, you the reader will probably now be able to list the potential pitfalls:

1. ill-trained, unprofessional set adviser
2. inappropriate choice of project
3. lack of support in the company
4. lack of time
5. mix of participants
6. lack of commitment by participants
7. all action and no learning
8. set dissolves into a talking shop

. . . much, in fact, that could go wrong on any other programme.

How these pitfalls can be eliminated or avoided

1. Use only trained set advisers; do not think you can take a line manager or even a trainer and turn them into a competent set adviser within the space of two days.
2. Make sure the project lies within the authority and scope of responsibility of the participants. The project should be neither so large as to swamp the participant, nor too small and simple. It needs to be something moderately difficult that the participant

hasn't tackled before and which they can get their teeth into.

3. Make sure there is senior management support for the programme and for the participants. Reg Revans's dictum of ensuring you pinpoint someone 'who knows, who cares and who can' rings very true here.

4. Ensure that the importance of time is taken on board at the planning stage. A programme should allow time for at least three or four (preferably more) monthly set meetings to last for a full day. There must be adquate time for the project to go from the incubation period to implementation, or at least for proposal stages to have been reached and further implementation agreed.

5. Ensure that set participants match each other, more or less, in terms of experience and level of responsibility.

6. Make sure participants are aware that it is in their own interest to commit to the programme and all its elements if they are to gain from it and be able to give to others.

7. Ensure that the emphasis is on learning and not just on action. In other words, ensure that projects (ie actions) are geared to participants' needs, and are not hijacked by senior mangers for their own ends.

8. Make sure participants are reminded of the 'action learning way of working' and keep to the processes of airspace and questioning in particular.

Comments from those who felt they had gained

Although participants had had problems in defining what action learning was, they were quite clear about what the experience had meant for them.

'It's a philosophy for life, not simply for work,' was how

one manager summed it up. 'The questioning goes to the heart of everything, to fundamentals. It's given me a set of tools to work with the unknown.' And a marketing manager described how 'the light bulbs went on. It brings you conscious awareness. It makes your brain work at a different level and speed.'

One young woman – who admitted to hating her experience of action learning because her set broke the rule of confidentiality and this inhibited her ability to work well, or even tackle the issue of no confidentiality – nevertheless said the process appealed to her. 'You can read till you're blue in the face, but until you start doing things the reading doesn't really mean anything. It's then you begin to learn.'

Others commented on the value of sharing: 'I've realized that if you rely exclusively on your own thoughts and presuppositions you come a cropper. I've so often failed to see others' points of view. Action learning stops that.' Another participant put it slightly differently: 'Others see things you don't . . . but it's the way you learn this that is the hallmark of action learning. You see this through listening and observing and hearing them talk and being non-judgemental, just taking things in.'

Many of the participants identified what they called an action learning spirit: 'What distinguishes the action learning spirit is that it's not about answers to questions or decision-oriented, but about questions and space to talk and think. Nor is it about getting advice or information.'

This was an observation that came up time and time again: the time and space to think and reflect. The programme legitimizes taking up others' time and gaining their insights, 'without feeling you're poaching or prying or encroaching on their territory.'

A nurse-manager was 'excited by its commonsense. It takes away the fear of ignorance – which instead becomes a strength, because you've identified what you don't know, and that's a first step to begin to learn, ask questions, and apply in the everyday situations you operate in . . .'

'The action learning discipline has given me a template of how people can work effectively. You sense the atmosphere when a group is working well – and I don't mean agreeing with each other. They're listening to each other and you know because you see how what they say relates to what the previous person said, and builds on it, rather than destroying it. And disagreements are approached constructively, by trying to work out where they spring form. Silences are OK, too, and body language tells you a lot.'

'I'll be encouraging my senior women managers to go on such a programme – to help them gain more confidence. Men, on the other hand, gain in different ways – usually to be more open and less authoritarian.'

'If only people at work would behave more like set members! Instead of being supportive and asking questions, you're given information and advice. Neither is very helpful.'

For a manager with a local authority, it was 'the challenge and the exploring that I found most useful. It was unlike the confrontations and the sense of being exposed that you get at work when you're questioned. It's really helpful to forage around as you can do in the set.'

'It's not only radical . . . it's the most dangerous course I've been on. Dangerous because it make you question everything.'

Many participants remarked on 'the discipline of that hour, of needing to do your homework, and report on what you've done, or just thinking about how you want to use the next meeting. It's something to take away with you into everyday life. You become more focused and disciplined.'

One academic,[8] defined action learning as 'like a "mobius strip" where the surfaces join up in one continuous strip imperceptibly – rather as action and learning are linked imperceptibly, and both part of the same "surface".'

And then there was the unusual experience of being listened to! 'That alone gives you confidence – and a sense of being valued . . . particularly when people agree with what you're doing or saying, or find it interesting . . . it gives you confidence to speak up elsewhere.'

Someone else commented that the set was 'like an elastic band that stretches you'. In a similar vein, a younger participant said, 'It's about empowering people. It pushes responsibility and duties – even power – back to staff.' Another young participant said, 'This may sound melodramatic, but I entered the programme as a boy and left as a maturer adult.'

SOME VISUAL IMAGES AND METAPHORS

As already mentioned in the introduction to this book, trying to unravel the experiences that participants described was like unravelling a complexly woven tapestry. But there were other images – both for participants and for me.

Metaphors are, for some, a way of trying to understand the process and to disentangle what they learnt, where, when and how. Images that participants drew on included: 'A big salad: you toss it around and come up with something that tastes good' and 'A lentil loaf – deep, crunchy and long-lasting.' Another participant was less flattering, and talked of 'knitting your own yoghurt'.

Interestingly, this image of action learning as being an activity belonging to the 'alternative' society – and closely resembling 1960s Californian 'experiments' – cropped up only once, when the managing director of a small firm referred to action learning as a 'new age activity'. He nevertheless attended all the meetings, and was very participative! His comments may well have been prompted by a need to protect himself. A few other managers admitted having grappled with the notion that anything 'supportive' which took place 'in a group' was going to be 'namby-pamby' and 'groupy-gropey'. One other participant – who has gone on to become one of action learning's most avid supporters – confessed, 'I was so scared of the idea when I first encountered it, I left it alone for two years.'

'Sitting in a balloon, and viewing the countryside below, with all the contours, rivers, trees,' was another version (not unlike the 'helicopter' image in popular use some years ago, although the balloon is a somewhat quieter means of transport, and those travelling in it are exposed to the elements). Another participant defined action learning as taking managers back to the coal-face. And, as though combining the previous two images, someone else described it as 'like an archaeological excavation of a buried and forgotten city. The first find could be the only one, or with the right tools and attitude the whole city can be uncovered.'

Scaffolding – a means of moving up and down, horizontally, vertically or at different angles – was another vivid image, conveying the flexibility and support offered by action learning.

One recurring image was derived from the theatre: the commedia dell'arte, in which actors in various roles were gradually able to drop their masks to reveal their true personas.

A number of men saw action learning as the 'feminization of management'. One went to say, 'I'm not sure the action learning way of working is suitable in a more masculine environment, which is aggressive, competitive, individualistic and ruthless.' This 'masculinity' also has connotations of doing rather than talking, of being crisp, clear and short-term. A 'feminine' organization, by contrast, was seen as more caring, more teamwork-oriented, building on networking, and more 'democratic' – where you were more likely to be listened to, and valued. As one member put it: 'I learnt a great deal from the women in the set. They're much better at teamwork and sharing responsibility with others, and generally using others to help them arrive at a decision.'

My own metaphors – which emerged after just a few interviews with participants, but which continue to be applicable – were these:

Initially, a bowl of spaghetti: spaghetti, because every time I tried to separate one aspect of action learning, it became entwined with other strands, so that it was impossible to separate one from the other. If I pulled too hard, the strands snapped.

The second – also culinary – image (I know not why!) was of a multi-layered chocolate cake. This image grew in strength (and layers!) as I realized the multi-layered complexity of action learning. I was also struck, though, that to achieve this richness, this complexity, several elements had to be present (see 'Is there a real McCoy? p. 305). Without them, the chocolate cake was nothing but a sponge cake, and the participants lost out on the breadth and depth that a well-managed action learning programme was able to offer.

A recipe for successful action learning[9]

Ingredients
- 6–8 people
- Commitment
- Trust
- Concern
- Time
- Experience
- Support
- Challenge
- Risk
- Facilitation
- Humour

Method

Take a liberal slice of time, and mix thoroughly with the lifetime experience of several committed people. Sprinkle a generous helping of concern for others, and add enough trust to mould the mix until it gels firmly together. An added catalytic facilitator may help it to bind. Season with a little risk. Add support and challenge, whenever necessary.

Leave to simmer indefinitely, stirring regularly as you feed with a variety of problems. An occasional dash of humour will prevent the mix from sticking.

Results

So, what do you get? The opportunity:

- to focus on particular areas of your professional life and to discuss at a level which, for a variety of reasons, you cannot do at work;
- of gaining new perspectives on such areas, based on the experiences of others;
- to develop and practise new skills in a relatively safe environment;
- for reassurance that others have 'been there before';
- for friendship

WHAT IS THE PLACE OF ACTION LEARNING IN THE FUTURE?

True to the spirit of action learning, let us end on a questioning note.

Action learning has its devotees, and those who decry it. Yet it is – after some years on the sidelines of management development and training – coming back to a point where, if not exactly centre-stage, it is at least widely recognized for what it has to offer.

Its prime strength is that it helps people focus on the practicalities of their everyday working lives, and gives them an opportunity to do something about the issues that concern them – and learn from that experience. It brings learning to the workplace, rather than separating the two.

Organizations, ie edifices which control the destinies of those who work within them, are increasingly seeking to create ways of involving staff, giving them an opportunity to contribute, to gain sense of achievement during the eight or so hours spent 'at work'. As organizations set about dismantling some of the old hierarchical structures, adapt to new market demands, and face competition worldwide, there may be a glint of hope for action learning.

Programmes are now being run across the world – in Australia, India, Nepal, Kenya, Japan and the USA; and in Europe, in Italy, Germany, Sweden, Ireland, the Czech Republic and Bulgaria.

If action learning is so powerful, why hasn't it taken the world by storm?

A good question! And there is no need to be defensive about an answer. In fact, participants themselves, from various organizations and from different functions, came up with a number of suggestions why it has been slow to catch on:

'It's too soft for the rigours of business today. It can be seen by more macho, autocratic managers – who are often those in senior positions – as being "namby-pamby" and a crutch for the weak.'

'It's too nice and cosy – not challenging enough.'

'For it to work – to take hold – the culture of the company is important. If it is authoritarian, fragmented and structured with egoistic managers, where someone is always blamed, and where mistakes are pushed under the carpet, then the programme is likely to ruffle feathers, and expose people who prefer to hide.'

'The culture of many organizations is the antithesis of action learning beliefs and principles – they're competitive, individualistic.'

'It's too revolutionary for many companies: it teaches you to ask questions.'

'Action learning threatens some people. If they are a little insecure they don't like to lose control. If they give people power they feel it reduces their authority. Some managers feel they need total control'.

'It's oversold as the panacea for all ills.'

'It's too vague for money-minded managers. Its benefits are not concrete enough – too hit and miss, not specific.'

'It fails to market itself.'

'The "literature" implies it is something everyone can do instantly – but that's not the case. It's not that simple.'

Some participants had the dilemma of not feeling able to use everything they had learnt back at work. One group said that, in their company, asking questions was 'taboo'. That just wasn't the game being played. In another, although the ostensible reason for the programme was to produce a new, enquiring breed of managers, only the select few on the programme were being actively encouraged to enquire, which created problems as they tried to gain access to information for their projects. Others talked of becoming disillusioned with their managers/bosses who pretended to know and have answers when they patently didn't. As many commented, wouldn't it be good if everyone at work behaved as though in a set, and adopted the same honest, open behaviour.

One participant, as long ago as 1978, had the following comments to make:

- lack of information and communication in organizations leads to problems and non-involvement;
- hierarchy and structure impede the taking of responsibility;
- management philosophy ossifies individuals' involvement, and devalues them;
- the raison d'etre for organizations is not clear – people lose their way into other avenues;
- change needs standard bearers;
- we may solve today's problems but there are new ones lurking around the corner.

Through action learning:

- we learn to communicate openly and freely;
- we learn how to solve today's problems and thereby gain insights on how to tackle tomorrow's;
- we learn to value and respect everyone;
- we learn to listen.

This may raise questions about the 'usefulness' of action learning in many organizations. On the other hand, it is only by people beginning to work in a different way that changes will come about. We have, in the end, to believe in our own power to influence, to start the ball rolling; we must have faith that small changes will lead to greater ones.

Inevitably there will be people who do not feel happy working in this open questioning way. This is not the place to analyse why. Suffice it to say that it is important that people opt to come on this type of programme; that they are told something about it beforehand, and exercise a choice.

But even some of those who choose to come may find, after experiencing it, that it isn't suitable for their needs, or they don't see how it can be applied back in their organization (if they have come on a mixed-company programme). Or perhaps some elements have not been professionally adhered to, so that the programme has been spoilt for them, or has missed its potential.

Action learning is also 'sold' as performing other tricks and magic. Its strength, however, lies in its potential to develop more thinking, questioning, challenging, yet sensitive and mature human beings.

Does action learning move us closer to creating learning organizations?

Well yes, it would appear that action learning can help organizations achieve that seductive notion of the learning organization. The concept of the learning organization has been around for a number of years, and a number of the progenitors of this elusive idea are themselves action learners, no doubt influenced in some of their thinking by their experiences of action learning.

Thus Pedler, Burgoyne and Boydell, the authors of *The Learning Company*, state:

In a learning company managers see their primary task as facilitating members' experimentation and learning from experience. It is normal to take time out to seek feedback, to obtain data to aid understanding. Senior managers give a lead in questioning their own ideas, attitudes and actions. Mistakes are allowed – if not exactly encouraged – for it is recognized that we will never learn if we don't try out new ideas, new ways of doing things, and these won't always work. We need to recognize that there is no such thing as a failed experiment – as long as we learn from it.[10]

Peter Senge, in his book *The Fifth Discipline*, defines a learning organization as '. . . [one] where people continually expand their capacity to create the results they truly desire, where new and expansive patterns of thinking are nurtured, where collective aspiration is set free, and where people are continually learning how to learn together.'[11]

And Bob Garratt, in a chapter entitled 'The Power of Action Learning'[12] states that action learning

. . . is a very powerful organizational tool for the reform of working systems and the subsequent restating of organizational objectives. Its power derives from releasing and reinterpreting the acccumulated experiences of the people who comprise the organization. The combination of this released energy and the act of moving the authority for problem solving to those people who must live with the consequences is a deliberate devolution of organizational power.

So there we have it. Action learning is one powerful way of creating a learning organization. And participants' experiences of action learning back up these more 'academic' musings.

Action learning: a step towards a learning organization

It develops people who:
- listen
- question self and others
- have a sense of self-awareness and confidence
- are willing to be open
- are willing and able to share, and to learn with and from others
- value and respect others
- understand the value of networking – and do so
- have a sense of energy, of being motivated, and wanting to achieve
- are aware of their own, and others', ability to change and develop

---

Peter Honey has defined what he thinks are the ten learning behaviours that organizations need to have present in their culture and their staff if they are to become such learning organizations.[13] Those behaviours are:

1 asking questions
2 suggesting ideas
3 exploring options
4 taking risks/experimenting
5 being open about the way it is
6 converting mistakes into learning
7 reflecting and reviewing
8 talking about learning
9 taking responsibility for own learning and development
10 admitting to inadequacies and mistakes

Many of these sound remarkably similar to behaviours that participants on the action learning programmes in my survey claim to have learnt!

In addition, in action learning, they acquire two other

important skills that are indispensable to an organization that is using all the accumulated experience of its staff:

- increased ability to network,
- recognition of the need for – and value of – time and space to stop and reflect

I would add one further quality – what Peter Honey and Alan Mumford have called 'being an opportunistic learner', ie someone who learns from any situation they find themselves in. In the words of one manager (quoted earlier), 'I've realized that everything is data from which I can learn.'

An opportunistic learner:

- can describe the learning process
- reviews experience
- recalls details
- shares experiences
- responds flexibly
- invests effort into learning
- asks questions
- listens patiently
- expresses thoughts
- is open to new angles
- identifies own development needs
- converts ideas into actions
- takes risks
- sees connections
- adjusts to the new/unfamiliar
- is intrigued by criticism, and converts it into suggestions for improvement
- asks for feedback
- accepts responsibility for self
- accepts all situations as learning opportunities
- believes you're never too old to learn
- explores alternatives

- accepts praise
- analyses successes, as well as mistakes
- feels exhilarated by change
- sits and thinks . . . without guilt or rush
- copes with ambiguity
- feels confident with strangers

Of course, these behaviours alone do not create a learning company. What is also needed is the will to use them: a culture which genuinely values such qualities, structures which encourage them, systems that reward them, and opportunities that will call for them. Many participants doubted whether their organizations could or would reach this stage.

But where organizations were willing to take the step, the model of the set could be a beginning – for in many ways the set is a learning company in microcosm. The way it values every member, allows airspace, gives space for thinking, reflecting and sharing, acknowledges mistakes as much as success in order to learn from both, builds people's confidence and self-awareness, and encourages a generally democratic and hence 'flat', non-hierarchical, non-authoritarian type of organization – these are all elements that a learning company needs. Can small beginnings lead to greater things?

PART 4

Putting an Effective Action Learning Programme into Practice

This final part of the book gives some guidelines on how to start up and run an effective programme. In the appendix you will also find a list of useful reading material that goes into greater depth on various aspects of action learning programmes that this book has neither the space nor intention to touch on, being intended as but a flavour of the multi-layered chocolate cake. With luck we have at least reached the icing – whether whisky-flavoured or not I leave to the readers' imagination and taste-buds.

IS THERE A REAL McCOY?

Yes . . . and no. Yes, there are certain elements that need to be present for an action learning programme to be considered the genuine article, as opposed to a pale imitation. Without these elements it cannot achieve the depth, breadth and complexity that an effective action learning programme can provide.

Thus, there are more or less purist versions – and to be truly purist we ought to eliminate set advisers, who were never part of Reg Revans's scheme of things. But there exist certain elements without which a programme is not action learning, depriving participants of what they could expect to gain from the real McCoy.

For me – in the light of participants' experiences and comments – these critical elements are:

- small sets, with (roughly) monthly meetings lasting a full day
- observing airspace and questioning processes
- a project or task to focus on and use as a vehicle for learning, and not solely for resolving senior managers' questions
- revisiting both action and learning with a competent set adviser, until the set is able to work without one
- the time factor – probably no less than 6 months
- an emphasis on the learning

The following pages contain various guidelines and notes on how to set up a programme. The guidelines given assume a programme of approximately six months' duration, with sets meeting for a full day, and participants focusing on tasks and projects for their learning.

BEFORE THE PROGRAMME

The person proposing to introduce the programme should:

- Understand its nature, be clear why they are proposing action learning, agree on an overall objective for the programme, and gain the commitment of senior managers to the programme. Make sure everyone understands how participants will change, and what qualities – and expectations – they will have at the end of the programme.
- Discuss the programme and its intention with potential participants, their managers and the clients, and development-training personnel.
- Ensure that everyone understands the time factor involved, the need for regular and relatively frequent set meetings, and the need for projects – when they are selected – to meet the learning needs of participants (and not some personal agenda of a senior manager!).

THE PROGRAMME

The person running the programme (not necessarily the same person who has proposed the programme or even the set adviser) should:

1 Be clear about the objectives of the programme and communicate them to all who are concerned and actively involved.
2 Ensure that everyone knows that the programmes will last for a minimum of 4–6 months, and that they are also aware of what other commitments it will involve (set meetings, a project, possibly a final written report).
3 Find a convenient location (or locations) for all set meetings, and ensure that all the necessary administrative arrangements are made (timing, rooms, food and refreshments).
4 Liaise with the set adviser.

5 Be available to sort out any misunderstandings that may arise during the programme.

6 Be clear what form of evaluation will take place, what will be evaluated, and who will be evaluating – and inform everyone.

THE PARTICIPANTS

Potential participants:

- should be selected in good time, and given a brief idea of the nature of the programme, and the reason why they have been selected;
- may be selected by their managers, by the personnel or training/development department, or by some other person who has a stake in their development; in some instances they may self-select;
- should be given the choice of whether to participate or not;
- should all – if they will be working together – be of approximately the same level of responsibility;
- can be either from the same function or different functions (and this may vary, depending on the objective of the programme);
- should be involved in selecting the task/project they will focus on during the programme. If they are working on a project, they should have identified it by the second set meeting at the latest.

CLIENTS AND OTHERS WHO NEED TO BE INVOLVED

Every participant (or set, if they work on a group project) needs to have a client (unless they are senior managers addressing their own tasks or quandaries).

- *Clients* should be senior managers who are in sympathy

with the programme, will champion it and the participants, and step in to resolve any misunderstanding over the programme between participants and their immediate manager (see pp. 139–40).

- *Managers* whose staff will participate in the programme need to be told what action learning is about, and should be involved in selecting a project for the participant. It is crucial that they understand both the amount of time that participants may need to spend on the programme, and the commitment required from participants in terms of attending set meetings.
- *Participants* need to agree with their managers and clients what their project will be, what 'action' outcomes are expected and what their intended learning is to be about. This would take place either just before, or on the introductory day(s) to the programme or immediately after.
- *Development/training* personnel, who may be the instigators of a programme, may be responsible for development programmes, or may have identified, through assessment centres, individuals who would benefit from action learning.

INTRODUCTORY DAYS

- Participants need to be introduced to action learning at the outset – in a one- or two-day introductory programme, usually by the set adviser;
- Clients also need to be introduced to action learning, and to their role as clients to the project(s) and champions of the participants and their learning;
- At the introductory days, participants and clients need to agree – if this is feasible – the intention and scope of the project(s);
- It may be helpful if the clients attend for part of the participants' introductory day, to publicly 'own' the programme.

Introductory days should involve:

- a short introduction to action learning by the set adviser;
- a short experience of it – with a *fish bowl*, or 'triad' exercise (see below);
- possibly other elements, eg mindmaps (useful for mapping out participants' relationships); lifelines (for focusing participants on their most effective learning experiences to date and what they involved); transactional analysis, to alert them to how certain behaviours trigger complementary behaviours in others;
- if the purpose of the programme is to build teamworking, an outdoor exercise, and possibly an introduction to Belbin's nine team roles (see p. 237);
- Honey and Mumford's learning styles questionnaire;[1]
- A Myers-Briggs questionnaire for participants is another useful tool (for those qualified to administer it).
- The first set meeting (see below).

The fishbowl

Five or six of those present form a 'set' and, sitting in a circle, they work with a set adviser while everyone else sits around the circle and observes the process. An empty chair is left in the inner circle; anyone from the outer circle wishing to participate on a point may join the inner circle by sitting in the empty chair. At the conclusion of the exercise, the set and the presenter are asked to comment on their experience, and then the discussion is open to everyone.

A triad exercise

Divide participants into threes or fours, and ask one member of each group to present an issue – a quandary, challenge, or irritation – but nothing too large.

Ask the presenter to hold onto their airspace for 15–20 minutes. Meanwhile the others should try to focus on asking questions, giving feedback, reflecting, and turning ideas or suggestions into questions.

When the time is up, ask each group to discuss the experience, beginning with the views of the presenter. Then bring everyone back into the larger group and discuss. First, ask the presenters what it was like to be the focus. Then ask the others how they experienced their role.

THE ACTION: PROJECTS/TASKS

What constitutes a project is described in detail on pp. 129–31.

1 Each participant needs to have an individual real-time work project or 'task', or a mini-project as part of a larger group project;
2 Projects may be within a participant's own work area or elsewhere;
3 Tasks for more senior managers should centre on or be directly related to issues central to the participant's working life: their own managerial issues, responsibilities, dilemmas and decisions;
4 A project should relate to, and give participants the scope to work on, their identified learning needs;
5 Projects should involve the participants in tackling something new to them, and something of importance to their section, department or their organization – something that will stretch them and something that will develop them in the ways identified earlier;
6 If projects include an implementation stage (an important stage in action learning), the participants must be given authority to carry this out;
7 Projects need ideally to last for the length of the programme;
8 Each individual and group project must have a client who expects results;

9 Participants need to be told at the outset whether they will be expected to produce a written report of their project and/or their learning, or if their efforts will be evaluated by some other means.

Action

- a project;
- a task; or
- a management/personal developmental issue, with a work-related focus.

Five stages in clarifying a project:

1 What I plan to do/what tasks to undertake/what experiences to try out.
2 What result/outcome I am anticipating/hoping for.
3 How I plan to go about it.
4 How I plan to review/evaluate it.
5 What I hope to learn.

THE SETS

Sets should:

- Consist of no more than five or six participants
- Be formed at the very beginning of the programme, on the introductory day(s)
- The membership of sets will depend on the objective of the programme, and may consist of people from different functions or just one. But members are most likely to be of approximately the same level of responsibility
- Be told that they will retain the same membership for the duration of the programme,

- Be told that they will be working with a set adviser (normally)
- Be told that they will be meeting for (ideally) a full day, approximately every month for a period of around 4–6 months

---

Helpful behaviour by a problem presenter

- prepare for meetings
- structure your time
- be clear what you would like – or would like the set – to focus on
- learn to ask for what you want
- learn how to get an empathetic response
- learn how to receive
- learn to generate action points

AT THE FIRST SET MEETING

The first set meeting will probably take place on the introductory day(s). At this meeting, set members should:

1 Create their own ground rules (see p. 105 for an example).
2 Agree on future dates for set meetings.
3 Create a learning agreement (if the programme demands one).
4 Help members think about a project – if they don't already have one.
5 Be told if they are required to – or if the set adviser thinks they would gain by – keep a diary or learning log.
6 Be reminded of any evaluation that will take place at the end of the programme.
7 Be told if they are expected to write reports or some other form of document on their project

Diaries/Logs

Some useful ideas on what to write up in them, using both the project/task and the set meetings themselves as the 'raw' data:

- What I planned to do
- How I prepared myself for it
- What took place
- Outcomes/what happened
- Was it what I'd anticipated?
  if yes, what went well?
  if no, what could have been done/said differently?
- My reflections on it:
  what was I thinking?
  what was I feeling?
  did I do/say what I'd planned to?
  if not, what was stopping me?
- What have I learnt/observed? What insights do I have about myself?
- What do I want to focus on next time/in future?
- Thoughts on how my learning is occurring

PROCESSES IN THE SET

These are the choices:

- airspace for everyone, ideally an hour at every meeting. If time does not allow, then set aside time for one or two people per meeting, either in rota or when someone needs airspace.
- asking questions
- challenging
- giving/asking for feedback
- giving insights/ reflecting

- sharing ideas and suggestions (in question form)
- trying out new behaviours (the set can be used as an 'experimental bubble')
- studying and learning from set processes
- brainstorming: the set give their insights and perspectives at the presenter's request and for a limited period only

Processes to avoid:
- giving advice
- having a general discussion
- criticizing and passing judgement

Some questions to help a presenter unpack an issue

Using 'how', 'what', 'where', and 'when' questions rather than 'why'.

1. Individual and the project/task
   - What is your position?
   - What's your issue/question? (draw it?)
   - What problems does that cause?/In what way is that a problem?
   - What isn't happening now?
   - What do you want to be different?
   - How would you like X to respond?
   - How do think that Y needs to be changed/altered?
   - What would you like to do – ideally?
   - How do you feel about that?
   - Can you tell us more about that?
   - Who have you consulted/talked to?
   - Who else might you talk to?
   - How does the other person/department see the issue?
   - Have you thought of . . .
   - What's stopping you?
   - What would happen if . . . you did/did the opposite/did nothing?
   - How will you go about it?
   - In what way will that help?

- Who else can you involve/get to back you?
- What else would you find helpful?

2. Individual and the set
   - What response would you like from the set?
   - How can we help you?
   - Can you tell us more about that?
   - I don't follow what you are saying
   - I don't understand that
   - Are we getting away from your question?
   - Do you want to tell us more?
   - What's at the back of your mind?
   - You sound . . .
   - Is this helpful?
   - How do you feel?
   - Have we helped you?
   - Are you being honest with yourself?

3. General process questions/statements
   - What is happening here now?
   - What are we doing at the moment?
   - Is it helpful/productive/getting us anywhere?
   - Why haven't we tackled . . . ?
   - What have we learnt?
   - I feel uncomfortable/confused/angry/helpless
   - You are stopping me from working
   - Please don't interrupt me

HOW TO USE SET MEETINGS

Options:

- Focus on shaping/progressing with the project
- How am I progressing?
- Am I achieving what I hoped?
- What is proving difficult?
- What else do I need to be doing?

- Focus on 'self':
  How am I doing?
  How am I feeling?
  How am I learning?
  How am I changing?

- Focus on the set:
  How can I/we use it?
  How is it helping me/us?
  What can I/we be doing differently?
  What are we learning?

- Focus on the processes:
  What am I finding useful?
  How are we working?
  What are we learning?
  How are we learning?

- Focus on other issues of mutual interest, to be jointly arrived at, and decide on form of work, ie whether discussion or dialogue
- Focus on what other processes would be helpful: eg brainstorming ideas

If set isn't helpful, have you:

- told them
- asked for help
- been clear
- attended regularly
- felt committed and involved yourself
- listened to others
- taken responsibility for working out 'why'
- helped the set or individuals to help you (by your own responses and feedback)

THE SET ADVISER

The role of the set adviser is discussed on pp. 205–18. The set adviser's main responsibility is to be preseent for the set meetings, and adhere to the principles of action learning throughout.

1 Should be 'trained' and understand his/her role to be that of a facilitator (not chairperson, group leader, tutor or lecturer);
2 Should have had some experience of action learning;
3 Should observe the ground rules of the set;
4 Should, if it is appropriate, organize short taught inputs on specific subjects of relevance to the set and their projects;
5 Should be competent and confident to work with the processes that are basic to action learning, ie airspace for every member, a focus on the task/projects in hand, a questioning approach, attention to listening, time for reflection, emphasis on learning, and avoidance of advice and judgement.

The role of the set adviser

- to help individuals learn
- to help the set learn
- to model helpful behaviour:

    to listen
    to ask helpful questions
    to give feedback
    to reflect
    to challenge
    to support
    to encourage dialogue, not discussion
    to express/admit to feelings

- to give members responsibility for their work and their learning

---

- to reflect back on the processes in the set
- to facilitate

and not to be:

- the expert
- a tutor
- the chairman
- the group leader

THE MEETINGS AND THE TIMING

- Should be at a place convenient for all participants – preferably away from work (to avoid phone calls or being called to other meetings);
- Should be regular, established at the beginning of the programme, and be adhered to, and attended regularly by all set members;
- The processes of the set should be observed at every meeting, unless the set – with the acquiescence of the set adviser – decides otherwise.

THE ASSESSMENT

Those responsible for running the programme should:

- Be clear and agree on – at the beginning of the programme – what form the assessment will take, eg will it be a written document, project report, a learning/reflective document, or some verbal presentation? Will both 'action' and learning be assessed? And by whom?
- Decide who will assess: will it be by self-assessment? Peer assessment? Or by participants' managers and clients?

- Be clear what will be assessed: the 'actions' achieved, or the learning and development achieved, or both.
- Communicate all this to everyone concerned – participants, their clients, the set adviser, the participants' managers, and possibly the training/development department.

FINAL MEETING

Most programmes have a final wrap-up meeting: to review the learning, to give verbal reports to clients, managers and others interested, and formally to end the programme.

Postscript

MY OWN EXPERIENCES – AND LEARNING

The material on which much of this book is based was gathered as part of a research project funded by International Management Centres – an action-learning focused business management school. Alan Mumford suggested that I should carry out the research in an 'action learning way'. I adopted a 'deductive' approach – ie with a broad picture in my mind which I adjusted as the data I collected shifted my view. I also kept a diary, which was lucky because without it, many ideas, thoughts, insights, reflections and questions would have disappeared.

I found the diary was more than a 'memory'. It became my partner for dialogue, my surrogate set. As I wrote, I found that I was putting ideas and thoughts down on paper – or rather on screen – that I had not known I had until I 'voiced' them in writing.

This mirrored what several participants said to me about the advantage of the set: that as you talk out loud, you hear yourself, and you answer your own questions, or realize what you're not doing that would be helpful.

My diary also provided a stream of comments on my 'findings'. What recurs is the feeling that so many programmes are not getting to what I came to call 'the breadth, depth and complexity of action learning'. They were, in several cases, pale imitations of the real thing.

My other major observation was that my research was a project, just as participants had their projects. I became more 'pragmatic' when organizing it in the early days – while at the same time complaining of the need to do this! I needed to talk to others to find in myself the energy to carry on – in the same way that set members described the energy they gained from talking to others. In this sense I had a 'telephone set' of people I talked to regularly. I confirmed my belief that I am a reflector, but reflect better following some 'action'. And that I learn through a combination of hearing myself talk, writing, drawing (visualizing) and listening. I also suspect that I am an 'opportunistic' learner – my diary confirms the ideas that emerged from a sermon in St Paul's Cathedral, a BBC World Service programme, a tennis match commentary, a Polish novel, and an Australian film!

I gained confidence by talking through some of my thoughts with others. Two or three of the most helpful ideas – and the ones I particularly remember – emerged as a couple of friends (non-experts) asked me some simple questions about action learning! But the insights of 'experts' were helpful in the early stages of the research, as I tried to formulate questions and develop structures, and latterly, as I tried to make some sense of the material I had gathered.

In the course of the research, I moved away from a 'questioning' approach to more of a 'dialogue' with the participants – though this dialogue was shaped by some initial questions, and with others loosely in mind. I found this more productive, and was reminded of one or two participants who talked of being 'in the firing line' of questions. But as I gained more insights from people through a dialogue with them (ie where I followed a train of thought they had begun and added some thoughts of my own) I began to wonder how useful it was to keep 'rigidly' to a questioning approach in action learning. I feel ambiguous about this, because some of the people I was working with, newcomers to action learning, found the questioning approach immensely helpful – an eye-opener, in fact. Is there a time for questions, and a time for dialogue?

I also wondered about questions in a set: whether the most helpful questions might be the ones which had a target in the questioner's mind – some picture. Yet if such is the case, how can a set – where any member may 'interrupt' such a train of thought – be accommodated in this process?

My acceptance of what constitutes 'action learning' is now broader than it was, while at the same time I am critical of much that passes under the name of action learning. For me, it's not enough for a programme to conform merely to the structure described in this book; it must also retain the processes and encompass the spirit.

As for my own 'processes': I gained more depth from individual interviews; I gained more sense of energy from set interviews. I found written responses to my questions stiff and in many cases only of limited value. The way people speak and the way they write are often poles apart. There are those who convey themselves well on paper, but some written pieces are so 'intellectualized' as to lose all sense of the person who is writing. That said, some participants' documents (particularly those associated with higher degrees) provided me with helpful analyses.

While undertaking this research I was asked whether the entire process of an action learning programme could not be undertaken by an individual working without the help of a set. The more I look at what people say about the set and its processes, the more I think it is a rare individual who can gain as much on their own as from working with others productively. It may be that some stages in an action learning cycle can be worked through alone – but the learning cycle in its entirety . . . ? Certainly, I began my research with a 'hunch' (a hypothesis?) that the set, with its processes and set adviser, would emerge as the vital element. I think this has been the case.

This research – and my experiencing of it – has in many ways paralleled or mirrored what happens in an action learning programme. This was something I hadn't anticipated. I've become aware, though, that I am not good at seeing my own journey around a learning cycle, although I follow one. It still has to be pointed out to me!

This issue of being reminded was brought back to me on several occasions when I was interviewing individuals or sets: they commented how good it was to be reviewing, or remembering what they had done and learnt. Wouldn't it be good, they'd say, to meet up again, to start something similar – perhaps another set. Is there a 'learning' point here? Do those of us who run action learning programmes need to re-gather participants to allow them to remind themselves of what they did and learnt?

I began my research with images, and they are still with me, and more have emerged. But the one I still like the most, which conveys the breadth, depth and complexity of action learning, is the many-layered chocolate cake (I have no idea why culinary images abound; maybe it has something to do with action learning feeding the body, mind and spirit!).

Further Reading

Books

B. Garratt, *The Learning Organization* (HarperCollins, 1987, 1994)

P. Honey and A. Mumford, *The Manual of Learning Styles* (Honey, 1986)

S. Inglis, *Making the Most of Action Learning* (Gower, 1994)

I. McGill and L. Beaty, *Action Learning, a Practitioner's Guide* (Kogan Page, 1992)

M. Pedler (ed), *Action Learning in Practice*, 2nd edn (Gower, 1991)

M. Pedler, J. Burgoyne and T. Boydell, *The Learning Company* (McGraw-Hill, 1991)

R. Revans, *The Origins and Growth of Action Learning* (Chartwell Bratt, 1982); *The ABC of Action Learning* (Chartwell Bratt, 1983)

Articles and short publications

L. Beaty, T. Bourner and P. Frost, 'Action learning: Reflections on becoming a set member', *Management Education and Development*, vol. 24, part 4, 1993

D. Boddy, 'Putting Action Learning into Practice', *Journal of European Industrial Training*, vol. 5, no. 5, 1981

R. Gaunt and R. Kendall, *A Short Manual for Set Members* (Greater London Employers' Association, 1985)

P. Honey, 'Establishing a Learning Regime', *Organisations and People*, vol. 1, no. 1, 1994

A. Lewis, 'An investigation into the long-term benefits, if any, of the action learning programme in the field staff operations of the Prudential Assurance Co. Ltd', research paper, International Management Centres, 1993

A. Logan and R. Stuart, 'Action Based Learning: Are Activity and Experience the Same?', *Industrial and Commercial Training*, March/April 1987

A. Mumford (guest editor), 'Action Learning', special issue of *The Journal of Management Development*, vol. 6, no. 2, 1987

A. Mumford, 'Learning in Action', *Personnel Management*, July 1991

M. Pedler and J. Boutall, 'Action Learning for Change, A Resource Book for Managers and Other Professionals' (NHS Training Directorate, 1992)

The International Foundation for Action Learning

The International Foundation for Action Learning, a membership organization, aims to identify and encourage a network of enthusiasts to support and develop the work of action learning worldwide.

The Foundation, based in the UK, collects and disseminates information; promotes research and case histories; publishes a newsletter three times a year; maintains a substantial library on action learning; runs a number of workshops and meetings during the year; and welcomes telephone and letter enquiries.

Membership is for both individuals and organizations

Address: 46 Carlton Road, London SW14 7RJ. Tel and fax: 0181 878 7358

Notes

Part 1: Action Learning in a Nutshell

1 Extracted from a research project by Alec Lewis into the benefits of action learning in the company in 1993.

2 In 1994 the following universities were running action-learning based management programmes: Brighton University, Glasgow University, Huddersfield University, Nottingham Trent University, Manchester Metropolitan University, Salford University, Stirling University, University of Northumbria, University of Wolverhampton.

Part 2: What is Action Learning? A Reflective Piece

1 Jean Lawrence, 'A Questioning Approach' in *Handbook of Management Development*, Alan Mumford, ed. (Gower, 2nd ed. 1986)

2 Mike Pedler, in *Action Learning in Practice*, M. Pedler, ed. (Gower, 2nd ed. 1991)

3 David Sutton, unpublished paper

4 Reg Revans's books contain much that is useful for anyone interested in action learning: *The ABC of Action Learning* (Chartwell Bratt, 1983); *The Origins and Growth of Action Learning* (Chartwell Bratt, 1982); and articles in *Action Learning in Practice*, M. Pedler, ed. (Gower, 2nd ed. 1991)

5 Tom Reeves who asked me this question has recently published a book, *Managing Effectively: Developing Yourself Through Experience* (Butterworth/Heinemann, 1994), which takes individuals through a self-questioning approach to try and achieve what a group in action learning would.

6 David Bohm, 'For truth try dialogue', *Resurgence*, issue 56, Jan./Feb. 1993

7 Jean Lawrence, op. cit.

8 Andy Logan and Roger Stuart, 'Action Based Learning: Are Activity and Experience the Same?' in *Industrial and Commercial Training*, March/April 1987.

9 Vaclav Havel, *Letters to Olga* (Faber & Faber, 1988)

10 M. Ferguson, *The Aquarian Conspiracy: Personal and Social Transformation in the 1980s* (Paladin, 1981).
11 Reproduced by kind permission of Jean Lawrence.
12 M. Pedler, J. Burgoyne and T. Boydell, *The Learning Company* (McGraw-Hill, 1991).
13 P. Honey, 'Establishing a Learning Regime', *Organisations and People*, vol. 1, no. 1, 1994

Part 3: The Experience of Action Learning

1 Devised by Roger Gaunt
2 My thanks to Alec Lewis for sharing this with me
3 Taken from 'Reflections on being a set member' by Liz Beaty, Tom Bourner, and Paul Frost in *Management Education and Development* (*MEAD*), vol. 24, part 4, 1993.
4 Adapted from an exercise used by Liz Beaty of Brighton University.
5 David Casey examines the role of the set adviser in two useful articles: 'The Role of the Set Adviser' and 'The Shell of Your Understanding' in *Action Learning in Practice*, M. Pedler ed. (Gower, 2nd ed. 1991)
6 M. Belbin, *Management Teams* (Paladin, 1981).
7 Reprinted with kind permission of Tricia Lustig of Lasa Management Training, and her colleagues.
8 Tom Bourner, Centre for Management Learning at Brighton University shared his metaphor of action learning with me.
9 Recipe devised by Dr Sheila Webb, Consultant in Public Health Medicine, 1992.
10 Pedler, Burgoyne and Boydell, op. cit.
11 Peter Senge, *The Fifth Discipline* (Century Business, 1990)
12 In M. Pedler (ed), *Action Learning in Practice* (Gower, 2nd ed. 1991)
13 Peter Honey, op. cit.

Part 4: Putting an Effective Action Learning Programme into Practice

1 In P. Honey and A. Mumford, *The Manual of Learning Styles* (1986).

Index

Sur/Petition

Edward de Bono

Creating value monopolies when everyone else is only competing.

Best selling author of *Lateral Thinking* and *Serious Creativity*.

'Edward de Bono jolts our minds into new pathways of thought.'
Success Magazine

Competition was fine once upon a time – but times have changed, and so has business. Now business must learn to exploit the vast potential of the integral values that surround the purchase and use of their products and services. Concepts, rather than technology, are coming to the fore. Competition is no longer the key to success – it's the bare minimum for survival. *Real* success requires a giant leap of the imagination to carry a business beyond competition and turn it into a market place leader.

No-one in business can afford to miss this amazing book by a major business strategist and the world's leading authority in the field of creative thinking.

Serious Creativity
Using the Power of Lateral Thinking
to Create New Ideas

Edward de Bono

The lack of fresh, constructive thinking is the vital missing ingredient in the way many businesses and people tackle the problem of the 1990s. With *Serious Creativity*, world-renowned Edward de Bono brings right up to date his landmark concept of lateral thinking, drawing on twenty-five years of practical experience on the deliberate use of creativity.

Creativity is becoming increasingly important for all businesses as competition intensifies, because it is the best and cheapest way to get added value out of existing resources and assets. New concepts are essential for the 'Sur/Petition' that is coming to replace traditional competition. Edward de Bono's *Serious Creativity* has undoubtedly become *the* standard textbook of creativity around the world, demonstrating that his techniques of lateral thinking do work for individuals *and* corporations.

With this step-by-step approach to creativity on demand, creative thinking at last becomes a usable skill instead of a matter of talent, temperament – or just luck.

ISBN 0 00 637958 3

Six Action Shoes

Edward de Bono

**A brilliant new way to take control
of any business or life situation**

'WALK THE TALK' *with* SIX ACTION SHOES

Most situations in business and life are ambiguous and confusing.
And confusion is the enemy of action. The brilliant yet amazingly
simple 'six shoes' framework lets us identify different situations so
that we can take control of them and respond in the most effective
way possible. Following routines, reacting quickly, responding
sensitively, bashing through obstacles, getting information, taking
charge – there is a shoe and an action made for every situation you
face.

Navy Formal Shoes – suggests routine and formal procedures.

Orange Gumboots – suggests conflict and danger.

Pink Slippers – suggests helping and caring.

Brown Brogues – suggests the sensible and the practical.

Grey Sneakers – suggests information and investigation.

Purple Riding Boots – suggests authority and judgement.

ISBN 0 00 637954 0

The Guide to Greatness in Sales

How to Become a Complete Salesperson

Tom Hopkins

GOT A *JOB* AND WANT A *CAREER* IN SALES?

Then you need to develop a successful sales *lifestyle*. Forget the swanky car and the prospect of loadsamoney, a *career* in sales must take you beyond the perfection of sales technique. Tom Hopkins, the sales trainer guru, talks about meeting career challenges – when you are not meeting customers – and guides you through landing your first good sales job to working effectively with peers to moving into management. This book will show you how to avoid a lifetime of career mistakes, and will open the door to a lifetime of career opportunities.

- Preparing for the tough interview
- Dealing with financial success and the inevitable slump
- Managing the rest of your life
- Sorting out what you want and where you want to go
- Courses and further education: the benefits
- Combating burnout and maintaining physical and mental health

'A must for anyone who is interested in a career in sales or improving their sales skills' Ken Blanchard, author of *The One Minute Manager*

ISBN 0 00 638228 2

The Official Guide to Success

Tom Hopkins's Own Personal Success Programme

Tom Hopkins

In *The Official Guide to Success*, Tom Hopkins, who made his first million at the age of twenty-seven, makes public his tried and tested motivational and inspirational techniques to help you achieve your goals. Whether you seek money, fame, personal happiness or another kind of success, you can use Tom's practical success formulas to become one of life's winners.

Learn how to:
- Overcome worry and use stress positively
- Increase your image and self-esteem
- Break out of the chains of the past
- Function creatively without a need for the approval of others
- Change negative behaviour patterns and create new success-orientated habits
- Unleash untapped mental and physical energies
- Set priorites and use self-discipline for quality time management
- Get happy and stay happy

ISBN 0 586 06315 3

How to Master the Art of Selling

Tom Hopkins

The Best Book Ever Written on Sales and Salesmanship

Tom Hopkins has learned and applied the best sales techniques there are and, in just three years, he earned over one million dollars!

How to Master the Art of Selling lets you into Tom Hopkins's secrets.

Do you think you're not selling anything? The truth is, you're always trying to sell quite a number of ideas, beliefs and goals, aren't you? Every successful person is good at selling himself or herself – they simply sell their ideas, beliefs and aims better than unsuccessful people do.

Showing you how to sell yourself successfuly is the aim of *How to Master the Art of Selling*. Tom Hopkins's know-how can be yours too.

ISBN 0 586 05890 6

Leadership and The One Minute Manager

Kenneth Blanchard

Leadership and The One Minute Manager goes straight to the heart of management as it describes the effective, adaptive styles of Situational Leadership. In clear and simple terms it teaches how to become a flexible and successful leader, fitting your style to the needs of the individual and to the situation at hand, and using the One Minute Manager techniques to enhance the motivation of others.

'Situational Leadership has been the cornerstone of our management training programme for the last five years. Now the model is available to everyone through this action-oriented book'
>   Mike Rose, Chairman and Chief Executive Officer,
>   Holiday Inns Inc.

'The lessons in this book work across cultures and countries. It is consistent with the Japanese philosophy of management'
>   Tomio Taki, President, Takihyo

ISBN 0 00 637080 2

Manage Your Time

Sally Garratt

The Successful Manager series
Edited by Bob Garratt

'The working day just isn't long enough . . . I never have enough time'

This, the distress call of so many managers, is something that can be cured. Solving your time management problems will not only make you more efficient day to day, but it will enable you to plan more effectively for your company's future, and spend more time enjoying your personal life.

Sounds impossible? Sally Garratt, who has run numerous personal-effectiveness courses for managers, shows that it can be done. She examines every area of time management – from the telephone and the 'open door', to the diary and setting priorities. She looks at how you cope with meetings, organize your office, the way you plan ahead and how you give work to your staff (if you give work to your staff!) There is an invaluable section on delegation, with advice on when you should and when you shouldn't delegate.

Practical, realistic, and packed with real-life examples, this book will open the door to more effective management of your time.

'It reminds managers of the things they know they should be doing and rarely do. I recommend it for all managers'
Michael Bett, President, Institute of Personnel Management

ISBN 0 00 638411 0

Managing Yourself

Mike Pedler and Tom Boydell

How well do you manage yourself?
Are you in control of your ideas, feelings and actions?
Does your life have purpose and direction?
Have you enough personal energy?

Anyone who wants to improve the way they manage others must first learn to manage themselves. Starting from the inside out, managers need to become more aware of what they are doing in the areas of:

- health – physical, mental and emotional
- skills – social and technical
- action – how you get things done
- identity – valuing and being yourself

This practical guide for the 'thinking manager' contains case studies and useful activities to undertake which are designed to help you increase your effectiveness in managing yourself and your life and in improving your performance both at work and elsewhere.

Published in cooperation with The Association for Management Education and Development.

ISBN 0 00 636892 1